Finding Your

with

Dyslexia and other SpLDs

'Understanding the impact that dyslexia/ SpLD has on our lives is an incredibly challenging undertaking which is wonderfully executed by Stacey and Fowler. They go beyond this by providing an intuitive guide for dyslexic individuals to help across all aspects of our lives, be it in everyday life or when applied to academic study. The design of the book enables any reader to choose their own path through the book with exercises, strategies, and suggestions helping facilitate understanding of how dyslexia and SpLDs affect us all.'
–**Thomas Hird**, *PhD candidate in Physics at University College London and Oxford University, and former SpLD student of Ginny Stacey, UK*

Finding Your Voice with Dyslexia and other SpLDs is an essential guide to living with dyslexia and other specific learning difficulties (SpLDs). The book provides readers with a practical guide to expressing and developing ideas and feelings.

Uniquely designed for dyslexic/ SpLD readers, this book discusses how individual people function and will help readers to:
• understand how they think
• know what they can do to maintain clear thinking
• know how they can positively contribute to any situation in which they find themselves.

When people with SpLD find their voice, they gain the self-esteem and confidence to tackle all elements of life (study, employment, general living) and to negotiate successfully with those around them. The book contains stories, insights, examples, tips and exercises, presented in a user-friendly way throughout. The book has also been designed for non-linear reading and each chapter includes a 'dipping-in' section to guide the reader.

The book does not have to be read as solid, continuous text from start to finish: it can be read more like a travel guide.

As well as providing vital assistance for people with dyslexia and other specific learning difficulties, this book will benefit anyone supporting, living or working with dyslexic/ SpLD people by helping them to understand more about the dyslexic/ SpLD world.

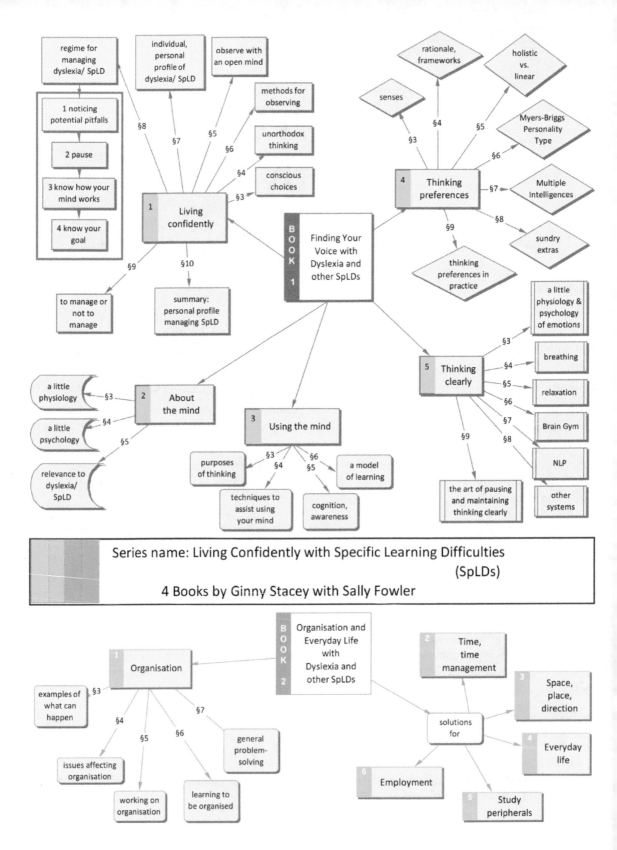

regime for managing dyslexia/ SpLD

individual, personal profile of dyslexia/ SpLD

observe with an open mind

1 noticing potential pitfalls

2 pause

3 know how your mind works

4 know your goal

methods for observing

unorthodox thinking

conscious choices

§8

§7

§5

§6

§4

§3

1 Living confidently

§9

§10

to manage or not to manage

summary: personal profile managing SpLD

BOOK 1 Finding Your Voice with Dyslexia and other SpLDs

rationale, frameworks

holistic vs. linear

senses

§3

§4

§5

Myers-Briggs Personality Type

§6

4 Thinking preferences

§7

Multiple Intelligences

§8

§9

sundry extras

thinking preferences in practice

a little physiology & psychology of emotions

§3

breathing

§4

5 Thinking clearly

§5

relaxation

§6

§7

Brain Gym

§9

§8

NLP

a little physiology

§3

2 About the mind

§4

§5

a little psychology

relevance to dyslexia/ SpLD

3 Using the mind

§3

§4

§6

§5

purposes of thinking

a model of learning

techniques to assist using your mind

cognition, awareness

the art of pausing and maintaining thinking clearly

other systems

Series name: Living Confidently with Specific Learning Difficulties (SpLDs)

4 Books by Ginny Stacey with Sally Fowler

BOOK 2 Organisation and Everyday Life with Dyslexia and other SpLDs

1 Organisation

2 Time, time management

3 Space, place, direction

examples of what can happen

§3

§7

§4

§5

§6

solutions for

general problem-solving

Everyday life

issues affecting organisation

working on organisation

learning to be organised

6 Employment

5 Study peripherals

Different, larger maps of each book: Book 1: p 25; Book 2: p 27

Contents p xviii   Where to start p viii

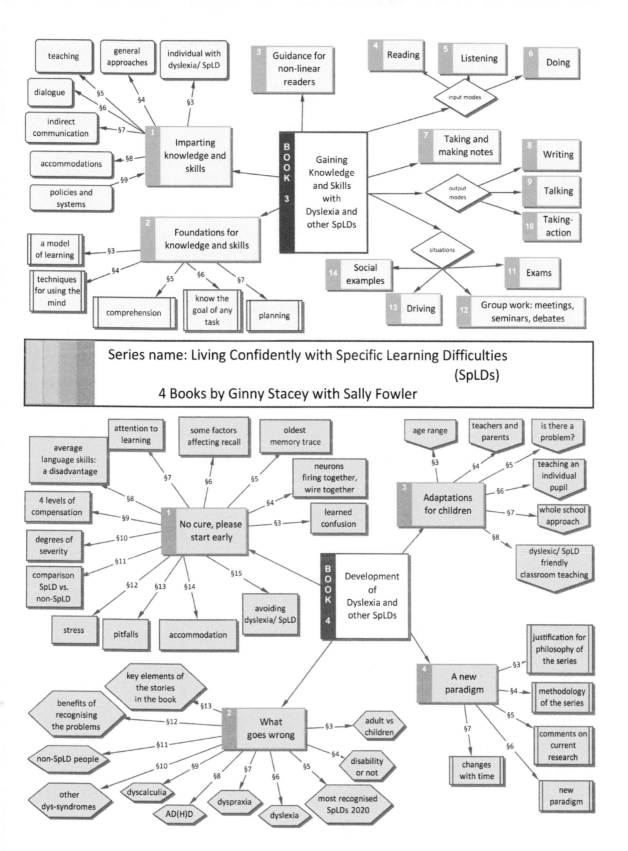

Series name: Living Confidently with Specific Learning Difficulties (SpLDs)

4 Books by Ginny Stacey with Sally Fowler

Different, larger maps of each book: Book 3: p 29; Book 4: p 31

Contents p xviii   Where to start p viii

Revised edition published 2021
by Routledge
2 Park Square, Milton Park, Abingdon, Oxon, OX14 4RN

and by Routledge
605 Third Avenue, New York, NY 10158

Routledge is an imprint of the Taylor & Francis Group, an informa business

First edition published by Routledge 2019

British Library Cataloguing-in-Publication Data
A catalogue record for this book is available from the British Library

Library of Congress Cataloging-in-Publication Data
Names: Stacey, Ginny, author. | Fowler, Sally (Dyslexia), author.
Title: Finding your voice with dyslexia and other SpLDs /
Ginny Stacey with Sara Fowler.
Other titles: Finding your voice with dyslexia/SpLD
Description: Revised edition. | London ; New York : Routledge, Taylor & Francis Group, 2021. | Revision of: Finding your voice with dyslexia/SpLD. 2019. |
Series: Living confidently with dyslexia and other specific learning difficulties (SpLDs) ; book 1 |
Includes bibliographical references and index. |
Identifiers: LCCN 2021020298 (print) | LCCN 2021020299 (ebook) |
ISBN 9781032066752 (hardback) |
ISBN 9781032066745 (paperback) |
ISBN 9781003203346 (ebook)
Subjects: LCSH: Dyslexia--Popular works.
Classification: LCC RC394.W6 S73 2021 (print) | LCC RC394.W6 (ebook) |
DDC 616.85/53--dc23
LC record available at https://lccn.loc.gov/2021020298
LC ebook record available at https://lccn.loc.gov/2021020299

ISBN: 978-1-032-06675-2 (hbk)
ISBN: 978-1-032-06674-5 (pbk)
ISBN: 978-1-003-20334-6 (ebk)

Typeset in Calibri
by Ginny Stacey

This book has been prepared from camera-ready copy prepared by the author.

Visit the companion website www.routledge.com/cw/stacey

Finding Your Voice
with
Dyslexia and other SpLDs

In the front cover image and the book icon,
the daisy represents growth.

Ginny Stacey
with Sally Fowler

Routledge
Taylor & Francis Group

LONDON AND NEW YORK

' "Know yourself" – that's the key message from this book. Images, both visual and written, analogies from maps to gardening, "insights" and movement ideas are used to understand dyslexia and other SpLDs. The layout helps us: clear font; text boxes; short blocks of text; mind maps; use of colour; glossary notes and clear routes or "pathways" through the different chapters which can be individualised. Lots of ideas here, so this book will help both dyslexic individuals and anyone who comes into contact with them – that is, all of us!'
– **Sally Daunt**, *SpLD support tutor, Liverpool Institute for Performing Arts, UK*

'*Finding Your Voice with Dyslexia and other SpLDs* is practical, personal and positive about dyslexic strengths, as well as providing ways to overcome the pitfalls. It offers a valuable balance of ideas, anecdotes and theory to enable the reader to work out the best ways to use their own individual thinking patterns. It has given me new insights into strategies to help my dyslexic students and I will be referring to it whenever I need inspiration in my teaching.'
– **Alex Brown**, *Specialist SpLD Support Tutor and Dyslexia Assessor, Member of Oxford SpLD Tutor Group, UK*

'What an amazing book! Ginny Stacey has been extraordinarily productive during lockdown with her series of 4 books. Here we have everything you could possibly need to find your voice as a dyslexic/ SpLD; impeccably organised in a series of mind maps and boxes to dip into. My dyslexic husband loved the plan!'
– **Angela Fawcett**, *Swansea University, UK*

Ginny Stacey is the author of these books. She discovered she was dyslexic in her 20s. She is a nationally recognised expert in the study of dyslexia/ SpLD. Committed to helping other dyslexic people achieve their potential, she has developed a range of highly effective techniques for supporting dyslexic students that are now widely used in universities and colleges. Ginny developed the dyslexia support system at Oxford Brookes University from 1991–2004 and held a post at Oxford University from 2005–2007. She has been a freelance dyslexia consultant since 1991.

Sally Fowler has been the back-up crew for these books. She discovered she was dyslexic in her 40s. She is an approved teacher for the British Dyslexia Association, with an MA in special education and has taught dyslexic children in schools and students at university. Sally taught at the Unicorn School in Abingdon, then a specialist school for dyslexia, and is a member of BDA and the Oxford SpLD Tutor Group. Since 2007, she has been a freelance support tutor.

Dedication

Dear fellow dyslexics,

The laughter we've shared tells me I'm on the right lines with my understanding of dyslexia. So do:

- the tears some of you have shed as you tell me your story and you know I hear
- the courage you've shown as you reveal your vulnerable side
- the joy you've known as you find ways to take charge of your dyslexia and run with it, not against it.

I hope this book will help many others to find their way through the trials and tribulations of dyslexia/ SpLD so that they can come out the other side to enjoy some of the good parts of being dyslexic/ SpLD.

SpLD = Specific Learning Difficulty
        dyslexia
        dyspraxia
        AD(H)D
        dyscalculia
see ⓖ p 350 for descriptions

Where to start:

- ## Linear readers, who like to read straight through:

In *Useful Preface:*

➢ Read *This Book: Finding Your Voice with Dyslexia and other SpLDs.*

➢ *The Series Living Confidently with Specific Learning Difficulties (SpLDs),* unless you have read another book of this series.

➢ Read sections marked with this book's icon.
Then read from Chapter 1.

- ## Non-linear readers, who prefer to move around a book:

A) Read the boxes in the *Useful Preface*
B) Choose one of these 5 suggestions:

1 Read the coloured boxes throughout the book and see what takes your interest.
2 Use the *Index* to find topics that interest you.
3 Use *Dipping-in to Try Out Ideas*, §1, in each chapter to find the most important topics.
4 Randomly move through the book to find what takes your interest.
5 Use the *Exercise: Initial Purpose for Reading* to create your own list of what you want to read first.

This Book: Finding Your Voice with Dyslexia and other SpLDs: p 19

The Series: Living Confidently with Specific Learning Difficulties (SpLDs): p 23

Useful Preface: p 0

Exercise: Initial Purpose for Reading: p 14

Tip: Reading Styles

It is useful to think about how you read.
See *Different Ways to Read:* p 9

---

§ = subsection

Ⓖ = *Glossary*

@ = Companion website
www.routledge.com/cw/stacey

Tip: This is a book to dip into. Solid reading is not necessary.

About the coloured boxes

Meaning of Box Colours

There are coloured boxes throughout the book:

 orange for stories

 orange for insights .

 green for exercises

 light blue for examples .

 purple for tips

dark blue for text and diagrams .

Contents of boxes:

> story: a narrative
> insight: story with added information; or an important point
> tip: contains a suggestion to help you make progress
> example: usually more general than a story; sometimes directly expanding
> on some part of the preceding text
> exercise: instructions to try out some idea(s)

Flow of boxes

The boxes are part of the text. They are often split across pages.

Tip: Finding Information

The *INDEX* is organised alphabetically, with some particularly useful groups of entries listed at the beginning.

The *GLOSSARY* Ⓖ has all the acronyms and symbols, as well as explanations of words and phrases. Page numbers are given for the different sections.

Summary of the chapters

Chapter 1 Living Confidently

Living Confidently as a dyslexic/ SpLD person often involves using thinking preferences (or unorthodox thinking) either unconsciously or consciously. When used consciously, there is the possibility to maximise your potential and minimise the effects of your dyslexia/ SpLD. A personal, individual profile of dyslexia/ SpLD is set out with four distinct elements. The chapter discusses different reasons for observing thinking with an open mind and ways in which it can be done. The process of building an individual profile is discussed. The chapter sets out a process for managing dyslexia/ SpLD. It ends with a summary of your individual profile and your personal regime for managing dyslexia/ SpLD.

Chapter 2 About the Mind

This chapter discusses some aspects of the brain and mind from physiology and psychology that are useful to know about in dealing with dyslexia/ SpLD.

Chapter 3 Using the Mind

The chapter discusses the purposes we have for using our minds and some techniques for using them better. The section on SYSTEMATIC REVIEWS is a method for exploring thinking preferences and developing them for individuals. Contributions from the faculty of knowing, cognition, are discussed. A model for learning concludes the chapter.

Chapter 4 Thinking Preferences

This chapter describes the thinking preferences that I have found useful while working with dyslexic/ SpLD people. It gives illustrations of strategies. It has stories and examples of how the strategies have been used. It describes some ways in which thinking can be unclear because a thinking preference is not used well.

Chapter 5 Thinking Clearly

The chapter discusses the interplay between different levels of being: mind, body and psyche (or spirit); and how work at both the physical and psychological levels can improve the clarity of thinking. Stories are told to help you relate to the ideas. Exercises and guidelines are given to help you maintain clear thinking.

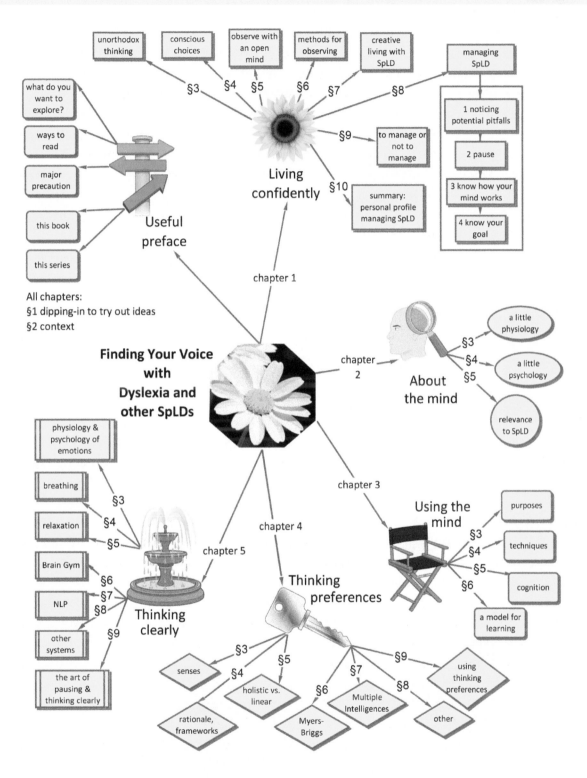

Acknowledgements

These books are the result of working with many, many dyslexia/ SpLD people since 1991. They have told me their stories; they have explored new ways of doing things; they have passed on the solutions they have found. I have worked with a few people with other disabilities or none. It has been a great adventure learning from them all.

I've also had conversations with many other people, sometimes deliberately, sometimes by chance – like a 20 minute conversation with a fellow passenger on a train. The books have benefitted from the ideas generated by the conversations.

My grateful thanks go to all these people.

I'd also like to thank colleagues in The Oxford SpLD Tutor Group, those at The University of Oxford and Oxford Brookes University for formal and informal exchange of ideas and experience. The network of support that we have between colleagues allows us to provide a high quality of support to the people we work with.

Several friends and colleagues have proof-read chapters for me in the final stages. Their comments have been very useful in clarifying the expression of my ideas. Sometimes their comments have re-enforced my view that the experience of dyslexia/ SpLD is foreign to the non-dyslexic/ SpLD world. If my expression occasionally seems strange to you, please wonder whether I'm saying something about dyslexia/ SpLD that is hard for a non-dyslexic/ SpLD person to understand since their minds simply don't give them the same experience.

I'm especially indebted to David Bullock who made 3 structures to lift my laptop, extended monitor, mouse and keyboard so that I worked standing and kept my brain's arousal system alert. Without these structures I would have struggled against the way words and my dyslexia send me to sleep. The final stages of preparing these books would have been months of awful struggle instead of the excitement I experienced.

I'd like to thank my family for their patience during the writing of these books. My husband deserves special mention for his encouragement, patience and his shed, which was my writing shed for many years.

Routledge and Taylor & Francis have been very patient with the time taken to convert the original single book into four standalone books. My commissioning editor, Lucy Kennedy, the assistant editor, Danielle Dyal, the production team leaders, Siân Cahill and Alison Macfarlane, and the proof-reader, Jackie Dias, have all done their best to understand and accommodate the unorthodox needs of dyslexic/ SpLD readers and my needs as a dyslexic author. My thanks to everyone who has been involved with this project.

I'd like to thank Carl Wenczek, of Born Digital Ltd., for tuition and much advice on dealing with my illustrations. I couldn't have managed all the visual components and figures without his guidance.

I have been extremely fortunate to benefit from Mike Standing's experience as a retired production manager of a printing company. He came and guided me through many details of the printing process as I undertook author typesetting of these books. Without his input, the typesetting process would have been a horrible struggle.

And finally, my thanks go to Sally Fowler who has accompanied me throughout the writing of the series. When I've been daunted or hit a blank patch, Sally's encouragement and enthusiasm have carried me through. Without Sally's belief in this work, the project would not have been finished.

Author typesetting revision

Do you ever find that you get to the end of doing something for the first time and you think:

> "OK. I get it now. I can see what it's all about.
> I know what to do. Please can I start again, for real?"

Many of us need to work our way through a system completely, to iron out all the hazards and incomprehensible non-dyslexic/ SpLD ways, and then go through the system in our own way.

Writing these books has been a bit like that. The first edition of this book showed up so many mismatches between my ideas to meet the needs of dyslexic/ SpLD readers and standard publishing expectations that Routledge and Taylor & Francis came to the conclusion we'd all be better off if the rest were author typeset. With some relief and optimism, I agreed.

It was a bit of an 'I wouldn't start from here' situation: MS Word is not designed for complex publishing, but that's what I'd used and all the text was basically written; it was only waiting to be put into the right layout – of course it got changed along the way. I'm now quite skilled at persuading Word to do what I want it to. I've also learned to manipulate images and create scalar vector graphics; these skills I'm delighted to have.

As I worked on the books, I knew I was making decisions that were based on significant experience of dyslexia/ SpLD – decisions that would be quite hard for anyone else to make.

In the first edition, some of the text ended up in surprising places; that has been put right. The title of the book has changed because computer searches didn't like the '/' in the original title. The book now follows the design details that characterise the other three books.

In working on this book again and while at the finishing proof stage of book 3, *Gaining Knowledge and Skills with Dyslexia and other SpLDs*, I realised that I hadn't thought through the use of our senses, their connection with thinking, and how they are used in reading and writing. I had linked reading and writing with the visual sense, which is ironic since some professionals regard the phonic element of dyslexia to have supreme eminence to the exclusion of all other possible contributing causes.

In education and communication, verbal and visual thinking abilities are well catered for. My students have shown me that kinaesthetic abilities need to be included as well. For some students, if kinaesthetic thinking is not engaged in their learning they find that learning very difficult.

In wanting to bring the kinaesthetic thinking to the fore, I wanted two means of communication that could be used in parallel with reading and writing, and with listening and talking.

So I had a neat table:

sense	acquiring	applying
visual	reading	writing
verbal	listening	speaking
kinaesthetic	doing	taking-action.

It was while I was tidying up this book in the author typesetting process, that I realised reading and writing are just as much verbal thinking as listening and speaking.

My understanding now is:
our physical senses are: visual, aural, touch, smell and taste
kinaesthetic sense: it is useful to expand the sense of touch by including our sense of the position of our body and movements
we process the signals from our senses in ways that are outside the scope of this book
there are differences in the ways we can think depending on connections with the various senses
we can usefully talk about three different sense-based memory and thinking systems: visual, verbal and kinaesthetic
those who show a preference for one of these sense-based systems can be called: visual thinkers, verbal thinkers or kinaesthetic thinkers; when appropriate, 'learners' instead of 'thinkers'

visual thinking and verbal thinking have been well researched and are included in models
  of working memory
the work with my students, and my own experience, have shown me the need to include
  kinaesthetic thinking.

My neat table remains but without the initial sense column:

acquiring	*applying*
reading	writing
listening	speaking
doing	taking-action.

I'm happy to say that this different approach has not fundamentally changed any of the
other information or insights in this series of books, though the change in terminology has
percolated into many different sections of this book.

Addendum

After this revision was submitted and before it went to the production department of T&F,
I was drawing figures of neurons firing and wiring together and I wanted to make sure the
figures were accurate. Reading further about neuron connections made me think about
situations in which neurons can be wired unequally. If there is a stronger influence that
prevents the learning that a dyslexic/ SpLD person is trying to achieve, the task of trying to
learn may generate the chaotic neural networks mentioned in THE PHILOSOPHY OF THE SERIES
(p 4).

The ADDENDUM: A ROLE FOR NEURONS (p 364) sets out my hypothesis that dyslexia/ SpLD
develops when constitutional elements and psychological characteristics of dyslexia/ SpLD,
through neurons firing-and-wiring and neuronal pruning, produce well established
neuronal networks that do not conform to the expected outcomes of education.
The hypothesis applies to all the syndromes of SpLD.

There is still debate as to whether dyslexia exists or not.   This hypothesis provides a
missing link that answers many of the questions about dyslexia and how to cater for
dyslexic learners.

I am very grateful to Lucy Kennedy, my commissioning editor, for allowing the inclusion of
the addendum.

Illustrations

Illustration acknowledgements and key to symbols

❖   Complete figures created using Inspiration® 9, a product of Inspiration Software®, Inc.

✍   Photos or drawings created by Ginny Stacey.

O   Material by Routledge/ Taylor & Francis.

⚐   Other figures whose sources are acknowledged in the text.

Throughout the book

❖   Mind maps for *USEFUL PREFACE* and all the chapters

O   The icons for the series, books and chapters were created by Routledge/ Taylor & Francis and inserted into the mind maps or other diagrams as appropriate

Front Matter

❖   The series mind map inside the cover   p ii, iii

❖   The book mind map   p xi

Illustrations in ADDENDUM are on page xxv

Contents

Useful Preface   This is worth reading

 Marks sections where some or all of the text is specific to this book.

Chapter 1 Living Confidently

Chapter 2   About the Mind

Chapter 3   Using the Mind

Chapter 4   Thinking Preferences

Chapter 4   Thinking Preferences *continued*

Chapter 5   Thinking Clearly

Chapter 5   Thinking Clearly *continued*

 Appendix 1   Resources

 **Appendix 2   Individual, Personal Profile of Dyslexia/ SpLD and
Regime for Managing Dyslexia/ SpLD**

Appendix 3   Key Concepts

 Appendix 4   Group Work

Glossary

List of Templates on the Website

Addendum   A Role for Neurons

Index

Addendum: A Role for Neurons   *Illustrations continued from page xvii*

Useful Preface
This is worth reading

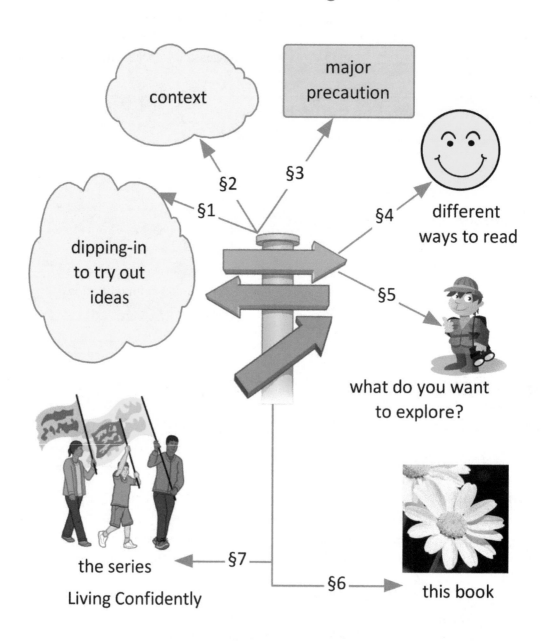

context

major precaution

different ways to read

§2

§3

§1

dipping-in
to try out
ideas

§4

§5

what do you want
to explore?

the series

Living Confidently

§7

§6

this book

Contents

Ⓖ p 350: SpLD: specific learning difficulty of which dyslexia is the best known and most widely researched

---

Insight: What to expect from this book

The book is not like a travel book: it doesn't tell you where to go, although it contains many suggestions.

It is more like a book telling you how to read maps and how to read the environment that you find yourself in.

So it's a book about finding your best ways to be, think and do.

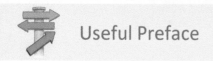

Useful Preface summary

This preface is similar in the four books.

 The book icon shows the sections that are particular to this book. The left margin blue line shows the length of these sections.

Templates on the website

TEMPLATES

COMPANION @ WEBSITE

A1   *JOTTING DOWN AS YOU SCAN*

A2   *BOOKMARK – PURPOSE*

A4   *JOTTING DOWN AS YOU READ*

A5   *COLLECTING IDEAS THAT INTEREST YOU*

Appendix 1 Resources

COLLECTING INFORMATION TOGETHER has ideas to help you be systematic about the way you gather information together.

COLLECTING INFORMATION TOGETHER: p 302

1   Dipping-in to try out ideas

Read *INSIGHT: WHAT TO EXPECT FROM THIS BOOK,* above.

Read *§3, MAJOR PRECAUTION.*

Do the *EXERCISE: AVOID MORE PROBLEMS WHEN LEARNING NEW SKILLS.*

Read the 3 boxes in *§2, CONTEXT.*

§3: p 7

EXERCISE: AVOID MORE PROBLEMS ... p 8

§2: p 3

2　Context

Story: Two dyslexic sailors

Scene: sailing on a yacht belonging to John. I had to learn the sequence for turning on the engine safely.

"I just can't do it that way! I know how my mind works. I've been teaching in the field for ages. You've got to listen to me! Let me ask my questions. Let me understand. Then I will be able to do it."

The frustration of being faced with another dyslexic person who WILL NOT LISTEN!

Both of us are fairly stubborn because we've individually worked out what we need to do to succeed and we're both teachers in different fields. We just don't happen to have the same thinking preferences.

In this situation, I'm slightly at a disadvantage because I'm the novice in John's field and there's no way either of us want me to go into my professional role to analyse his strategies.

We simply both want me to learn to switch the engine on.

If I hadn't found my voice, there was no way I could find my way through my friend's view of how to learn (but see *Margin Note*).

Margin Note:
I appreciated John's approach when he used it to help me up and down a 604m climb beside a Norwegian fjord.

As we learn we change the workings of our minds. There are changes at the neuron level of the brain. Efficient learning results in good neural networks.

Ⓖ p 353:
neural networks

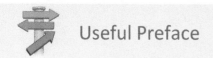

The following analogy helps you to think about neural networks.

Insight: Park paths and pruning neurons

If a park has no fences round it, people will walk across in many different directions.

If a park has 2 gates on opposite sides of the park, people will walk across in a straight line between the gates. A definite path will show where the grass is worn away.

If the park has several gates either side, there will be a series of paths linking the various gates.

When a baby is born, the brain is like the unfenced park: few routes have been established through the brain to respond to the world around.

As a result of good learning, definite neuronal networks become established with use; this is the result of neuronal pruning. The single path is the analogy for non-dyslexia/ SpLD.

The park with several gates either side and many paths linking them is the analogy for dyslexia/ SpLD.

Ⓖ p 353: pruning, neuron

This analogy is also used in the *ADDENDUM:* p 364

Neuronal pruning: Kolb (1995)

The philosophy of this series

The philosophy of this series of books is that we, dyslexic/ SpLD people, can work out how our minds work, we can direct our thinking so that it is as effective as possible and we can enjoy contributing to the situations that we find ourselves in (see *MARGIN NOTE*).

We then have ownership of our thinking and actions. We can achieve to the level of our individual potential. We can confidently take our place alongside everyone else in the situations in which we find ourselves. We know how to *MANAGE*

MARGIN NOTE: As so often, this is good practice for everyone, but VITAL for dyslexic/ SpLDs.

OUR DYSLEXIA/ SPLD. We can co-operate with others to minimise the effects of our dyslexia/ SpLD on our own lives and on the lives of those who live, work or engage in action with us.

Dyslexia/ SpLD is not seen as a static phenomenon, like short-sightedness that only slowly changes with time. Dyslexia/ SpLD is seen as a collection of chaotic[1] neural networks that can exist alongside more useful networks, see MATURED DYSLEXIA/ SPLD.

Once the chaotic neural networks have established, dyslexia/ SpLD has developed. The chaotic neural networks are not destroyed when the more useful networks are established; they can lie dormant for a significant amount of time; they can be triggered into use in different ways. However well you manage it, you are always at risk of being as thoroughly dyslexic/ SpLD as ever.

The collection of chaotic neural networks will vary from person to person, even with the same dyslexia/ SpLD label.

Underlying the networks is a constitutional level of difference, which, when ignored, leads to the establishment of the chaotic neural networks. The constitutional level of difference is the permanent part of dyslexia/ SpLD. The chaotic neural networks are the source of the observed, problematic behaviours.

A child born with the differences at the constitutional level is 'at risk' of dyslexia/ SpLD. When recognised early in the development of learned networks, the constitutional differences do not have to lead to chaotic neural networks, though it may be impossible to prevent all of them. The unorthodox thinking processes that many successful dyslexic/ SpLDs enjoy will still develop, since they

REGIME FOR MANAGING DYSLEXIA/ SPLD: p 71

MATURED DYSLEXIA/ SPLD: p 369

For further exploration of these ideas, see ADDENDUM: p 364

Ⓖ p 353: neural networks

---

[1]Chaos theory: when asked to spell a word, many dyslexic people have a collection of possibilities, for example sense, sens, cens, sns, scens. Each of these possibilities is the product of neural networks that connect the prompt to spell the word to the action of spelling it. By practice of the 'correct spelling' these alternative spellings are expected to be reduced (pruned) to only one, resulting in a stable neural network to achieve the correct spelling. That dyslexics continue throughout life with the variable spelling, shows this pruning isn't working for them and the implied collection of neural networks behind the variations is what I mean by 'chaotic neural networks'. The idea comes from my understanding of chaos theory (Gleick, 1997).

Ⓖ p 353: chaos theory

are needed very early in learning to prevent establishment of the chaotic neural networks.

John is typical of many successful dyslexic/ SpLDs who have got through life without any special attention. They may have used:

John is in *TWO DYSLEXIC SAILORS*: p 3

hard work

sheer determination (John: bloody-mindedness)

winging it

the gift of the gab

secretaries, parents, spouse or partner, children, friends

one or two teachers with just the right approach

pot luck

apprenticeships, or other routes to the top from the shop floor, etc.

'other' (always a necessary option).

Whatever the route, they succeeded and they don't see what all the fuss is about now. They are the lucky ones; they made it to success. Many of their contemporaries didn't achieve very much; they can be dissatisfied with life and what they contribute.

Dyslexia/ SpLD, education and beyond

The educational system used to have elements that suited dyslexic/ SpLDs better than current systems do, and it was possible to get promotion without having to produce certificates that showed what qualifications you had.

There are changes afoot, but not ones that look likely to take us back to a regime that will suit most dyslexic/ SpLDs.

Society, workplace practices and education may change to be more sympathetic to dyslexic/ SpLD people (and to those with other disabilities); assistive technology allows access to modern communication systems; but without finding your own voice you aren't fully the person you could be; in using that voice to communicate with others you need listeners who can hear what you are saying: these last two objectives are the main aims of this series.

Proverb: 'Give a man a fish and you feed him for a day; teach a man to fish and you feed him for a lifetime.'

3 Major precaution

Protection from further dyslexic/ SpLD problems is an important aspect of managing dyslexia/ SpLD.

Insight: Anything 'new' needs care

You need to be very careful in the initial stages of a subject, or situation, even before you start to make sense of it. You can too easily create an unhelpful memory that interrupts your thinking for a very long time.

Example: A problem created at an initial stage

After some 20 years of playing the guitar, my sight reading is still impaired by an early mistake.

One note (B on the treble clef) is an open string for a beginner, i.e. no left hand finger is needed to play it. In musical notation, this note is a blob with a line through it (it is the middle line of the treble clef).

'Blob on a line' equated to 'finger on a string' when I first met it, and it still does. I still have to work really hard to remember the note is an open string; I have to work hard to stop myself putting a finger on a string.

I didn't know then how to manage my dyslexia. Now I know that I have to be careful, particularly at the beginning of something new.

**Exercise: Avoid more problems
when learning new skills[2]**

- What were the skills you learnt most recently?
- How did you learn them?
- What task was involved?
- How important are the skills to you?
- What made them easy to learn?
- What was hard about learning them?
- How easily have you been able to adapt the skills to other uses?

Reflection question: Is it a good idea to try out something new on tasks that are really important to you?

- It is OK if you can easily make changes to the way you do something later.

- It is not OK if you find the first way you tackle something leaves a strong impression.

- If this is your experience, try out new systems or skills on tasks that you don't mind about too much but that you are quite interested in.

- It is not OK if you are likely to think: "Can I trust this new approach? Will it muck up this task or topic?" Doubt like this will not allow you to explore the new approach freely.

- If in any doubt, use a task or topic that doesn't matter too much first; struggling with dyslexic/ SpLD tangles is such a pain, it's worth avoiding new problems.

- You won't give a new skill or system a fair trial, if you are worried about it or the task.

This green colour is recommended for colour blind people on the website of Okabe and Ito (Accessed 12 Feb 2021)

---

[2] The way many dyslexic/ SpLD people have to pay attention to learning may mean first learning makes more of an impression than it does for other learners.

4 Different ways to read

You may not like reading. Many dyslexic/ SpLD people don't.
Do take notice of the message in *Something Goes Wrong with Reading*: the author's style can cause problems.

Something Goes Wrong with Reading: p 11

Tip: Margin

You can use the right-hand margin to jot down your ideas as you scan or read the book.

I have used it for cross-referencing and for references to help you find these when you want them.

The books in this series are written with several different styles of reading in mind.

Margin Note: the different ways of reading relate to *Thinking Preferences:* p 188 and in *Index*

You need to decide what your style of reading should be; do *Exercise: Reading Style*. You may find a new style that suits you. Different styles might suit you at different times or for different purposes.

Exercise: Reading Style: p 11

	The reading style is in green; the writing styles in this book are in blue.
Linear readers	People who read easily, starting at the beginning of a book.
	The books are written with a flow of information that can be read from beginning to end.
Spatial readers	People who would read best by moving about a book, finding the most relevant parts first.
	Each chapter starts with a *Dipping-in* section that helps the reader choose the best way to dip-in.
Framework readers	People who need an overview to be able to understand. Some people's brains don't retain information unless they have thought about the framework, or schema, that holds it all together.

Ⓖ p 353: framework, schema

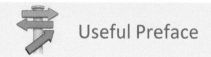

Framework readers continued	The *Philosophy of this Series* is one framework of the series.	*Philosophy of this Series:* p 4
	Each chapter has a contents list and a mind map at the beginning to help people understand the author's overview.	
	Rationale or Framework discusses the importance of establishing a schema.	*Rationale or Framework:* p 216
Sense-oriented readers	Some people's understanding is dependent on the sense(s) they use. They may not use the senses equally. Vision, aural and the kinaesthetic sense are the most commonly used ones in education. People vary: of these three senses, sometimes one or another is very much more used, or one may be decidedly less used than the other two. Smell and taste are also senses and may need to be considered.	Senses: visual, aural, kinaesthetic (G) p 353: kinaesthetic *Margin Note:* kinaesthetic processing uses touch, body perception and physical movement to good effect
	1) Visual: different layouts are used to indicate different types of information. For example: exercises for the reader are in green boxes. Cartoons and figures are used.	
	2) Verbal: the language is direct, not complicated, but elegant (at least that is the intention).	*Visual Thinking:* p 200 and in *Index*
	3) Kinaesthetic: there are exercises for the reader which should engage the kinaesthetic sense; as should the anecdotes about the actions of others.	*Aural and Verbal Thinking:* p 201 and in *Index* *Kinaesthetic Thinking:* p 206 and in *Index*
Interest-oriented readers	Some people use their strongest interests in order to understand; they cannot retain information if these interests are not actively engaged.	
	1) Any reader for whom interest is a key issue should use the *Myers-Briggs Personality Type* and *Multiple Intelligences* sections of *Chapter 4*, to work out what their innate interests might be and deliberately use them while reading these books.	*Myers-Briggs Personality Type:* p 227 *Multiple Intelligences:* p 239

Interest-oriented readers *continued*	2) Material can be written bearing in mind different interests by presenting different perspectives. The suggested *ROUTES* on the *WEBSITE* for various reader groups are examples of catering for different perspectives.
Further comment	If two or more people are using the book together, the different styles of reading should be accommodated.

ROUTES

4.1 Exercise: reading style

Exercise: Reading style

Consider which styles of reading might suit you:

> Why might they suit you?
>
> Which have you tried already?
>
> Which work most of the time/ sometimes/ never?
>
> Which sound worth experimenting with?
>
> What do you know already about your way of reading?

See examples in *DIFFERENT WAYS TO READ:* p 19

4.2 Something goes wrong with reading

If you are struggling with reading, it is important to check whether there is anything that can be done about it.

For example, going to sleep over reading can indicate that the brain is taking in too much material that has not been understood properly.

There are many approaches to make reading effective that do not involve the mechanics of reading. The full discussion of reading is in *Gaining Knowledge and Skills with Dyslexia and other SpLDs* (Stacey, 2021b). The discussion includes ways in which an author's style of writing is unhelpful to dyslexic/ SpLDs.

Stacey (2021b)

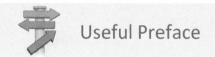

Insight: External factors hamper reading

Reading difficulties can be made a lot worse by the way the text is written or presented. They aren't just from your dyslexia/ SpLD.

Insight: Word changes cause doubt

Some authors don't like to repeat the same word too many times, so they change the word even though the idea hasn't changed.

Do you ever find that you then start to doubt your reading ability? It's as if your mind is worrying because you may have missed some significant detail that the change of words indicates. Then gradually, your reading skill deserts you; you struggle; you end up sleeping over the text, even when you are very interested in it.

Sometimes in this series, I have deliberately not changed words, even though the repetition is rather tedious.

5 What do you want to explore?

One key tactic for making reading easier is to prime your mind, rather like warming up muscles. No serious sportsman would start their sport without warming up their muscles. The mind can be looked after in the same way.

Tip: Know your reason for reading

When you identify your main purpose for reading anything, you give your mind some guidelines for understanding what you are reading.

You then allow yourself to explore the text, looking to satisfy your purpose; reading is much easier.

Dyslexia and the other specific learning difficulties (SpLDs) have wide-spread impact on our lives.

Ginny Stacey and Sally Fowler are both dyslexic, in different ways!

This book is worth reading because:

- it covers many different aspects of being dyslexic/ SpLD
- it allows you to find your best way of managing your dyslexia/ SpLD
- it teaches you some ideas about the mind that help with dyslexia/ SpLD
- it teaches you some useful mental techniques
- it allows you to find your thinking preferences
- it helps you to keep building your best way of managing your dyslexia/ SpLD.

Any of these topics in the book could be part of your purpose for reading.

5.1 Initial purpose for reading

The following exercise is designed to help establish any reader's initial purpose: you are effectively creating your own dipping-in list.

Exercise: Initial purpose for reading

1 Use the TEMPLATE: *A1 - JOTTING DOWN AS YOU SCAN* to keep track of ideas.

   1.1 Remember you are scanning for this exercise, not reading. You are finding the sections most interesting to you now.

TEMPLATES

2 Scan the following places to find ideas that catch your interest:

   2.1 point 1.1 above, to remember to scan

   2.2 the orange insight boxes in this chapter

   2.3 the *TABLE OF READER GROUPS, §5.2*

   2.4 the themes in *§5.3, READING TO FIND OUT ABOUT A THEME*

   2.5 *§6, THIS BOOK: FINDING YOUR VOICE WITH DYSLEXIA AND OTHER SpLDS*

   2.6 *§7, THE SERIES: LIVING CONFIDENTLY WITH SPECIFIC LEARNING DIFFICULTIES (SpLDS)*

   2.7 the *CONTENTS* of the book

   2.8 the *INDEX*.

§5.2: p 15
§5.3: p 18
§6: p 19
§7: p 23

CONTENTS: p xviii
INDEX: p 379

3 For each idea that catches your attention:

   3.1 note where in the book the idea is

   3.2 why the idea interests you

   3.3 how important the idea is to you immediately and in the longer-term.

4 Think about your life:

   4.1 What issues to do with dyslexia/ SpLD do you want to understand or solve?

   4.2 What situations in everyday life, employment or study are affected by your dyslexia/ SpLD, or might be affected?

NB: you are creating your personal dipping-in list.

5 Look at the list of ideas you have made.

   5.1 Are there any common threads that could be grouped together? Use *TEMPLATE: A5 - COLLECTING IDEAS THAT INTEREST YOU* to gather the common threads.

TEMPLATES

5.2 Number the ideas in the order that you would like to explore them now.

5.3 Write the ideas on the *Template: A2 - Bookmark – Purpose* in the order that you want to explore them. The *Bookmark – Purpose* will remind you what you have decided to explore.

6 Start reading. Use *Template: A4 - Jotting Down as You Read*, or any other template, to capture insights as you read.

 ## 5.2 Reader groups

One way of giving your mind the guidelines that assist reading is to recognise why you want to acquire any new information.

I have thought about different reader groups with slightly different reasons for reading this book. These are shown in the table *Reader Groups.*

This section gives the profile of each group.

The *website*

has further reader groups for the whole series.

Reader groups
A   Dyslexic/ SpLD readers wanting:
A1   to understand what happens to them
A2   to solve problems
A3   to apply how they think best.
B   Non-dyslexic/ SpLD people wanting:
B1   to understand more about ways dyslexic/ SpLDs manage their lives
B2   to use the many ideas that are good practice for all while being VITAL for dyslexic/ SpLDs.

Decide which reader group(s) you belong to.

Why do you choose the group(s)?

What information are you looking for? Use *Reading to Find Out about a Theme*, below, and *Aims, Outcomes and Benefits* to help you decide.

Aims, Outcomes and Benefits: p 21

A1-A3: Dyslexic/ SpLD people

These groups include those who have formal diagnostic assessments and those who suspect they belong to the dyslexic/ SpLD group. They need to know as much as possible about themselves in order to gain autonomy.

The groups are distinguished by three approaches:

- wanting to understand what happens
- wanting to solve problems
- wanting to apply how they think best.

As far as final outcomes are concerned, there is no difference between these three groups. The initial approach is likely to be quite different.

B1: Non-dyslexic/ SpLD people

wanting to understand more about ways dyslexic/ SpLDs manage their lives

The art of living with differences is fundamental to good relationships between people across the dyslexic/ SpLD and non-dyslexic/ SpLD divide.

Non-dyslexic/ SpLD people who live with dyslexic/ SpLDs often feel they don't understand how the dyslexic/ SpLDs function. There can be considerable tension when communication is not straightforward. Knowing much more about the impacts of dyslexia/ SpLD should help to improve the quality of communication.

Those working with dyslexic/ SpLDs or engaging with them in other everyday activities (i.e. 'in action with') may need a good understanding of dyslexia/ SpLD, though there are times when communication works well regardless. Reactions due to lack of clear communication could be easier to deal with when the people involved are not living in the same place.

People in the media have an important role. Knowing more about the wider impact of dyslexia/ SpLD, they could help change attitudes towards these syndromes.

autonomy: control over your life by self-determination: acting and thinking for yourself; independent; free; self-governing

MARGIN NOTE FOR READER GROUPS A1-A3: the world around you needs to understand what is happening to you.

16

We need a culture in which:

- dyslexic/ SpLD people encountering a difficulty can talk openly about it
- there is a willingness to look for alternative approaches to problems and to develop solutions
- there is a relaxed acceptance of differences
- there is a focus on potential achievement and not difficulties.

Good signage and communication styles can make a significant improvement to the ease with which dyslexic/ SpLD people can gain information. Communicators should know the techniques, often simple, that improve the clarity of communication for dyslexic/ SpLD people.

There are people whose communication and dealings with dyslexic/ SpLD people can have long-lasting effects on the lives of the dyslexic/ SpLD people. It is really important that any impact of the dyslexia/ SpLD is clearly and fairly dealt with.

Misunderstandings and difficulties in communication may be obvious to both sides but they can also be hidden because neither group of people is paying any attention to differences in thinking styles and different interpretations during the communication.

Dyslexia/ SpLDs are hidden: you cannot look at one of this group of people and say, "That person has dyslexia/ SpLD, I need to be aware of that." Much of the general approach to dyslexia/ SpLD is about courtesy between people; an increase in courtesy would be beneficial to society at large.

Policy-makers and politicians, especially, need to be well informed at a general level of interest because policies built on incomplete knowledge can be harmful and expensive.

B2:   Non-dyslexic/ SpLD people
        to use the many ideas that are good practice for all while being
        VITAL for dyslexic/ SpLDs

There are many ideas that apply to people in general. Non-dyslexic/ SpLD readers can find ideas to improve their approach to many tasks or situations.

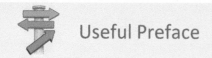

5.3   Reading to find out about a theme

Dyslexia/ SpLD impacts on the whole of life.

There may be a particular aspect of your life that you want to explore first.

In thinking how a dyslexic/ SpLD person might approach the material, I put together several different themes.

The themes relevant to this book are listed below. The full list of themes in the series is on the *WEBSITE*, with where to find the discussions.

THEMES

 The themes that are relevant to this book include:

> Finding your voice

- Objective observation
- Living confidently
    - o Collecting together a regime for managing dyslexia/ SpLD
    - o Building an individual, personal profile
    - o Gaining insights
- Using the mind well
- Thinking preferences
- Pausing and maintaining clear thinking

The themes for the rest of the series come under the general headings of:

> Everyday life, education, employment including:

- Pitfalls of dyslexia/ SpLD
- Accommodations for dyslexia/ SpLD

> Thinking, knowledge and skills

> Understanding and dialogue

6 This book: *Finding Your Voice with Dyslexia and other SpLDs*

6.1 Different ways of thinking

Story: Different ways of thinking

Pacing about he said,
"I don't think in straight lines."

He sat down, shut his eyes and drew with both hands, in the air at face level,

"The theory about cities is somewhere in the middle. Over here on the right is everything known about the Ubaid culture[3]: the houses, relationships, farming, crops, …. It's all in 3-D. Over here on the left is Uruk, connected to the Ubaid, but different. It develops quite differently."

and his hand moved to a lower space on the left.

"Then you have to expand to take in the whole region and it all joins up with theories about cities."

His hands took a wide sweep just above the desk and came back up to the level of his face where he had started with the theory of cities.

As he spoke, I drew symbols on an A3 page.
Sam opened his eyes, looked at the shapes I'd drawn and said:
"The shapes need to have pictures or symbols".

Sam is dyslexic and dyspraxic. He needs to know how he can organise his thoughts and how to use mental pictures to make his thoughts vivid. When he's speaking or writing, he needs to focus on his mental construct and let the words follow the route he takes through it. He will get in a muddle if he tries to think about the words too early or if he tries to create a linear plan.

---

[3] Ubaid and Uruk are early periods of civilisation. Sam was studying archaeology.

Dyslexic/ SpLD people don't all think like Sam. They each have their own style and own experiences, but knowing how they each think well and being able to use that method to manage their dyslexia/ SpLD is an essential element to minimise the effects.

Dyslexic/ SpLD people are also different from the majority of people. You can't take for granted that there is a shared experience of how the world works, of how everyday living progresses. It can be difficult to find the right vocabulary to convey ideas and experience to those who don't have the same quirks of mind or instincts. It is as if you have no voice to speak with.

FINDING YOUR VOICE WITH DYSLEXIA AND OTHER SPLDS is about living with dyslexia and various other specific learning difficulties. 'Voice' in this context indicates the ability to express your ideas and feelings; it is more than the ability to produce words through your mouth or a computer.

Insight: How you function

You can get to know what helps you to function as a person by:

- understanding how you think,
- knowing what you can do to keep your thinking clear,
- knowing how you can contribute to any situation in which you find yourself.

You gain self-esteem; you gain confidence to tackle what life (study, employment, general living) brings you; you find out how to negotiate with those around you so that life flows more satisfactorily both for you and them:

You Find Your Voice.

Once you have found your 'voice' the adventure of living life to the full can be undertaken with a different integrity.

MARGIN NOTE: The Ship That Found Herself by Rudyard Kipling (1898) is a good story that illustrates the integrity of finding yourself.

6.2   Aims, outcomes and benefits

Understanding how to think well has an impact on learning well. Most of learning can be fun while still requiring effort and practice. I still enjoy learning, but if I feel I am putting in a lot of effort without much progress, I stop and look at how I'm learning and see what I can do to alter the progress-to-effort balance. The same is true for almost any situation in everyday life or during employment: if you know how you think well and you can keep your thinking clear, you have the best chance of making the most of the situation.

Margin note:
The *Addendum: A Role for Neurons*: p 364, describes a new hypothesis about dyslexia/ SpLD which it is hoped will contribute significantly to our understanding.

Insight: Gardening analogy for good thinking

Getting yourself to think well can be helped when you know:

- how you might use the processes of the mind in conscious ways

- what your thinking preferences are, and whether you need to pay attention to them

- how to keep your mind functioning in the best possible way.

These three aspects of thinking well can be compared with growing plants well, which includes:

- knowing how plants grow well

- choosing the plants to grow

- improving and maintaining best growing conditions.

Chapter 2, About the Mind, and *Chapter 3, Using the Mind*, are equivalent to knowing how plants grow well; *Chapter 4, Thinking Preferences*, is equivalent to choosing the plants to grow; and *Chapter 5, Thinking Clearly*, is equivalent to improving and maintaining the best growing conditions.

To complete the analogy, *Chapter 1, Living Confidently*, is equivalent to tools and a garden shed.

About the Mind: p 86

Using the Mind: p 138

Thinking Preferences: p 188

Thinking Clearly: p 254

Living Confidently: p 38

These are not linear steps in either thinking or gardening. In gardening, you need to know about your growing conditions (e.g. what sort of soil you have) at the same time as you think about your plants. Similarly with thinking, you need to be aware of all three aspects together.

The ideas in this book can be useful to anyone, with or without a specific learning difficulty. Those without usually find their minds develop good thinking naturally, i.e. without deliberate effort on their part. Those with dyslexia/ SpLD usually only develop good thinking with conscious attention to thinking processes themselves.

6.3   Caveat about the theories used in this book

The work in this book is essentially practical and varied. Certain theories have been used to provide a language for discussion, but the discussion is not dependent on any of the theories being 'true' for all people all of the time. If the theories are extended or disproved then some other system of language will be needed for discussion of the things that happen.

At the time of finishing this book, 3 theories might be queried: Left-Brain Right-Brain, Brain Gym, and Myers-Briggs Personality Type. In all situations, you use what suits a particular dyslexia/ SpLD person, you ignore anything that doesn't work for that person and you always have the option 'other' available to ensure an open mind.

Ⓖ p 353: 'other'

Holistic vs. linear is often used now instead of Left-Brain, Right-Brain. Some of the books using the old terminology are still worth reading.

Movement can be beneficial in a variety of circumstances. Brain Gym can be used as a deliberate injection of movement for a break.

Myers-Briggs Personality Type (MBPT) can be mapped on to Multiple Intelligences (MI) theory reasonably well. MBPT is based on 8 pairs of contrasting behaviour patterns which are very useful for discussing some of the problems that occur when working with dyslexic/ SpLD people; these contrasting patterns are not part of MI theory.

7 The Series: *Living Confidently with Specific Learning Difficulties (SpLDs)*

7.1 Readership/ audience

Living Confidently with Specific Learning Difficulties (SpLDs) is a series of books that look at the whole of the experience of living with these specific learning difficulties.

Descriptions in ⓖ p 351 of 4 SpLDs:
dyslexia
dyspraxia
AD(H)D
dyscalculia

The ideas described in this series draw on work over 25 years helping individuals to find out how their minds work and how to use them effectively in study or everyday life.

Finding Your Voice with Dyslexia and other SpLDs and *Organisation and Everyday Life with Dyslexia and other SpLDs* are both written addressing dyslexic/ SpLD people.

Gaining Knowledge and Skills with Dyslexia and other SpLDs and *Development of Dyslexia and other SpLDs* both address people in roles alongside a dyslexic/ SpLD person.

Each book can be used on its own, but there are some concepts that spread over the four. The KEY CONCEPTS are summarised in APPENDIX 3.

APPENDIX 3: p 328

7.2 Summary of the series

Life is a journey. We need to find our way through it.

We need our own voice to help us navigate.

Living Confidently with Specific Learning Difficulties (SpLDs) is about living life to the full and enjoying the journey, each person using her maximum potential and minimising the effects of her dyslexia/ SpLD.

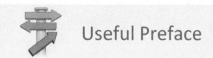

Book 1: *Finding Your Voice with Dyslexia and other SpLDs* (Stacey, 2021a)
The book is written for dyslexic/ SpLD people and contains:

- building a personal, individual profile
  - thinking preferences
  - pitfalls
  - ways to pause well
  - accommodations

- four steps for managing dyslexia/ SpLD
  - recognising your pitfalls
  - pausing
  - using your thinking preferences
  - knowing your goal

- ideas from physiology and psychology that
  - relate to dyslexia/ SpLD
  - help make sense of some effects of dyslexia/ SpLD

- techniques for using the mind well
  - mind set
  - chunking
  - recall
  - memory consolidation
  - concentration
  - metacognition
  - objective observation
  - reflection
  - making connections
  - prioritising

- thinking preferences
  - sense-based: visual, verbal, kinaesthetic
  - framework or rationale
  - holistic vs. linear thinking
  - Myers-Briggs Personality Type, especially motivation
  - Multiple Intelligences

- thinking clearly: techniques for using maximum mental capacity
  - emotional hi-jacking
  - emotional states of mind
  - confidence
  - self-esteem
  - breathing
  - relaxation
  - Brain Gym
  - Neuro-Linguistic Programming (NLP)
  - the art of pausing and maintaining clear thinking.

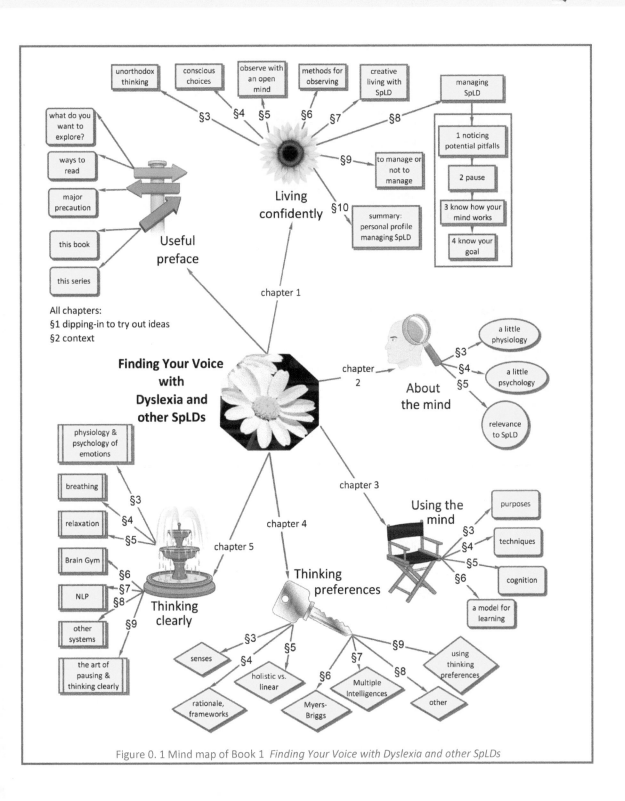

Figure 0. 1 Mind map of Book 1 *Finding Your Voice with Dyslexia and other SpLDs*

Book 2: *Organisation and Everyday Life with Dyslexia and other SpLDs* (Stacey, 2020a)
The book is written for dyslexic/ SpLD people and contains:

- a model for working out issues to do with organisation
  - materials and methods for working on any ideas
- general problem-solving
- solutions applied to
  - time and time management
  - space, place and direction
  - everyday life
  - study peripherals
  - employment.

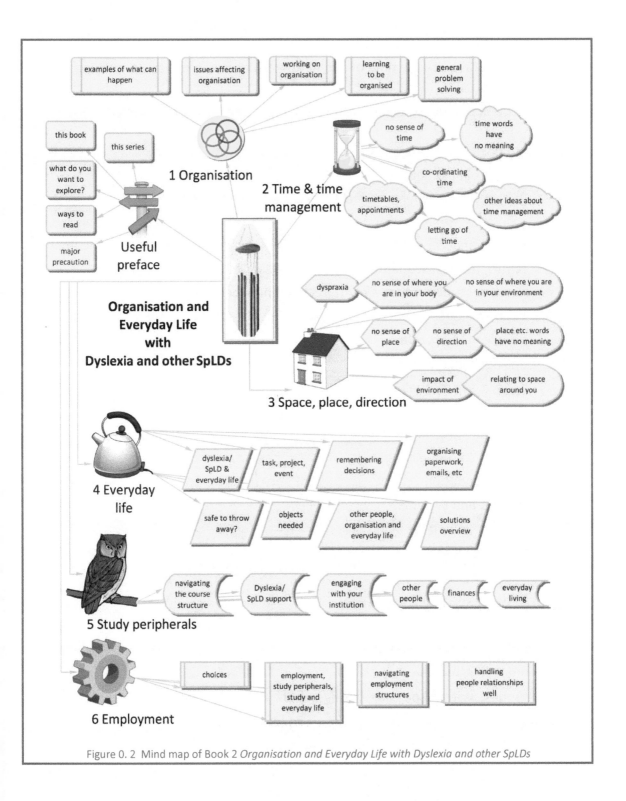

Figure 0. 2 Mind map of Book 2 *Organisation and Everyday Life with Dyslexia and other SpLDs*

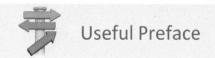

Book 3: *Gaining Knowledge and Skills with Dyslexia and other SpLDs* (Stacey, 2021b)
The book is written for people who assist dyslexic/ SpLD people to gain knowledge and skills, which includes everyone:

- when you tell someone the time of day or how to cook an egg, you are passing on knowledge and skills
- you can't immediately tell whether the person you are talking to is dyslexic/ SpLD.

The book contains:

- different roles people have:
    - 1-1 support teachers, subject teachers and lecturers
    - employers, managers and supervisors
    - professionals in positions of influence and authority: healthcare, legal, financial
    - family, friends, acquaintances, work colleagues
    - designers and producers of indirect communications
    - policy-makers
    - people in the media
- imparting knowledge and skills:
    - general approaches
    - teaching
    - dialogue
    - indirect communication
    - accommodation
    - policies and systems
- foundations for knowledge and skills:
    - model for learning
    - comprehension
    - knowing the goal
    - planning
- input modes: reading, listening, doing
- taking and making notes
- output modes: writing, speaking, taking-action
- situations: exams, group work (meetings, seminars, debates), driving
    - social examples: travel, job applications, eating out, finances.

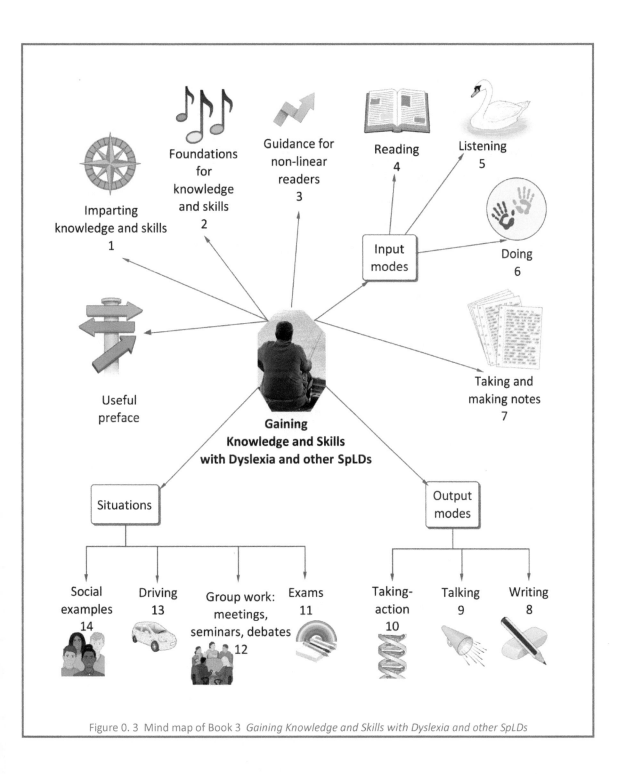

Figure 0. 3 Mind map of Book 3 *Gaining Knowledge and Skills with Dyslexia and other SpLDs*

Book 4: *Development of Dyslexia and other SpLDs* (Stacey, 2020b)
The book is written for those alongside dyslexic/ SpLD people and contains:

- ideas about the persistence of dyslexia/ SpLD and reasons to take dyslexia/ SpLD into account earlier rather than later, including:
    - learned confusion
    - neurons firing together, wire together
    - the persistence of dyslexia/ SpLD
    - problems masked by average language skills
    - levels of compensation
    - degrees of severity
- what goes wrong
    - discussion about the different SpLDs
    - discussion about similar problems experienced by non-dyslexic/ SpLD people
- adaptations of the ideas for younger children
- how to approach matching an individual's learning to what they are good at.

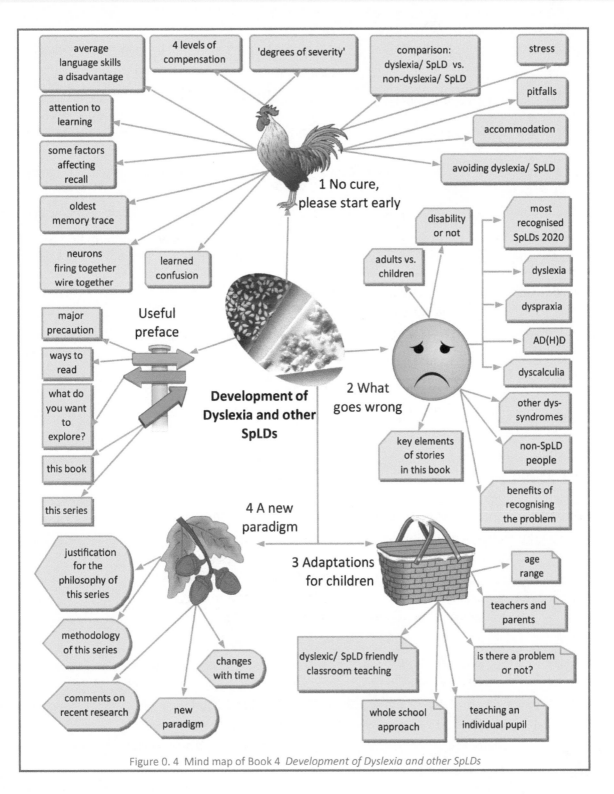

average language skills a disadvantage

4 levels of compensation

'degrees of severity'

comparison: dyslexia/ SpLD vs. non-dyslexia/ SpLD

stress

pitfalls

attention to learning

accommodation

some factors affecting recall

avoiding dyslexia/ SpLD

oldest memory trace

1 No cure, please start early

disability or not

most recognised SpLDs 2020

neurons firing together wire together

learned confusion

adults vs. children

dyslexia

major precaution

Useful preface

dyspraxia

ways to read

AD(H)D

what do you want to explore?

Development of Dyslexia and other SpLDs

2 What goes wrong

dyscalculia

other dys-syndromes

this book

key elements of stories in this book

non-SpLD people

this series

benefits of recognising the problem

justification for the philosophy of this series

4 A new paradigm

3 Adaptations for children

age range

teachers and parents

methodology of this series

changes with time

dyslexic/ SpLD friendly classroom teaching

is there a problem or not?

comments on recent research

new paradigm

whole school approach

teaching an individual pupil

Figure 0. 4 Mind map of Book 4 *Development of Dyslexia and other SpLDs*

Applicable to all books in the series

Series website

- has material to assist with using the books:
    - templates and check-lists
    - recordings of some exercises
    - different ways to select the material most useful to you.

Useful Preface

- is mostly the same for each book
- the sections particular to each book are marked by the book icon and a blue line on the left-hand margin.

It contains:

- the philosophy of the series
- a warning to avoid further dyslexic/ SpLD traits developing as new things are learnt
- some suggestions to make reading easier
- information about the book in question
- information about the series.

Appendix 1 Resources (The same in all 4 books except for referencing.)
will help you collect information together, decide on priorities and monitor progress.

Appendix 2 Individual, Personal Profile and Regime for Managing Dyslexia/ SpLD
        (The same in all 4 books except for section 1 and referencing.)
will help you build the information about your dyslexia/ SpLD and how you manage it.
Section 1, *LIVING CONFIDENTLY*, starts by stating the aim for dyslexic/ SpLD people to be as autonomous as possible. In books 2 - 4, a summary of the material in book 1 is included so that these books can be used independently of each other.

Appendix 3 Key Concepts (The same in all 4 books except for referencing.)
In order to allow the separate books of the series to be used on their own, summaries of the key concepts of the individual books are given in Appendix 3. These are the concepts I think are most important for living confidently with dyslexia/ SpLD.

 Appendix 4 Group Work
has suggestions for using some of the material in the book with groups.

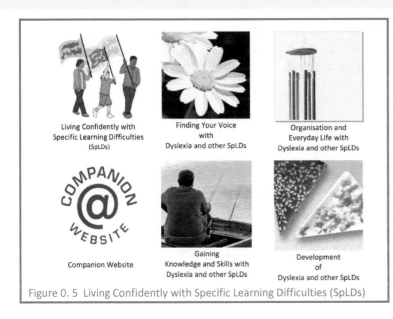

The book cover images:

The daisy represents growth.

Wind chime music represents life flowing well when organisation suits the individual concerned.

The fisherman recalls the saying: 'Give a man a fish and you feed him for a day; teach a man to fish and you feed him for a lifetime'.

The slices of cake represent changing 'That's the way the cookie crumbles' to 'It's a piece of cake'.

Figure 0. 5 Living Confidently with Specific Learning Difficulties (SpLDs)

7.3 Aims and outcomes

The first group of aims of this series is that dyslexic/ SpLD people can:

- find out what their best ways of thinking are, how to use them and maintain their use
- understand how their specific learning difficulty affects them
- be able to pause when they recognise a pitfall has occurred
- know how to deal with the pitfall
    - by using best ways of thinking
    - knowing what needs to happen
- negotiate with those around them so that they are able to fulfil their potential in any situation and so that the dyslexic/ SpLD effects are minimised.

The general attitude at the end of the process is almost:

- OK, I'm dyslexic/ SpLD; I really enjoy the way I process information and the way I am
- everyone has some problems, mine just happen to have a label
- it's no big deal; I'll do well 'with a little help from my friends'.

In order to achieve this group of aims, a group of specialist support providers will need in-depth knowledge of dyslexia/ SpLD. Their knowledge and experience are usually a major contribution to the progress made by any dyslexic/ SpLD person.

The second group of aims is that:

- non-dyslexia/ SpLD people can understand better what the issues are for the people with dyslexia/ SpLD
- communication between the two groups can be improved to the benefit of all parties.

These two sets of aims produce different outcomes depending on whether you are dyslexic/ SpLD or alongside a dyslexic/ SpLD person. The *Website* has *Outcomes* for various reader groups more finely classified.

They have been divided into:

- the Skills and Knowledge
- the Benefits, including changes of behaviour
- and some thoughts about the Potential Possibilities.

There can be a lot of laughter and joyful living once good communication is established across the differences of dyslexia/ SpLD.

7.4   Distinguishing between the different SpLDs

Most of the series is not marked as more or less relevant to a particular SpLD. People are so varied even when their problems are given the same labels. The clearest separation I know is that organisation is the major problem for dyspraxic adults when it comes to thinking (the motor side of dyspraxia is not covered). But even in this group, I'm aware of one student with no dyslexic problems who needs to be aware of his thinking preferences in order to do justice to his knowledge.

Out of respect for the overlap of experiences (problems and solutions), this book makes no distinction between the different SpLDs.

7.5   The way forward

The whole series is about the autonomy that allows dyslexic/ SpLD people to get out from under the difficulties. These difficulties have a label, may have various labels, but they aren't the only difficulties that people face. Negotiating accommodations should be done with understanding of the issues for all parties involved. The way forward could benefit many groups of people.

ⓖ p 353: autonomy

What I hope people will get from the series:

Dyslexic/ SpLD people:

> a systematic way of observing strengths and weaknesses and using the strengths to help you manage the problems you face because of your dyslexia/ SpLD; the confidence to contribute to work, life, in your study, in a way that fulfils your innate potential and which is not masked or hampered by your dyslexia/ SpLD.

Those in supporting roles, whether in a 1-1 relationship or in a more general type of relationship:

> resources to understand the impact of dyslexia/ SpLD on the whole lives of dyslexic/ SpLD people and ways of making necessary adjustments to facilitate better communication.

Those who have to think about public communication and use of public spaces:

> an understanding of the difficulties encountered by dyslexic/ SpLD people and a recognition that making communication and access easier for them will also help many other people.

Politicians, other policy-makers and people in the media:

> an understanding that dealing with dyslexia/ SpLD effectively as early as possible is the right thing for society to do; that done well it has cost benefits in many different ways and is therefore worth carrying through properly; that mutual respect and consideration between all members and levels of society are enhanced through the best approaches to dyslexia/ SpLD.

What I hope will happen for dyslexic/ SpLD children:

> that adults will listen to them and observe them so that they can grow up with maximum autonomy and management of their dyslexia/ SpLD; that many of the recognised problems might not develop for them.

What I hope will happen in general education is that the new paradigm I have put forward (Stacey, 2020b) will be seen as teacher-friendly, effective, sensible, satisfying and cost saving.

Ⓖ p 353: paradigm

(Stacey, 2020b)

The new paradigm is:

- that systems are developed, and used, to explore how individuals, children and adults, learn
- that learners have the opportunities to tailor their learning tasks so that they can achieve the knowledge and skills being taught
- that teaching programmes are flexible enough to accommodate all learner approaches.

Final comment

When people are confident of their skills and not afraid to own and manage their weaknesses, they have many of the tools necessary to face the various situations in their life, see the *Tool Box for Living Confidently*.

Tool Box for Living Confidently: p 319

The voice is found; the potential is unlocked; living with dyslexia/ SpLD is done with confidence.

References

Gleick, James, 1997, *Chaos, The Amazing Science of the Unpredictable*, Minerva, London

Kipling, Rudyard, 1898, *The Day's Work,* MacMillan and Co., London

Kolb, Bryan, 1995, *Brain Plasticity and Behaviour,* Lawrence Erlbaum Associates, Mahwah, NJ

Stacey, Ginny, 2020a, *Organisation and Everyday Life with Dyslexia and other SpLDs*, Routledge, London

Stacey, Ginny, 2020b, *Development of Dyslexia and other SpLDs,* Routledge, London

Stacey, Ginny, 2021a, *Finding Your Voice with Dyslexia and other SpLDs*, Routledge, London

Stacey, Ginny, 2021b, *Gaining Knowledge and Skills with Dyslexia and other SpLDs*, Routledge, London

Website information

Okabe, Masataka and Ito, Kei, 2008, *Color Universal Design (CUD) - How To Make Figures and Presentations That Are Friendly to Colorblind People,*
http://jfly.iam.u-tokyo.ac.jp/color/ Accessed 12 February 2021

Series website: www.routledge.com/cw/stacey

1 Living Confidently

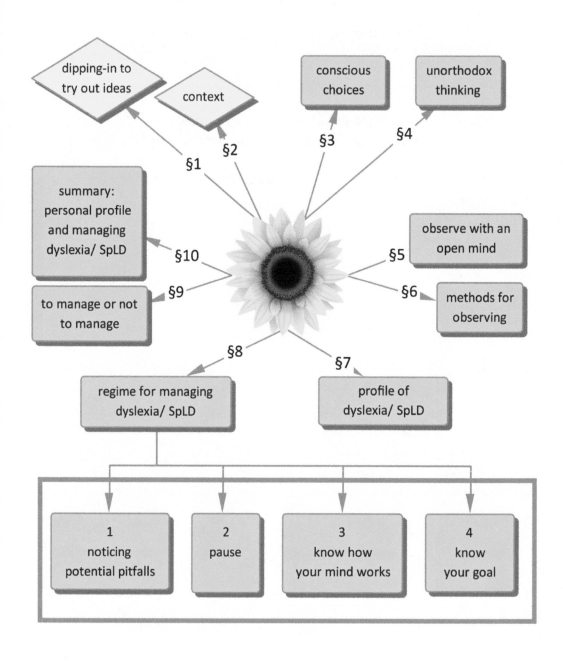

dipping-in to try out ideas

context §2

§1

conscious choices §3

unorthodox thinking §4

summary: personal profile and managing dyslexia/ SpLD §10

§9

to manage or not to manage

observe with an open mind §5

§6 methods for observing

§8

regime for managing dyslexia/ SpLD

§7

profile of dyslexia/ SpLD

| 1 noticing potential pitfalls | 2 pause | 3 know how your mind works | 4 know your goal |

Contents

Vital for dyslexic/ SpLDs, good practice for all

This chapter is about making choices and taking control, which can be useful to anyone.

To make accurate choices you need to observe objectively, so the section on *Methods for Observing* would come under the heading of 'good practice for all'.

Regime for Managing Dyslexia/ SpLD has ideas that can be readily adapted to deal with many problematic situations, and also is in the category of 'good practice for all'.

The rest of the chapter is specifically to do with dyslexia/ SpLD.

People supporting dyslexic/ SpLDs should know this material too.

Methods for Observing: p 55

Regime for Managing Dyslexia/ SpLD: p 71

Working with the chapter

Collect ideas together that interest you and relate to your experience. The templates and *Appendix 2* will help you build your *Individual, Personal Profile of Dyslexia/ SpLD* and construct your *Regime for Managing Dyslexia/ SpLD*.

Appendix 2: p 314

Templates on the website

In the initial stages of working with this chapter use:

A1   *Jotting Down as You Scan*
A2   *Bookmark – Purpose*
A4   *Jotting Down as You Read*
B1   *Collecting ideas That Relate to You*

As you test out your insights, record what happens and reflect on them to alter them as need be:

B3   *Compare Expectations and Reality*
B4   *Actions, Results, Next Step*

Check your understanding using:

B11   *Monitoring Progress*

Templates:

Build your insights into your *PERSONAL, INDIVIDUAL PROFILE OF DYSLEXIA/ SPLD* and your *REGIME FOR MANAGING DYSLEXIA/ SPLD* using *APPENDIX 2*.

APPENDIX 2: p 314

All the *TEMPLATES* suggested in this chapter are shown in the *LIST OF TEMPLATES*.

LIST OF TEMPLATES: p 326

Appendix 1 Resources

APPENDIX 1: p 300

This appendix will help you collect information together, decide on priorities and monitor progress.

Appendix 2 Individual, Personal Profile and Regime for Managing Dyslexia/ SpLD

APPENDIX 2: p 314

This appendix will help you build the information about your dyslexia/ SpLD and how you manage it.

Appendix 3 Key Concepts

APPENDIX 3: p 328

This appendix has a summary of the key ideas I cover when doing an audit of skills and knowledge with a dyslexic/ SpLD student. It shows which of the 4 books in the series covers each idea in full.

1   Dipping-in to try out ideas

If you want to read examples that might tally with your experience,
> Start with *OBSERVE WITH AN OPEN MIND, §5.*

§5: p 45

If you want to collate your strengths and weaknesses,
> start with *AN INDIVIDUAL, PERSONAL PROFILE OF DYSLEXIA/ SPLD, §7.*

§7: p 64

If you want to deal with your dyslexia better,
> start with *REGIME FOR MANAGING DYSLEXIA/ SPLD, §8,* and move around the chapter as your questions prompt you.

§8: p 71

If you want to explore how you think,
> start with *METHODS FOR OBSERVING, §6,* and move around the chapter as your questions prompt you.

§6: p 55

2 Context

Story: Playing classical guitar

I became interested in dyslexia when I wanted to learn to play the classical guitar in my 30s.

In my early 20s, I had found out that some of the peculiar things I do belong to the phenomenon of dyslexia. By then I'd completed an undergraduate degree and acquired a doctorate in physics, both at The University of Oxford. My dyslexia had affected me, but I could always find a way round problems.

Learning to play the guitar was the first time my dyslexia had to be confronted. There are neither spell-checkers nor proof-readers, you have to play the right note at the right time to make music.

I gradually became aware of how I was thinking and what made a difference to my guitar playing. From there, I grew interested in how other dyslexics managed their thinking and started working with dyslexic students at university.

In its simplest form, the philosophy that underpins my work with students is that:

it is possible to:

- maximise your potential
- minimise the effects of your dyslexia/ SpLD.

Full philosophy:
PHILOSOPHY OF THIS SERIES: p 4

These goals are achieved by:

- you observing and exploring the way you think
- you using your varied, unexpected, unorthodox ways of thinking
- you using strategies that get round the pitfalls from your dyslexia/ SpLD
- accommodations being put in place for any effects of your dyslexia/ SpLD for which you have no strategies.

This chapter is about

1   the processes of observing thinking and many things that happen
2   building an individual, personal profile
3   outlining a regime for managing dyslexia/ SpLD.

Some final thoughts in this opening section:

Everyday life is full of learning.
Learning is hard work; you are altering the patterns your brain uses, no-one else can do it for you.

Tip: Only you can eat an apple

One teacher friend of mine used to tell his pupils: "If you are hungry and there's an apple on the table, you have to eat it; I can't eat it for you. Learning is the same."

However, there is enjoyment to be had when you use your mind well while you are learning.

3 Conscious choices

FIGURE 1.1, LIVING CONFIDENTLY WITH DYSLEXIA/ SPLD, shows three routes for living confidently, one that happens unconsciously and two routes that involve conscious choices.

Via the unconscious route, people are free to contribute their insights, their problem-solving, their intelligence, their creativity without more ado; they unconsciously and confidently use their unorthodox ways of thinking. This is a very good route and dyslexic/ SpLD people who find it are fortunate.

Others have to achieve the same confidence by conscious choice:
1) to use thinking preferences
2) to manage dyslexia/ SpLD.

These are not alternative routes to confidence. You may need to be working on both fronts together.

Both these routes depend on careful observation and both use very similar approaches.

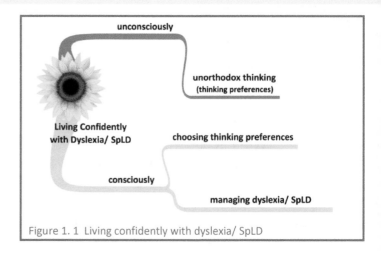

Figure 1. 1 Living confidently with dyslexia/ SpLD

As you accumulate the observations, you can build them into your personal, individual profile and your own regime for managing dyslexia/ SpLD. The profile and regime allow you to make conscious choices that contribute to living confidently.

This chapter is about making the deliberate choices. Other chapters are about the options from which you can choose. The final chapter, *THINKING CLEARLY*, is about maintaining your choices.

THINKING CLEARLY: p 254

4 Unorthodox thinking

Some of these comments are specifically about dyslexic people since more research has been done on dyslexia than on other forms of SpLD.

Many successful dyslexics recognise that their dyslexia has contributed to their success. Some see their way of thinking as being fundamental to them and that, if being dyslexic is the price to pay for their unorthodox thinking, it was a price worth paying. Often they are not very specific about the way they think, but they just get on and do it.

Dyslexics are often valued for their ability to think 'outside the box' and solve problems; some firms and institutions deliberately recruit dyslexics for these qualities. Tom West (1991) has written and spoken extensively about successful dyslexics.

West (1991)

From the varied careers of and contributions from these successful dyslexics, it would be surprising to find that they all had the same unorthodox ways of thinking. Listening to some of them speak[1], I find myself speculating which of the THINKING PREFERENCES explored in this book would be the ones they use.

THINKING PREFERENCES:
p 188

Many times when a student and I have been working on his thinking preferences, he has recalled times in the past when he recognised that he was using the same ways of thinking. When confidence is not strong, students won't pursue their instincts: "I wanted to do it that way, but I didn't dare."

Often dyslexic/ SpLDs don't want to be different. As children, they think that adults must know best and if no-one has suggested these alternatives, they can't be worth following. The lucky ones are encouraged to try different ways of thinking and 'taking-action'.

Ⓖ p 353:
'taking-action' is used in this book to mean: 'applying knowledge and skills in a practical way'.

One way to fully engage your thinking preferences is to choose jobs and subjects that are interesting to you. The interest and the best thinking preferences working together can help you over the pitfalls of dyslexia/ SpLD. A job or subject that is safe as far as dyslexia/ SpLD is concerned could be so boring that the dyslexia/ SpLD gets worse anyway.

Ⓖ p 353: pitfalls

5   Observe with an open mind

I have discussed observing with an open mind in terms of variations between individuals, within one individual both from time to time and from one task to another.

In my experience of dyslexia/ SpLD nothing is ever static; you rarely get to a point where you can think everything is in place and there will be no more problems (which is true for most of humanity, too), but you can get to a point where you have constructive, personal approaches that are fairly robust.

---

[1] A web search on 'Orlando Bloom dyslexia' finds several interviews with him. He describes some of the processes that have helped him. From the same search there will be links to other interviews with other famous people.

Tip: Observing yourself

Often there are gut feelings and gut reactions that have been overridden for years.

Take the opportunity now to see them in a new light and let yourself follow their lead.

Record insights about yourself. *COLLECTING INFORMATION TOGETHER* has suggestions of ways to record insights and to gather them together usefully.

COLLECTING INFORMATION TOGETHER: p 302

The major points for the discussion about observing are in the following sections:

§5.1   You have to listen to yourself

§5.2   Explore how you think best

§5.3   Tasks not going to plan are useful

§5.4   Best thinking varying at different stages of a task

§5.5   Progress improved

§5.6   No progress when best thinking is not used

§5.7   Absence of best thinking magnifies the problems of dyslexia/ SpLD

§5.8   New situations or tasks undermine dyslexia/ SpLD management

§5.9   Stress increases the effects of dyslexia/ SpLD

§5.1: p 47
§5.2: p 48

§5.3: p 48
§5.4: p 49

§5.5: p 50

§5.6: p 52

§5.7: p 53

§5.8: p 54

§5.9: p 54

Objective observation allows you to see what's at the heart of a situation, as in the story in the box below. You then find opportunities and approaches that you can use to establish your personal profile and regime for managing.

5.1 You have to listen to yourself

Insight: You have to listen to yourself

Dyslexic/ SpLD people do not all process information in the same way, for example:

- some dyslexic people use mind maps very well, others can't use them

- some remember very well what they have done, others remember what matters to other people (for other ways people remember well and think well, see *Thinking Preferences*)

Thinking Preferences: p 188

nor is the problem presented necessarily the one that needs to be addressed:

- One student asked for help writing her essay; she just couldn't find her usual fluency. Everything I suggested, she either had tried, or she came back with a reason why it wouldn't work. She kept repeating the word, "Can't".

  We brainstormed around 'Can't'. She was a mature student, several hundreds of miles from home during the week and her teenage daughter was at home with her husband. It wasn't working for the daughter to be so far from Mum and the worry was undermining the mother's management of her dyslexia.

  Once she recognised the problem and what needed to be done, her language fluency returned and there was no problem with writing.

The third bullet point in *Insight: You Have to Listen to Yourself* was essentially resolved using part of *Finding the Root Cause of a Problem* (Stacey, 2020a)

Listening attentively to yourself is essential in order to find out what is happening, which ways of thinking work best for you and whether something quite unrelated is causing problems.

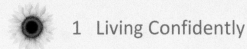

5.2   Explore how you think best

The following are some ideas about the processes involved in finding out what your thinking preferences are and how you can build on them.

BUILDING UP INSIGHTS:
p 316

- Exploring thinking is an iterative process in which knowledge of thinking is refined:
    o   by trying some way of thinking
    o   reflecting on the results, working out why that way worked well or why it didn't
    o   building on the insights gained to modify the thinking and start the cycle again.

- You work with what you do well, and it can be anything. You reflect on how and why that task goes well. And then you think about what could be applied to a task that is currently being problematic, see *USING CHALLENGES*.

USING CHALLENGES:
p 288

- You improve solutions that work. In doing so, you find out more about the way you think well.

- Solutions that don't work are just as useful. Use why they don't work to give more information about the way you think best.

- The mind exercise in *KNOW YOUR OWN MIND* can be used to find out the characteristics of your thinking. You need to probe behind the obvious comments to find the context, which will give a better indication of your thinking

KNOW YOUR OWN MIND:
p 56

- *MIND SET: MENTAL PREPARATION* and *RECALL AND CHECK* can be used to explore how you think.

MIND SET: MENTAL PREPARATION: p 152
RECALL AND CHECK: p 62

5.3   Tasks not going to plan are useful

TEMPLATES:

It is important to use the times when something doesn't work as expected. You need to find out why something didn't work. You can record what happened using the *TEMPLATE: B4 - ACTIONS, RESULTS, NEXT STEP*. The insights gained can be added to the way you build your *PERSONAL PROFILE* and your *REGIME FOR MANAGING DYSLEXIA/ SPLD*.

INDIVIDUAL, PERSONAL PROFILE OF DYSLEXIA/ SPLD: p 64
REGIME FOR MANAGING DYSLEXIA/ SPLD: p 71

Example: MBPT motivation and memory recall

A group of student historians were presenting their mini projects to each other. The idea was that they all did research in depth about a small section of the topic and learnt the whole topic through the work of everyone. The dyslexic student of the group came to me because she had difficulty in understanding some people's work.

We brainstormed the whole session. She described the style of presentation of the various sets of students within the group. Those who did something dramatic in their presentation made an impression on her and she could remember what they said; those who read an essay without expression or who presented a dense well argued set of ideas made no impression on her memory.

The failure highlighted her need for connections to people in her work. She can't rely on others to supply that every time, so it is up to her to recognise when the personal element is missing and to make sure she includes it.

 p 350:
MBPT

(MBPT) Motivation:
p 232

5.4   Best thinking varying at different stages of a task

stages of a task (e.g. learning):
A Model of Learning:
p 178

Example: Best thinking varies

A person will use colour coding to separate different parts of a topic in order to understand it. The understanding then provides a schema for the topic. It is the schema that is then used for recall and the original colour coding plays no part in recall.

Ⓖ p 353: schema

5.5 Progress improved

Example: Progress using thinking preferences

A final-year chemistry student needed to know the periodic table. It is not something that students are usually asked to learn.

However, she could understand the chemical behaviour of different positions in the periodic table; she simply couldn't remember which name went where and which set of chemical behaviours belonged to the many different names.

This lack of knowledge would rule out a lot of questions in her finals paper. If she could learn the periodic table, she would be able to answer many questions.

We went through the whole table and devised methods for her to use for different sections. She came back the next week having learnt all of them without much effort.

The methods for her were:

- some recognised from school; no new method needed
- some were known from practical work
- some were easy to learn from patterns in their names
- 2 long lists of names were learnt through mnemonics the student made up.

The last 2 are worth describing.

MARGIN NOTE: the periodic table has all the chemical elements, more than 110, grouped by chemical properties.

ⓖ p 353: mnemonics

From the patterns in their names:

In the way the table is arranged, 6 elements are in a block as shown in the margin. The student knew the names and the letters for the elements of the 2nd column; she could not remember their order.

Block of 6 elements from the periodic table

We noticed that:

the top 2 are in alphabetical order, R>S;

the middle 2 are in the opposite order, C<B;

the bottom 2 have 2 'r's in the middle, FrRa.

She felt she could remember those links.

known	Un-known
Rb	Sr
Cs	Ba
Fr	Ra

Mnemonics to remember a long list of names:

She wanted to learn 2 of the groups of transition elements.

In the periodic table the first of these rows is:

Sc	Ti	V	Cr	Mn	Fe	Co	Ni	Cu	Zn

The full names of the elements are: scandium, titanium, vanadium, chromium, manganese, iron, cobalt, nickel, copper and zinc.

Either way looks impossible to learn.

The mnemonic she devised was: 'sweet Tilly valiantly climbed mountains for Chris never counting zebras'.

There was a similar mnemonic for the second line of the transition elements. She was grinning happily at the end of the session.

Within a week, she knew the periodic table, and was confident about sitting her exams.

There is a range of different thinking preferences in this story. It was a question of playing until we found the right one for each part. The story is one of many examples where the right way of thinking has made so much difference to the individual's performance.

5.6 No progress when best thinking is not used

Example: Reverting back to not managing

One university final-year student was making very good progress with her subjects. We were finalising her support because we thought she didn't need it any more: she knew how to use her mind.

Then one day she couldn't come to see me because she had an essay crisis. It turned out that she had been struggling with a new module for several weeks. Her underlying lack of confidence had surfaced when she was struggling and she didn't think to bring the problems to the support sessions, nor to question the way the subject was being presented. She thought the lack of progress was her fault.

MARGIN NOTE: essay crisis signifies a time when a student has very little time to write or finish an essay before it has to be handed in.

The most important aspect of any subject for her was the underlying schema for it. Once she had understood the schema, she had no problem learning the material.

MARGIN NOTE: Needing a schema is part of *RATIONALE OR FRAMEWORK:* p 216

The new subject was an emerging field and there was no schema for it as yet. She seemed to be presented with random material to memorise, a task often beyond dyslexic/ SpLD people.

We decided a pattern from research could act as a schema.

1) You have a question you want answered

2) you do an experiment

3) you analyse the experiment and get results

4) the results usually provoke more questions

5) the results may start to contribute to a theory.

There is a cycle that gets repeated until the subject is understood.

She was able to link the seemingly random information to the cycle; see a sense to it; and so, remember it and work with it. She did very well in the subject in her finals exams.

This story demonstrates how important it is to make sure your best way of thinking is engaged in any task that is proving difficult.   You need to be aware of the progress you expect to make and just check all your options when progress is slower.

5.7   Absence of best thinking magnifies the problems of dyslexia/ SpLD

Example: Cheating or dyslexic problems?

A student was accused of cheating when writing his major dissertation. The tutors were very concerned that there were two different styles of writing throughout the thesis. One was competent, well argued and without too many errors; the other was rambling, showed little understanding and was full of errors. The tutors were convinced that two different people had written the thesis.

There were family circumstances that meant the student had no access to a library at a critical moment in his research. As he was working to a deadline, he had no way of addressing that (the story belongs to the era before the internet).

He was fascinated by the practical parts of the dissertation material, and he had hands-on experience of it. He could find no way to think clearly about the theoretical parts.

When he understood the subject he could write fluently and you would not have expected him to be dyslexic; when he tried to write the theoretical part his language showed considerable dyslexic problems, so much so that the tutors found it hard to believe that the same person had written all of the thesis.

When your fluency with language is not at its best, check:

- how you are thinking about the subject and
- whether you need to use any of the Techniques in THINKING CLEARLY.

THINKING CLEARLY:
p 254

53

5.8   New situations or tasks undermine dyslexia/ SpLD management

- 'Hot-desking' in an office is equivalent to coming to a new work situation each time you come to work. You can't set out your work environment so that it suits your dyslexia/ SpLD management easily, nor the computer arrangement nor the many other minor parameters that just mean the dyslexia/ SpLD is kept under control. Without these arrangements in place you are highly vulnerable to dyslexia/ SpLD episodes.

MARGIN NOTE: 'hot-desking' is the practice whereby an employee doesn't have his/ her own office space, but shares it with others or moves around the office depending on free desks.

- A new teacher with a different style of working can disrupt your thinking. The danger here is that the disruption is likely to be right at the beginning of a teaching cycle and subsequently the dyslexic/ SpLD person may always struggle with that topic.

Just be observant when anything is new, and deal with dyslexia/ SpLD issues as early as possible.

5.9   Stress increases the effects of dyslexia/ SpLD

For most people, stress makes anything in life harder to deal with. For dyslexic/ SpLD people stress can increase the effects of the disability (Miles and Varma, 1995, Stacey, 2020b) and it is no good trying to solve a secondary problem without tackling the root cause; see 3rd bullet point in *INSIGHT: YOU HAVE TO LISTEN TO YOURSELF*.

Related Section:
A LITTLE PHYSIOLOGY AND PSYCHOLOGY OF EMOTIONS: p 260

Miles and Varma, (1995)
Stacey (2020b)

INSIGHT: YOU HAVE TO LISTEN TO YOURSELF: p 47

There are those for whom the extra buzz of stress is needed to energise them. Careful observation will show where you fall in the stress spectrum, from benefiting from stress at one end, to being paralysed by it at the other.

Once you decide from the observations which level of stress helps you to function effectively, you need to manage your life so that you have the optimal level of stress.

6 Methods for observing

Look at the drawing of the LADY IN A HAT, FIGURE 1.2. Shading and the background are put in; they are what tell you this is a 'Lady in a hat'. Very few lines belong to the hat, lady or chair. Observing how someone else thinks is a bit like this drawing: you can't directly make observations; you have to use indirect means. With practice, you can become much more aware of how you think yourself and what you are feeling.

When I started to try to explain the effects of my dyslexia to other people, I knew I would not believe what I was saying if I had not learnt to observe how I was thinking and what I was responding to.

Figure 1. 2 Lady in a hat

Once observations have been made, they need to be checked to see that they have been understood correctly and further explored to see how they can be incorporated into what you want to achieve.

The first four of the following sections are about observing THINKING PREFERENCES:

- KNOW YOUR OWN MIND, §6.1

- HOW DO YOU TEACH OR PASS ON INFORMATION? §6.2

- WHAT PERSPECTIVE COMES THROUGH THE WAY YOU SPEAK OR THE LANGUAGE YOU USE? §6.3

- HOW DO YOU DO A TASK? §6.4

- TAKING-ACTION AND THINKING PREFERENCES allows you to make observations through taking-action; particularly for those people who work with actions rather than words.

- CYCLES OF OBSERVATIONS is about checking understanding and exploring the observations further.

- TRIGGERS INTO DYSLEXIA/ SPLD deals with the observations about the pitfalls of dyslexia/ SpLD.

6.1 Know your own mind

This mind exercise comes from yoga originally (Wood, 1962). It has been published in the dyslexia context since 1992 (Stacey, 1992). It allows you to develop awareness[2] of mind and so become an observer of how you are thinking and feeling.

Wood (1962)
Stacey (1992)

One word of caution:
The mind exercise could allow you to be conscious of thoughts and feelings you have buried. If you find yourself becoming negative about your observations, use ideas from *NEURO-LINGUISTIC PROGRAMMING (NLP)* to maintain a positive, healthy attitude. You may need to seek professional help from someone who understands dyslexia/ SpLD.

NEURO-LINGUISTIC PROGRAMMING (NLP): p 279

You can use *TEMPLATE: B2 - KNOW YOUR OWN MIND* for the following exercise. If you don't like mind maps: you could draw, or choose some art work for the central object; you could record your ideas instead of writing; someone else could write down your ideas; you could use a series of lists.

TEMPLATES:

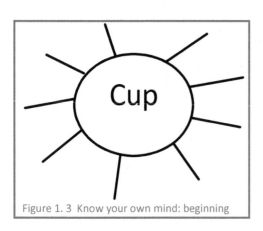

Figure 1. 3 Know your own mind: beginning

Figure 1. 4 Know your own mind: example based on cup

---

[2] Awareness: 'we aim to have voluntary attention, so that we may properly awaken or grow, and properly reproduce things on the screen of imagination for the purposes of thought' (Wood, 1962, p 64). Mindfulness is another name for awareness.

RECORDINGS:

Exercise: Know your own mind

Choose any object or idea, e.g. 'cup' or 'red'. Write it in the middle of a page, see
FIGURE 1.3, KNOW YOUR OWN MIND: BEGINNING.

Draw a circle round it.

Write associated ideas round the circle, like spokes of a wheel.

After each associated idea, bring your mind back to the central idea.

The ideas that you write around the central focus should all be directly connected to
that focus. You should not allow your mind to wander away.

In *FIGURE 1.4, KNOW YOUR OWN MIND: EXAMPLE BASED ON CUP*, all the surrounding ideas are
directly related to 'cup' by me. I did not spiral out by going beyond the first associated
idea.

- 'Granddaughter' could have spiralled out to 'drinking', 'present', and 'next visit'
- 'forgetting' could have gone to 'offering cups of tea', 'memory techniques' and
  'embarrassment' (I frequently forget that I have offered a cup of tea to someone,
  if I don't need a drink myself; I use various memory techniques to avoid
  embarrassment).

When you analyse the collection of ideas using *THINKING PREFERENCES,* you find they stem
from different triggers. In this example, 'sport' and 'medals' come from the news
current as I wrote; 'china' and 'granddaughter' both relate to people close to me; all
the others are connected to things I do.

Further examples of collections of ideas and interpretations are given in *EXAMPLE: MIND
EXERCISE FROM A WORKSHOP.*

THINKING PREFERENCES: p 188
EXAMPLE: MIND EXERCISE FROM A WORKSHOP: p 194

In the yogic scenario, you would stay focused on the central idea for
about 5 minutes after the last association came into your mind. You
would be using the practice to increase awareness; you would not
need to record anything (Wood, 1962).

Being able to focus and to direct your mind can be useful skills when it
comes to managing dyslexia/ SpLD. The skills develop in this exercise
as you learn to monitor your thinking while it happens. You learn to

Wood (1962)

focus of mind: the
ability to bring your
mind back to the
selected topic rather
than letting it wander
following random
associations.

notice when you are having difficulty with some task, and you start to realise that shifting your thinking a little bit will enable you to avoid getting stuck in a dyslexic/ SpLD frame of mind, or it will help you get out of a difficulty faster than previously.

Example: Directing your mind to avoid a dyslexic/ SpLD problem

Dyslexic people frequently can't find a word they want.
If you think in diagrams, you can learn to pay attention to your ideas as a diagram and you let the words flow from the diagram. That way, you explain your idea much more coherently than by struggling to find the right word.

You can put much more complex ideas at the centre in order to gauge your understanding of a topic, or where something might be a problem. At that level of complexity, you tend not to be concerned about the way you are thinking; you would allow the pattern of ideas to develop away from the centre. Used in this way, the exercise can be a very powerful one; it can be more than a mind map because it allows you to see:

1   how you are thinking
2   how your thinking is developing
3   what you are feeling about the subject.

The mind exercise is more than a mind map of a topic; a mind map stays at the level of what is known about a topic whereas doing the exercise allows you to

know your own mind

because you are observing your mind as it thinks.

6.2   How do you teach or pass on information?

Another way of deciding how you think well is to teach someone something and to observe how you do it.

You could teach someone:

      a computer game or a card game
      to cook a dish
      to use equipment or an electronic device
      to use a software package
      a subject at school or at any other formal education setting.

What materials do you use to help the other person understand what you are saying?
What type of activity would you prefer to teach?

The interpretation of the choices needs the understanding of different ways of thinking, as discussed in *THINKING PREFERENCES*.

THINKING PREFERENCES: p 188

6.3 What perspective shows through the way you speak or the language you use?

Observing the way you speak, or listening to the language you use, can indicate something about the way you naturally think.

If you move your hands around a lot while you are speaking, it is worth exploring whether you think best by doing, or by thinking from a doing perspective.

You might talk from a people point of view, or by using sound or visual analogies.

      Example: Thinking preferences and style of speech

In a lecture, a teacher described a reading session with a boy. She told him to go forward in the book. He asked, "Do you mean forward to the back of the book or backwards to the front of the book?"

The question indicates a logical mind or a precise one or even a down-to-earth here-and-now one; it points away from a mind that picks up nuances.

6.4   How do you do a task?

Any task can also be used to observe how you think well.

Exercise: Doing a task and thinking preferences

Choose a task you like and do well.
Describe the task.
Use some questions to help you reflect on what you do, such as:
>   What do you like about it? Why?
>   Are you organised or do you do it in a spontaneous way?
>   How are you setting about the task?
>   How do you feel about the task when you've finished it?
>   What motivation is satisfied at the end of the task?

Use *TEMPLATE: B6 - RECORDING TEMPLATE - 2*
Headings:
>   A = part of the task   C = details
>   B = question for reflection   D = reflection

What do you observe about the way you think from your reflections?

TEMPLATES:

6.5   Taking-action and thinking preferences

If you are a kinaesthetic thinker, someone whose attention is on action, use your actions to learn about yourself.

You have to think in order to take-action. Trying to find out how you think might be too abstract a process for you to engage with. Whereas, focusing attention on what you do, how you do it, why you do it that way is likely to be much more interesting.

Ⓖ p 353: take-action

You will also learn more about yourself while you try out ideas in this book.

If you collect your observations using *TEMPLATES: B3 - COMPARE EXPECTATIONS AND REALITY* and *B4 - ACTION, RESULT AND NEXT STEP*, you can use the last columns, Comment and Next Step respectively, to focus on actions.

One possible way of collecting the details is to use the *TEMPLATE: B7 - RECORDING TEMPLATE - 3*. The headings would be:

TEMPLATES:

      A = Date, place, situation,

      B = What was happening,   C = Details re dyslexia/ SpLD

      D = What you were doing   E = Insight code/ key words.

You can then keep the records in a file or ring binder.

You might want to avoid writing words. On a computer you could use clip art, or draw diagrams using software.

Another way would be to have a note book and to use the headings suggested above as headings in your notes. You could highlight the headings so that you can find them more easily. You could draw, or make collages.

Use any method that captures your observations in a way that suits you.

Tip: Don't lose your system

Whatever system you use, put it down on paper or in a computer. Make sure you can find it again, even several years later. You want to avoid designing different systems every time you have something to record.

6.6 Cycles of observation

As you gather insights about yourself, you will find that there are changes. There will be cycles of observation as you interpret your observations and as you let skills and knowledge develop. You need to know that your interpretations are working for you.

MONITORING PROGRESS: p 62

MONITORING PROGRESS is about recording details so that you accurately see your progress.

RECALL AND CHECK: p 62

RECALL AND CHECK is a process for working with your interpretations about your *THINKING PREFERENCES* and how well they work for you.

THINKING PREFERENCES: p 188

6.6.1 Monitoring progress

It can be very satisfying to see how you are making progress with what you want to achieve. If you capture sufficient detail you can see:

- which ideas really are helping

- which things are not helping as much as you thought they were and why

- when you are skipping part of a process that is key to what you want to do

- what is a waste of time and should be abandoned.

Recording details, however you do it, allows you to pay attention to everything and not miss something that is significant.

Use *Monitoring Progress* in *Appendix 1*, or see what that achieves and devise your own system.

Monitoring Progress: p 311

6.6.2 Recall and check

Thinking Preferences: p 188

Thinking Preferences has ideas as to how to interpret the observations you make about the way you think. The ideas are also relevant to observations about taking-action.

Then, you need to know that your interpretation is good.
The 'proof of the pudding is in the eating', *Figure 1.5:* How well can you use the *Thinking Preferences* when you need to?

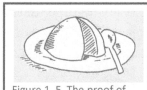

Figure 1. 5 The proof of the pudding

Exercise: Recall and check

One test to see how well you have uncovered your *Thinking Preferences* is:

1   to find something you don't care about[3] but which is similar to material you would like to remember (not always a possible option)

2   understand it and organise it in a way that seems to fit the topic

Templates:

you can use
B7 - *Recording Template - 3*
with headings:
A = date
B = topic
C = observations
D = thinking preferences
E = how good

---

[3] When you have become familiar with these steps, they can be used on material that you would like to remember. For the reason to choose unimportant material to start with, see *Major Precaution*: p 7

3   convert the important parts into notes; use any method of making notes that suits you; it is quite good to leave about 10 minutes between the end of working on the topic and making the notes

4   the next day, see how much you can remember and why; check against the notes you made

5   think about the links between ideas or items that you remember and
   o   try to work out any relationships between them
   o   work out their relationship to you

6   look at the ideas or objects that you didn't remember
   o   see what you could adapt from the things you did remember
   o   see whether you are bored or have some other adverse reaction
   o   alter the way you think about these things so that they are hooked into your memory more firmly

7   keep assessing what you are learning about your way of thinking through this mechanism.

Tip: Developing the thinking preferences of your profile

You can repeat the process many times.
What you don't remember is helping you to observe how you think well.

6.7   Triggers into dyslexia/ SpLD

As you explore how your mind thinks well, you will also be able to observe the pitfalls that trigger you into dyslexic/ SpLD behaviour.

Ⓖ p 353: pitfalls

You need to collect the insights as near as possible to the time that they happen.

> Record the date and where you were.

> What was happening at the time you were triggered into dyslexic/ SpLD behaviour?

> What did that behaviour involve?

These *Pitfalls* are part of your profile of dyslexia/ SpLD.

Pitfalls: p 69

7   An individual, personal profile of dyslexia/ SpLD

Your profile of dyslexia/ SpLD is a summary of the information about you that is important in relation to dyslexia/ SpLD. It represents the information that is known about your dyslexia/ SpLD: tools and problems. It is an integral part of how you will most easily manage your dyslexia/ SpLD.

profile: represent in profile, draw in cross-section; outline; give a summary description ('profile, v. 1a and 3c' OED Online, 2020)

Personal profiles will vary but important ingredients are:

- individual thinking preferences
- specific pitfalls from your individual dyslexia/ SpLD
- strategies that help you to pause and to stay in control
- areas that need to be accommodated, and how the accommodation can be done.

Ⓖ p 353: pitfalls

These ingredients are the four areas of the *Templates in Section C: Individual, Personal Profile of Dyslexia/ SpLD.*

Templates:

Thinking Preferences: p 188

The options for thinking preferences are discussed in *Thinking Preferences*. The strategies that allow you to pause are in *Thinking Clearly*. *Pitfalls* and *Accommodations* are discussed in this section. They also emerge in working with the other books of this series (Stacey, 2020a, b, 2021).

Thinking Clearly: p 254

Pitfalls: p 69
Accommodations: p 71
Stacey (2020a, b, 2021)

7.1   Your profile may change over time

While working with a book such as this one, or having specialist support during education, quite a few insights and experiences are likely to happen in a relatively short length of time. They won't come in a planned order. Some may come when you don't expect there to be any issues with dyslexia/ SpLD. Once most of the profile has been built, you can still find that new insights emerge. They need to be added to the profile.

Insight: Individual profiles develop over time

A profile is unlikely to be fixed for all time. You can get to a stage where your profile serves you well in most of your life and then you find a new task or situation is bringing back dyslexic/ SpLD problems again (Stacey, 2020a). You should go back to exploring your profile and see what you need to add to cope with the new situation or task.

Add the new insights to your profile.

MARGIN NOTE: EXAMPLE: REVERTING BACK TO NOT MANAGING, p 52, is about dyslexia triggered by a new course.

Stacey (2020a)

7.2 Developing your profile

The practical resources for building and updating your profile are in *APPENDIX 2*. The material there runs through the whole series of the 4 books. I have put it into the appendix so that it will be consistent from one book to another.

APPENDIX 2: p 314

- You observe objectively, collecting and recording stories and insights
- you reflect on the material you have collected
- you test your observations
- you update your profile whenever new insights emerge.

You need to collect the information in a systematic way so that you can use it effectively. You need detail so that you have evidence to back any statements you want to make. You will probably find it useful to reduce the detail to key words or themes.

Example: Detailed information that is likely to be useful

Key words	Details
Event 1	
date, place, situation	dd/mm/yy. Support tutor's office. Work on revision for exams.
Revision posters information linked I need to understand	Discussion about the way I work and the implications for dealing with dyslexia. I was describing my revision posters. It became obvious that I'm remembering the ones where I've linked the information together and I understand it. Some of the other posters are just dim. Got to talking about classes and how I ask all the questions. It fits with what happens.
Event 2	Recalled after discussion in Event 1
date, place, situation	dd/mm/yy. college, class in a group of 5.
I ask questions uncomfortable others don't know we all gain	I was asking a lot of questions. The others didn't have any questions. I felt uncomfortable asking all the questions. As the discussion went on with the tutor, it was clear that the others didn't understand as much as they should. By the time my questions had been discussed and answered, we all knew the subject so much better.
strategy for dealing with my dyslexia/ SpLD	What came from the revision posters: I need to link information together. I can use colour and space to aid the linking. On their own, space and colour don't work.
gain in confidence self-esteem	Asking all necessary questions is part of my regime for managing dyslexia. Others can benefit from my questions. I don't need to feel uncomfortable about the questions, but see them as for us all.
insight for profile	Thinking preference: in order to learn I need to thoroughly understand a topic, and make links.

Insight: *RECALL AND CHECK* **used to develop a profile**

A student wanted to know how to revise for exams. She had
learnt to use some of the techniques for note-taking. She had a
set of full notes that she was reducing to one or two pages of A4.
She was putting boxes round sections of information.   Sometimes,
she used diagrams to illustrate concepts.

She was testing herself by recalling the A4 sheets. She reported
that the recall was not working very well, but that it was better
when there was a diagram.

RECALL AND CHECK: p 62

MARGIN NOTE: Further
ideas in *RECALL:* p 157
and
*MEMORY
CONSOLIDATION:* p 160

She demonstrated the recall process to me for several of her
sheets. She was using the position of her notes on the A4 page:
"There's something down in the left hand corner" and that
reminded her of information. She was remembering some of the
diagrams.

We looked at what was wrong or missing. We thought about what
had already emerged about her thinking strengths:

> to use visual aids
>
> to question information
>
> to use kinaesthetic processing.

The main problem was that she was trying to 'learn by rote' and
she was not engaging her questioning mind to check that what she
was remembering was true. She hadn't really understood and
organised the material effectively, so getting that right was the
first step towards improvement. Some of the diagrams were
helping; others were too incomplete to trigger all the information.
The use of lines round different topics was helping.

The most important gain was to realise that rote learning wasn't going to work and that she had to understand a topic in order to use the links between the information as part of the recall process.

The insights gained for her profile were:

> thinking preferences: frameworks are needed;
> > visual aids help but are of secondary importance
>
> pitfall: rote learning
>
> accommodation: teaching must include explanations;
> > learning must include understanding
> > learning should include the kinaesthetic processing.

As you become certain which are the significant key words, or phrases, for you, they can be accumulated on the *TEMPLATES: C1* or *C3 - INDIVIDUAL, PERSONAL PROFILE OF DYSLEXIA/ SPLD (SPATIAL* or *LINEAR)*.

Examples from work with students are given in *TEMPLATES:*

> *C4 - 2 EXAMPLES OF INDIVIDUAL, PERSONAL PROFILES (LINEAR),*
>
> *C2 - EXAMPLE INDIVIDUAL, PERSONAL PROFILE OF DYSLEXIA/ SPLD (SPATIAL)*
>
> *E3 - EXAMPLE: TABLE OF THINKING PREFERENCES.*

In the end you want to have a clear picture of your individual, personal profile of dyslexia/ SpLD as far as you know it to date. You want to be able to update it in the light of new experiences.

Details, similar to *EXAMPLE: DETAILED INFORMATION THAT IS LIKELY TO BE USEFUL,* allow you to remember how you built your profile. These details can have several benefits.

- It's helpful to see your progress.

- Your confidence is likely to increase when you scan the progress you've made.

- You will have a body of information that you can use in discussion with others.

TEMPLATES:

EXAMPLE: DETAILED INFORMATION THAT IS LIKELY TO BE USEFUL: p 66

- The details in the information you collect will trigger your memory, improve your accuracy and probably enhance the discussions you have with others.

- You don't want to repeat anything that didn't work, unless you are testing to see whether something new will bring new insights.

7.3 Pitfalls

The processes that allow you to see your strengths also allow you to be specific about the pitfalls of your dyslexia/ SpLD.

pitfall: a hidden or unsuspected danger, drawback, difficulty or opportunity for error ('pitfall, n. 4' OED Online, 2020)

Insight: The art of managing is to diminish pitfalls

The more you inspect the pitfalls of your profile, the more you learn how to deal with them.

The symptoms of dyslexia/ SpLD vary:

- from one person to another, both with the same professionally assessed syndrome

- for one person from time to time.

This variation doesn't help with the dialogue with those who have no dyslexia/ SpLD.

Keeping records of your observations will help you to understand what happens to you and will help you to explain to others. Your records should also include:

- any experiments you have done to find ways round your various pitfalls

- how you manage your way round the pitfalls.

With this information, you can show what you can achieve by minimising the effects of your dyslexia/ SpLD.

Other people may still be bemused, but as your confidence grows, there is often a good way of working or living together.

Example: Detailed information about a pitfall

Information	Example
date, place, situation	4th August 2010, Chester, wedding
what was happening	group of 8, my family, conversation about holidays
details re my dyslexia/ SpLD	I was moving my head to see Aunt T's hat in line with the palm tree behind her. It made a delightful pattern. Aunt T asked me a question; she was trying to include me in the cousins' talk. I was so embarrassed that I was too off-hand and hurt her feelings. I couldn't remember what we were talking about; I couldn't find any words that I wanted. My mind went a blank. I couldn't talk easily for the next couple of hours.
reflection	I frequently move my head like that. I don't know I'm doing it until I'm tripped up. 1) I like Aunt T and she would respond well to a card from me. 2) Find a safe occasion and try to be open about the distraction. See what that feels like.
insight code/ key words	pitfall/ visually distracted; no verbal recall.

Recognising that it happens allows you to watch out for it. Knowing that this pitfall gets you into difficulties, you then have the opportunity to do something about it. You can record what happens in several different situations to decide: 1) when it is serious and when it doesn't much matter; 2) whether there is anything you can do to see such a moment coming and take avoiding action. Without observing and keeping records, you limit your choices of keeping out of the ensuing dyslexic/ SpLD moments.

As well as showing a pitfall, this insight suggests visual thinking is strong and verbal isn't. You can test that by using visual strengths in different circumstances and see what impact the visual thinking has on what you want to do.

7.4 Accommodation

Pitfalls can be divided into hazards and obstacles. A hazard is something that you need to take particular care about, but you can work your way around it: you have strategies. An obstacle is something you have no method to deal with. You will need accommodations to deal with obstacles.

Accommodations are part of your profile of dyslexia/ SpLD because they can be negotiated in advance of being used: they are part of the known package that your profile represents.

NEGOTIATING ACCOMMODATION: p 324

You will be asking other people to put something different in place for you: extra time in exams is one well-known accommodation in education; typefaces without serifs (the projections on letters in some fonts) are quite common in communication.

Collecting evidence is part of negotiating with those who need to organise the accommodation. This time your evidence will be showing:

- how your dyslexia/ SpLD is hampering your performance
- anything you have tried as a way to deal with the pitfall
- why other strategies you have don't work for this pitfall
- that you are capable of the task when the pitfall is taken care of.

You may need someone to support your request for accommodation; it can be quite difficult to negotiate on your own behalf.

8 Regime for managing dyslexia/ SpLD

Being dyslexic/ SpLD, you cannot assume your mind is going to function well all the time, see *ASPECTS OF DYSLEXIA/ SPLD*. The nature of SpLDs is that the effects are going to be intermittent and will occur unpredictably. Therefore, skills for managing dyslexia/ SpLD need to be developed and built into a regime for managing dyslexia/ SpLD.

ASPECTS OF DYSLEXIA/ SPLD: p 342

Developing the necessary skills is not easy, especially if you experienced lack of understanding and progress while a child.

The psychological scarring from childhood can be deep and possibly never goes away. If anything happens to trigger the memory of a painful episode, dealing with a current situation can become more complex.

Insight: Mental energy to manage dyslexia/ SpLD

By using thinking preferences and various strategies, it is possible to function at a level that is comparable to your best intelligence.

For a dyslexic person that means using language at a level that is much better than the dyslexic language, see *FIGURE 1.6, MENTAL ENERGY TO MONITOR*.

However, the dyslexia/ SpLD doesn't get removed. It is still there in the mind and you can be triggered into using those thought processes.

Mental energy often has to be reserved to monitor progress in order to stay out of your dyslexic/ SpLD processing.

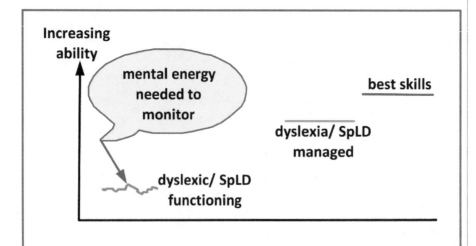

Figure 1. 6 Mental energy to monitor

The following steps are useful in deciding how to manage dyslexia/ SpLD:

Step	Step details	Section	Further discussion
1	to see potential dyslexic/ SpLD pitfalls	8.1: p 74	*METHODS FOR OBSERVING:* p 55
2	to pause and keep thinking clearly	8.2: p 76	*THINKING CLEARLY:* p 254
3	to know how your mind works	8.3: p 77	*THINKING PREFERENCES:* p 188 *USING THE MIND:* p 138
4	to know what your goals are	8.4: p 78	*KNOW WHAT YOUR GOALS ARE:* p 78

Managing dyslexia/ SpLD uses the information in a personal profile of dyslexia/ SpLD.

- It will be a question of knowing which pitfall from your profile is alive in any given situation, or whether you are facing something new.
- The most suitable way of pausing and keeping thinking clear will be chosen from the profile.
- Thinking preferences will be used from the profile.

Managing situations may reveal new insights that can be added to these sections of a profile.

- Knowing your goal in any situation is a combination of several different thinking skills.

Goals are specific to a situation or task. They are not part of your profile. The skills to identify a goal are part of your regime for managing dyslexia/ SpLD.

The details of the accommodation element of a personal profile are usually put in place in advance and are part of any situation that has to be managed. As they are used, new experience may show how they need to be adjusted to be more effective.

The next 4 sections discuss each step of managing dyslexia/ SpLD. The 5th section deals with developing the skills and building them into a regime of good practice that suits you.

8.1 See potential dyslexic/ SpLD pitfalls

In building your profile, you pull together all the likely pitfalls from your dyslexia/ SpLD. In knowing them more objectively, you give yourself the opportunity to learn to recognise them. One of the benefits of becoming more observant is that you can recognise pitfalls while you can still do something about them. But not all pitfalls are known in advance and not all can be seen coming towards you.

AN INDIVIDUAL, PERSONAL PROFILE OF DYSLEXIA/ SPLD: p 64

The first story below is an example of a predictable pitfall, the second of an unpredictable one:

Story: Pitfall turning off a yacht engine

The steps in turning off the engine on a yacht need to follow a certain sequence. One dyslexic sailor, Anne, learnt them by doing the sequence; another, Bob, by numbering the steps and knowing what was important about each step. At one point a black knob is pushed down: Anne just did it; Bob needed to know that the fuel was being reconnected for future running of the engine . The potential pitfall is that Bob would get the sequence wrong if he followed Anne's method of learning the sequence.

Story: Unpredictable pitfall

A dyslexic colleague and I were working with a group of dyslexic students in the early afternoon. The students were sitting at tables in rows. I was giving out the handouts, walking round the room and putting the handouts on the tables in front of the students. The way I put the handout on a desk in front of my colleague brought back memories of being in an exam. The memory triggered her dyslexic functioning. For the rest of the afternoon she could not get out of being dyslexic: in reading, in timekeeping and in her organisation.

Comments on the first story:

You need to take responsibility for the way you learn and be clear about why you are using the approach you adopt. Not taking responsibility could have led to dyslexia taking over the thinking processes of Bob as he turned off the engine. Anne could not see the point of Bob's need for information.

It can be difficult when two dyslexic/ SpLD people have to work together, because they may not realise, any more than non-dyslexics, that you have to work with the differences rather than fight them. The stress from the lack of confidence in knowing the sequence could have been the cause of a dyslexic episode and a potential danger out in the ocean.

Comments on the second story:

Two approaches can help. One is to be aware of how you are functioning. The other is to know a lot about dyslexia/ SpLD so that you can put such an episode into perspective and not take any difficulties personally.

Know how you are functioning:
METHODS FOR OBSERVING: p 55

Other examples of situations when both the foreseen and unforeseen pitfalls are likely to occur are: sitting exams, presentations, roadworks, shopping ...

There are times, sitting exams is one, when it is important to reserve some mental attention just to keep an eye on progress and keep checking that all is well. No matter how well you know your material for exams, there is the potential to get stuck in dyslexic/ SpLD functioning and extra time is often used as the buffer time to sort out the problems.

> **Tip: Recognising pitfalls**
>
> As you observe objectively, you will be able to describe pitfalls that occur for you in terms of:
>
> - any dyslexia/ SpLD issues
> - what you notice as advance warnings
> - any reactions in your body
> - other signs you come to know.
>
> Add anything useful to the pitfall section of your profile.

Gradually, pitfalls lose some of their power to derail you, and become part of life's rich fabric. You can get to a point where most of the time you can think:

> "OK, this [...] has happened. No big deal. That's the way the cookie crumbled. Let's pause and decide what's best to do!"

There are also times when you are not derailed at all. Something happens that is characteristic of your dyslexia/ SpLD but you notice it immediately and can undo what's happened without any difficulty. Such moments are dyslexic/ SpLD glitches.

Ⓖ p 353: glitch

8.2 Pause and keep thinking clearly

There is an on/off switch between a state of panic and deep breathing:

- in a state of panic you will be breathing rapidly and with the upper chest
- if you switch your breathing to be deep and rhythmic, you will switch off the panic and your thinking will be clearer.

See *THINKING CLEARLY* for techniques of breathing and relaxation, and other ways of pausing to good effect so that your thinking remains clear.

THINKING CLEARLY: p 254

My own thoughts are that you have to practise any technique and get it well established before trying it out for real; then you need to build up trust in it by using it in mild situations first. Further, if you are not clear about what to do or think next, the panic will set in again, hence the next two steps of managing dyslexia/ SpLD.

Tip: Pausing well

As you practise ways of pausing, notice which ones work well for you and in what sort of situations they work.

Add the information to both your profile and your regime for managing dyslexia/ SpLD.

8.3 Know how your mind works

Once you've recognised something which is going to tax your dyslexia/ SpLD and you've paused to reflect on it, you have to think how to deal with it. Deliberately using your thinking preferences helps you to use your mind effectively. Very consciously employing good mental strategies also helps you to think effectively.

The next three chapters of this book are about learning how your mind works; you will find those choices that make the most difference to the way you think.

next 3 chapters:
ABOUT THE MIND: p 86

USING THE MIND: p 138

THINKING PREFERENCES: p 188

Tip: Your mind can work well

Enabling your mind to work well is a combination of knowing your thinking preferences and knowing a range of techniques which help with thinking. You can gather the ones that suit you best into the appropriate section of both your profile and your regime.

The application of good thinking preferences and techniques will gradually improve your self-confidence and you will find it easier to negotiate your needs with other people.

8.4 Know what your goals are

- You've recognised something that presents a pitfall to your dyslexia/ SpLD.
- You've stopped to give yourself a chance to deal with it.
- You've collected your mental strengths.

If you don't think about what you need to achieve, you could end up doing totally the wrong things, or lapsing back into the pitfall.

Story: Goal: To find the right environment

A dyslexic and dyspraxic student has to find the right place to revise, work and live. To revise for finals, she was given a separate room to work in. She could mount her revision charts on the walls. These were large and very pictorial. She could spread out her books and notes on the floor and all the available surfaces. She could leave everything in place, knowing nobody would move anything.

This arrangement was essential for her style of working. Her goal was to have a space in which she could function at her best.

I have supported her during courses after her finals. She has been through several places of living and work. It's as if she journeyed through different habitats: a forest, a desert, a downland...

When she ignores the goal for her to be in a space that works for her and she lets other aspects, such as low rent, become priorities, she doesn't manage her dyslexia and dyspraxia at all well. Life definitely goes pear-shaped again.

Just taking the care needed to think things all the way through can make a big difference to you feeling you have achieved the right outcome, rather than feeling that it has all gone horribly wrong again.

Exercise: What is your goal?

You have paused to manage a situation or task.

What is the task facing you? or the situation?

What do you want to do?

How much time do you have?

What resources do you have?

Define your goal as clearly as possible.

What PITFALL has caused you to pause? Is it a hazard or an
 obstacle?

How do you want to cope with it?

How is it impacting on your goal?

What is the next step for achieving your goal?

PITFALL: p 69

Tip: Skills for defining your goal

As you practise defining goals, notice which strategies you like
using best and what kind of topic or situation they work for. Build
these strategies into your regime. It is probably worth making a
note of those that work for you, even if they are not the very best
for you. You may need them as well.

8.5   Building your regime

Developing management skills is a process of building up knowledge
of how you think and take-action well and how you avoid the pitfalls.
By being systematic in the way you build up this knowledge, you will
gain patterns of behaviour that you can draw on and develop further.
You can summarise the skills into a regime for managing dyslexia/
SpLD.

Ⓖ p 353: take-action

As you develop your skills, you need to interpret your observations and test them to make sure the interpretations fit together.

Exercise: Developing skills for managing dyslexia/ SpLD

RECORDINGS:

1   Make a list of recent situations or events that you think were affected by your dyslexia/ SpLD.

2   Decide: how well you can remember them
                     how you feel about each one now
                     how often something similar happens.

3   From your list choose a situation:

a   for which you don't have a strong emotional reaction, or you have the least emotional reaction

b   which you remember well/ best.

4   To capture your memory of the situation, use the TEMPLATES:
D1 - MANAGING DYSLEXIA/ SPLD (SPATIAL) OR
D2 - MANAGING DYSLEXIA/ SPLD (LINEAR).

TEMPLATES:

5.   To understand further what was happening, use material listed under INDEX entries:

          pitfalls, pausing, thinking preferences and goals.

INDEX: p 379

6   Look for answers to the following questions:
          What do you think triggered your dyslexia/ SpLD?
          What was the dyslexic/ SpLD problem that was triggered?

Did you use any skills for pausing?

How effective were they?

What would you use another time?

What thinking preferences did you use?

How effective were they?

What would you do another time?

How well did you recognise your goal?

Did you stay focused on it?

Was it the right goal to help you?

7   Decide on any skill you would like to practise for a future event. Work out a timetable for practising it.

Using this exercise on a regular basis with different situations affected by your dyslexia/ SpLD will enable you to build your regime for managing dyslexia/ SpLD.

You should be able to finish with a summary such as *TEMPLATE: D5 - EXPERIENCES FOR MANAGING DYSLEXIA/ SPLD - EXAMPLE*.

TEMPLATES:

Choose headings for your experiences that suit your life circumstances, for example 'work' or 'hobbies' instead of 'study', which is in the example.

Your regime will probably change over time as your life circumstances change and as methods of communication change. Be flexible and try new ideas in situations where you can afford to be adventurous.

9 To manage or not to manage

You need to find the level of dyslexia/ SpLD management that suits you best.

Some dyslexic/ SpLDs thoroughly enjoy being very well organised with the SpLD always (as much as possible) under control.

Others can tolerate things going wrong and yet again others love the adventure of never quite knowing what will happen.

It does have an impact on those around us, because they often operate quite differently and find it hard to come to terms with the way we are, so their needs should be taken into consideration.

The different experiences of non-dyslexic/ SpLD people are of sufficient importance that there is an item in the *INDEX*.

INDEX: p 379

Managing your own dyslexia/ SpLD is much less dangerous than relying on the help of others.

When you are the manager: you gain in self-respect and confidence; you have resources to draw on when things go wrong, as they inevitably will. (Remember, things go wrong for most people in some way at some time.)

When you rely on others, there comes a time when the helper isn't around and you get stuck without resources, which is not nearly such a good position to be in as being able to manage your dyslexia/ SpLD yourself.

**Tip: Responding to the remarks of others
– good, bad or neutral**

The remarks from others are likely to keep coming. Gradually you can find a way of deflecting the remarks while maintaining your confidence in your way of doing things.
You may have to find a phrase you feel comfortable with such as:
"I'm choosing to function and not be chaotic!"

A parallel situation is how I wear ear muffs even on a warm summer day. I can get really tired of people remarking on them. I've taken to saying, "Ear-ache or ear muffs. Which would you choose?"

Creative living without dyslexia/ SpLD

'Creative living' includes the effective way you deal with life as much as being artistically creative or scientifically inventive or a distinct problem solver.

As you learn to manage your dyslexia/ SpLD, you enjoy creative living.

Sometimes, life has no challenges and you can simply get on with living.

Sometimes, you will deal with a challenging situation without any need to deal with dyslexia/ SpLD. Parts of your profile of dyslexia/ SpLD and regime for managing it will be useful:

- there is an element of conscious choice in the way you bring your strengths to the situation
- you may have to maintain the application of your thinking strengths using TECHNIQUES TO ASSIST USING YOUR MIND and THINKING CLEARLY techniques.

You will probably be using thinking preferences that the majority of other people ignore. Others often notice your contribution, and you may well find yourself being extremely capable.

You can grow in confidence and self-esteem by choosing to live creatively using your thinking strengths and the skills of managing dyslexia/ SpLD.

10   Summary: your personal profile and your regime for managing dyslexia/ SpLD

A personal profile of dyslexia/ SpLD comprises:
> thinking preferences
> pitfalls (due to dyslexia/ SpLD)
> pausing and maintaining clear thinking
> accommodations

A regime for managing dyslexia/ SpLD includes:
> recognising the pitfalls
> pausing
> using your best thinking
> knowing your goal

MARGIN NOTE: One outcome from working with this book is that a dyslexic/ SpLD person has a *TOOL BOX FOR LIVING CONFIDENTLY:* p 319

Both will develop over time and probably will always be evolving.

The profile is all that is known to date. The accommodations can be put in place in advance of their use.

The regime for managing dyslexia/ SpLD is about the instantaneous skills for dealing with life as it happens. Part of managing dyslexia/ SpLD involves using the personal profile well.

References

Miles, Tim and Varma, Ved, 1995, *Dyslexia and Stress,* Whurr, London
Stacey, Ginny, 1992, *A Taste of Dyslexia (Video),* Oxfordshire Dyslexia Association, Oxford
Stacey, Ginny, 2005, *A Taste of Dyslexia (DVD),* Oxfordshire Dyslexia Association, Oxford

Stacey, Ginny, 2020a, *Organisation and Everyday Life with Dyslexia and other SpLDs,* Routledge, London

Stacey, Ginny, 2020b, *Development of Dyslexia and other SpLDs,* Routledge, London

Stacey, Ginny, 2021, *Gaining Knowledge and Skills with Dyslexia and other SpLDs,* Routledge, London

West, Thomas, G, 1991, *In The Mind's Eye,* Prometheus Books, Buffalo, NY

Wood, Earnest, 1962, *Yoga,* Penguin Books, Harmondsworth

Website information

OED Online, December 2020, Oxford University Press. Accessed 12 February 2021.

Orlando Bloom: search on "Orlando Bloom" and "dyslexia" to find interviews with him and links to interviews with others.
e.g.: Orlando Bloom – Made by Dyslexia
https://www.youtube.com/watch?v=-_ij_ZyDwVI
Accessed 12 February 2021

Series website: www.routledge.com/cw/stacey

2 About the Mind

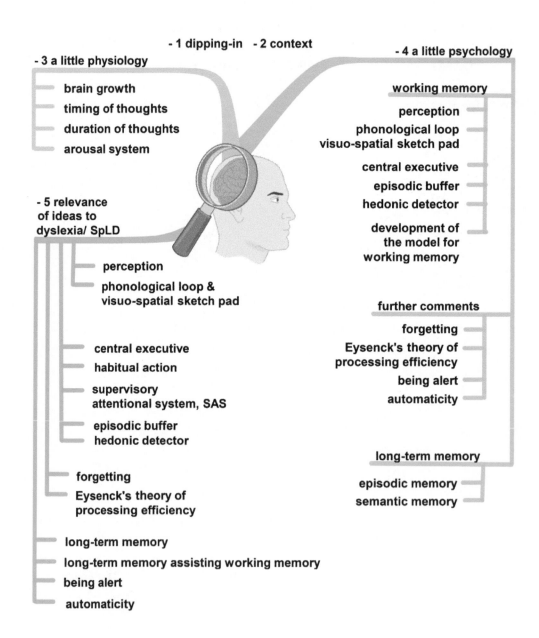

- 1 dipping-in   - 2 context

- 3 a little physiology

- brain growth
- timing of thoughts
- duration of thoughts
- arousal system

- 5 relevance
of ideas to
dyslexia/ SpLD

- perception
- phonological loop &
visuo-spatial sketch pad

- central executive
- habitual action
- supervisory
attentional system, SAS
- episodic buffer
hedonic detector

- forgetting
- Eysenck's theory of
processing efficiency

- long-term memory
- long-term memory assisting working memory
- being alert
- automaticity

- 4 a little psychology

working memory

- perception
- phonological loop
visuo-spatial sketch pad

- central executive
- episodic buffer
- hedonic detector

- development of
the model for
working memory

further comments

- forgetting
- Eysenck's theory of
processing efficiency
- being alert
- automaticity

long-term memory

- episodic memory
- semantic memory

Contents

Interconnecting sections:

This chapter has many interconnected sections (§).

The page numbers of the connections are given in the margin.

The text used in §3 & §4 is: '*RELEVANCE:*§ number & p number'.

     in §5: '*PHYSIOLOGY* or *PSYCHOLOGY:*§ number & p number'.

Vital for dyslexic/ SpLDs, good practice for all

The concepts from physiology and psychology in this chapter are some of the ideas that have made a significant difference to dyslexic/ SpLD people with whom I've worked. Knowing these ideas can enhance your self-esteem and confidence. The chapter icon and a gold margin line have been used to pick out the significant ideas.

Much of the basic physiology and psychology applies to everyone, so it can be interesting and helpful to anyone.

Working with the chapter

Collect the information that relates to you. See how knowing more about your brain and mind can change the way you deal with dyslexia/ SpLD and how you feel about yourself.

Templates on the website

A1   *JOTTING DOWN AS YOU SCAN*
A4   *JOTTING DOWN AS YOU READ*
B1   *COLLECTING IDEAS THAT RELATE TO YOU*
B3   *COMPARE EXPECTATIONS AND REALITY*

TEMPLATES:

Appendix 1 Resources

MONITORING PROGRESS could help you build on ideas that relate to you.

APPENDIX 1: p 300

MONITORING PROGRESS: p 311

Appendix 2 Individual, Personal Profile of Dyslexia/ SpLD and Regime for Managing Dyslexia/ SpLD

Add anything that helps you with your dyslexia/ SpLD to the best place in your profile or regime.

APPENDIX 2: p 314

Appendix 3 Key Concepts

This appendix has a summary of the key ideas I cover when doing an audit of skills and knowledge with a dyslexic/ SpLD student. It shows · which of the 4 books in the series covers each idea in full.

APPENDIX 3: p 328

1 Dipping-in to try out ideas

- Look for sections that match your experience
    - use the chapter icon and gold margin strip and use the coloured boxes
    - start with RELEVANCE TO DYSLEXIA/ SPLD
- As you find sections of interest, follow the connections in the margin to other related sections in the chapter.

RELEVANCE TO DYSLEXIA/ SPLD: p 120

Skim any sections you don't read now, so that you know what's in them and can come back to them when they are relevant to you.

2 Context

FURTHER READING:
Baddeley (1982, 2007)

Rattray Taylor (1979)

Stein and Stoodley (2006)

Wolf (2008)

The brain-mind is fascinating, at both the physiological and psychological levels. I have listened to scientists talking about the brain and mind, and read their work. I wanted to make sense[1] of the experience of dyslexia/ SpLD, both my own and that of people I have worked with for more than 20 years.

The findings from physiology and psychology are important because:
- they make sense of some experiences dyslexic/ SPLD people have
- they help you to decide how to proceed in the future
- they give adults more confidence to talk about their experiences.

The more we contribute in this way to the general understanding of dyslexia/ SpLD, the more we will improve our own situation:
- the better employers will understand our needs and make any adjustments that will let us contribute fully
- the better families and friends will accept who we are and what we bring to life
- the more children will have a chance to be listened to.

---

[1] Caveat. It is difficult to write about subject areas that you haven't studied properly. I recognise that I am neither a physiologist nor a psychologist. However, I have found that these ideas have helped me to use my dyslexic brain-mind, which is the only one I have. I wrote this chapter in the hopes that the ideas will help others.

2 About the Mind

Many of the difficulties of dyslexia/ SpLD can be avoided. Adults' and children's self-esteem and confidence can remain high when there is greater understanding of differences in the way we all think.

Physiology studies the brain: its structures, the neurons, the chemical reactions, etc.

Psychology studies the mind and behaviour.

In *FIGURE 2.1, USING THE MIND*, working memory and long-term memory are part of the psychological functions of the mind while thoughts, actions and personal memories are the processes of the mind.

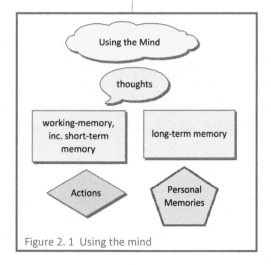

Figure 2. 1 Using the mind

This is how I think of the brain, mind and psyche:

- Brain is the physical material: the structures of the brain, the neurons, the chemical reactions, etc.
- Mind is the thinking processes: the products or results of what happens in the brain.
- Psyche is the complexity of thinking and feeling that contributes to an individual person's characteristics.

Ⓖ p 353: brain, mind, psyche

 I have met many dyslexic/ SpLD people with difficulties that have grown and multiplied from some very early memories. It is as if something about the memory has become fixed in an incomplete or erroneous way. The memories are stored in the brain structures; they are part of the psyche and they contribute to the workings of the mind.

Story: Pronunciation error

'Hyperbole' was pronounced as 'HYper- bowl'[2] by one dyslexic English teacher until he was 40 years old; then he realised others were saying 'high-PER-b-lee'. To this day, the correct pronunciation requires careful attention by the teacher, since his original pronunciation has not been erased.

 Whether new information is being used in the short term or is intended for longer term use, it can be really important that your mind is being well used right from the start, either as an adult or as a child.

Story: A psychologist's view on how people think

Thinking preferences are not included in assessments.
I once asked a psychologist whether the methods people use for thinking were ever included in psychological assessment; he told me: "No, that would be too subjective."

Grant (2005) and Jefferies (2008) are two psychologists who have taken note of the comments of those they assess. Stacey (2020b) Ⓖ p 353: subjective vs. objective

Yet my students often came back from their diagnostic assessment expressing disquiet because they had the feeling that the tests were not assessing their thinking accurately (Stacey, 2020b). I think it is really important that adult dyslexic/ SpLD people contribute their understanding of their dyslexic/ SpLD experiences to psychology, especially when it doesn't fit the perceived wisdom.

---

[2]'HYper-bowl'. One way to show pronunciation is to use a well recognised spelling to give the sound of each syllable and to use capitals or bold font to show the stressed syllable, i.e. the part of the word that is most noticeable.

3   A little physiology

I have only included the ideas from physiology that I have found particularly useful when discussing dyslexia/ SpLD; I have included why or how the ideas relate to dyslexia/ SpLD.

The *INSIGHT: PARK PATHS AND PRUNING NEURONS* has an analogy for pruning neurons and the *PHILOSOPHY OF THIS SERIES* sets out my view of dyslexia/ SpLD in terms of neural networks. Some of the comments in this section may make more sense if you read these two boxes first.

INSIGHT: PARK PATHS AND PRUNING NEURONS: p 4

PHILOSOPHY OF THIS SERIES: p 4

The ideas included are:

- brain growth, pruning, neural connections and neural networks
- timing of thoughts and myelin layers
- duration of thoughts, electrical and chemical changes and changes to proteins
- the arousal system and alertness.

FURTHER READING:
Russell (1979)

Baddeley (1982)

Rattray Taylor (1979)

These possible physiological explanations offer the chance of reflecting on your own experiences and developing the best solution to the various problems encountered. They are not reasons to give up.

3.1   Brain growth

This section discusses why the early years are so important for minimising dyslexic/ SpLD problems.

The brain goes on growing after a baby is born in that the number of neural connections is still increasing. Between 4 months and a year, the baby has twice as many connections as he/she will have as an adult (Eagleman, 2015, p 7). At birth, a baby's brain weight is about 25% of that of the adult brain. At about the age of 5 the child's brain weight is about 90% of that of the adult, but 90% of the connections that were made during the first 2 years are pruned away later because they don't prove useful. The majority of growth happens before 5 years old, but pruning and optimisation of connections still goes on until you're old. Learning in adults as in children still involves changes in these connections (Russell, 1979, p 23).

Eagleman (2015, p 7)

Russell (1979, p 23).

As the child learns, the neural connections that help make sense of the world are used more than others. Those that are not used die through lack of use, in the pruning process (Eagleman, 2015, p 7). Pruning is useful; it strengthens and selects the most used neural connections and produces consistent neural networks for representing the world and accomplishing tasks; the neural networks are what mediate learned skills.

(G) p 353: pruning

Eagleman (2015, p 7)

As a result of pruning, many tasks become automatic and can be done without conscious thought, for example spelling a word. Confusion can result if a single neural network is not established, but several conflicting pathways persist that could be used to carry out a task, see *PARK PATHS AND PRUNING NEURONS*.   I sometimes wonder whether pruning is incomplete for dyslexic/ SpLD people: spelling and reading don't settle to accepted patterns as they do for others.

See *PARK PATHS AND PRUNING NEURONS*: p 4

Differences in brain structures of dyslexic people's brains were reported in 1985 (Galaburda et al.) when deceased people's brains were examined. Current research uses non-invasive techniques, such as functional Magnetic Resonance Imaging (fMRI). Finn et al. (2014) showed that the connectivity in dyslexic readers' brains is significantly different from that in non-impaired[3] readers' brains. Their research also reports that the dyslexic readers use alternative circuits (neural networks) to those used by non-impaired readers.

Galaburda et al. (1985)

Finn et al. (2014)

In the process of thinking, signals pass through the neural networks, see *MARGIN NOTE*.

MARGIN NOTE: It has not yet been established how signals passing through the brain become thoughts, but they are obviously related.
This analogy doesn't represent the whole of thinking, but it can be a useful picture to have.

Insight: Analogy for thoughts – metro map

My mental image, or analogy, came from the way you could find a route on the Paris Metro system: The whole system set out as a map represents the brain for me. If it represented a child's brain at birth there would be connections directly between most of the stations, but since only certain stations are connected by the different lines, the metro map represents a brain after pruning has happened and neural networks have been established.

---

[3] 'Non-impaired' is the terminology used by Finn et al.

You selected the beginning and end of your journey and, as you pressed the buttons on those stations, the stations in between lit up. When you selected a different journey, other stations lit up. The whole system was there, but it was not all lit up at the same time.

I see this as similar to the way thinking sends signals through some parts of the brain and while that thinking is going on energy, of some sort, is flowing through certain neural networks and leaving memory traces.

As all children are learning, it can be easy to overlook the signs of different processing in a few children amongst a whole class. However, it is really important that the early learning is right for each child, as the networks laid down at the early stages can persist for some children much longer and with greater strength than is expected; see *OLDEST MEMORY TRACE*.

OLDEST MEMORY TRACE: p 342

Insight: Hazards of dyslexia when learning

I am particularly careful about the way I learn something new when the hazards of my dyslexia will be involved. I realise that I need carefully to establish the most useful neural pathway, and I need to avoid any possible alternatives so that they can die away and not contribute confusion.

By way of contrast, my dyslexia does not affect my sense of space and direction; my mind registers information about where I am without me having to try; I can afford to get lost in most places because I can be confident of finding my way again, see *MARGIN NOTE*.

MARGIN NOTE: 'No sense of direction' is usually recognised as characteristic of dyslexia, but there are some, like me, who have a good one.

One of the tragedies of dyslexia/ SpLD is that the importance of the early stages is overlooked. Is that what happened for you? Were your parents told you would grow out of the early stage difficulties? Some parents don't recognise that their child could make more progress if taught a different way and, without question, they accept that their child isn't learning.

3.2   The timing of thoughts

The timing of thoughts may impact on effective processing by the mind.

As the neural system and brain develops, the axons of neurons gradually become coated with myelin (a process called myelination), see *FIGURE 2.2*. The myelin enables signals to be passed along the axon at greater speeds.

For simplicity, *FIGURE 2.2* shows only a few connections, synapses, at the end of the axon. There is a vast number of other synapses, including ones which input to the neuron. When the net input from all the synapses takes a neuron over a certain threshold, it fires, which means it sends a signal down the axon.

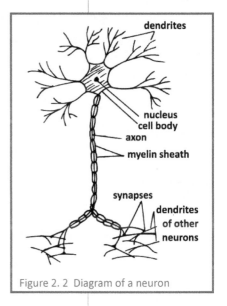

Figure 2. 2 Diagram of a neuron

Ⓖ p 353: neuron firing

The visual system in the brain was developed, in evolutionary terms, much earlier than language and there is some specialisation of cell function that could result in the visual system being faster than the verbal.

I find it helpful to know that there are processes in the brain mechanisms that can affect the timing of transmission, and hence of thought, and that different thoughts might get out of sync.

Insight: Malsequencing not mis-spelling

As you write you can be aware of the order in which letters or words flow to the paper or computer; you can see that certain letters are frequently getting to the text out of order; the same happens with words. Newby, who is dyslexic, has argued that 'mal-sequencing' aptly described the experience of dyslexics and that 'conflicting signals get in the way in such areas as spelling'.

Newby in Miles and Varma (1995, p 106)

Insight: Mind and hand out of sync

Students have reported that their minds are racing on with their ideas while the hand is dragging behind; they find words belonging to ideas in the mind get written in amongst the words that the hand is trying to write[4]. Fast touch-typists should have less of a problem with this than slow typists or those who write by hand. To be a fast touch-typist many of the movements will have been learnt to the point at which they become automatic and the typing process will be much better able to keep up with the production of ideas.

---

[4] We have a disagreement with a friendly non-dyslexic psychologist over the descriptions in these stories and insights. These are just the types of insights that dyslexic/ SpLD people need to share with each other to build up a body of case histories that can more accurately represent what is happening in our brain/ minds. This is the evidence that dyslexic/ SpLD adults can provide to contribute significantly to the research into dyslexia/ SpLD.

Insight: Difficulty with word finding

A persistent and commonly shared problem of dyslexia is difficulty with finding the right words. The rapid naming task is one of the most reliable tests in the assessment battery. It tests the speed of naming certain objects in pictures.

Insight: Being aware: speed of thoughts – part 1

The more you become aware of your thinking the more you can see that some of your thoughts have significantly different speeds. Russell (1979, p 172) states that thoughts dealing with concrete information are far faster than those dealing with abstract information.

Speed of thoughts: see also: *INSIGHT: SPEED OF HOLISTIC THINKING*, p 223

Russell (1979, p 172)
Ⓖ p 353: concrete

It has been argued (West, 1991) that dyslexic people think well on the right side of the brain, which is more involved with spatial thinking, while the left is more involved with language processing. There can be considerable problems if the differences in speed of your ideas and your language are not managed well. As part of building your *REGIME FOR MANAGING DYSLEXIA/ SPLD*, you can gather together your strategies for dealing with the problems you encounter.

West (1991)

REGIME FOR MANAGING DYSLEXIA/ SPLD: p 71

> **Insight: Being aware: speed of thoughts – part 2**
>
> Several thoughts are usually needed to make a decision or to take action. They may not arrive for processing in your mind in the order expected by others based on their own experience. You may need to put in much more effort to arrive at an outcome that seems reasonable to others. You may need to spend time and energy to explain your thinking to others.
>
> The unexpected timing of one thought with respect to another may cause misunderstandings and is another factor to watch for in dealing with dyslexia/ SpLD.

Anecdotal evidence suggests that the timing of thoughts is an important factor. There are ideas from physiology that raise questions about timing of thoughts. The important point for managing dyslexia/ SpLD is to observe what is happening for you and work out strategies to minimise any disruptions while enhancing your useful contributions.

3.3 Duration of thoughts

We all have a tendency to expect everyone's thinking patterns to be the same as ours. The result can often be false expectations and frustration. Accepting that people's thoughts last for different amounts of time can be part of defusing tangled situations.

For complex thinking, you need to work with a lot of different thoughts all at the same time:

- you need your thoughts to exist for some length of time
- you need some storage for thoughts (memory)
- you need access to your thoughts.

The length of time a thought is accessible affects whether you can use it or not.

Insight: Too many thoughts to keep in mind together

It can feel like juggling when too many thoughts have to be kept in mind together: you have to keep going round them to keep them 'alive' long enough to work with them.

For a major dissertation, one dyslexic had this problem after he had done all the research and needed to plan how the dissertation would be put together and written. He had to write out the significant information on Post-it notes. He stuck the Post-it notes on large pieces of paper which he laid out on the floor, *FIGURE 2.3*. This way, all the notes were visible and none could be overlooked (out of sight is out of mind). He then moved the notes around until the dissertation had a structure that could be written.

Figure 2. 3 Post-it notes for planning

Signals relating to thoughts pass along the axons of neurons; they cross from one neuron to another by either changes in electrical potential across the gap between neurons, the synapse, or the release of transmitters in the synapse (Russell, 1979, p 35), see *FIGURE 2.4*.

The signal along the neuron is electrical, as are the changes in an electrical synapse; the transmitters in the synapse are chemical. With time, the electrical and chemical changes reset: the signal stops, or the thought passes. Without rehearsal, a thought lasts not much more than 18 seconds, (Baddeley, 1982, p 154). With some rehearsal, the time that the thought persists can be lengthened to the order of minutes, and again when the electrical and chemical conditions are reset, the thought has disappeared.

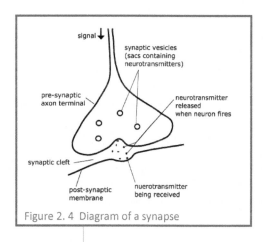

Figure 2. 4 Diagram of a synapse

Russell (1979, p 35)
Baddeley (1982, p 154)

3.3.1 Long-term memory

Long-term memory can last for a few days or for decades (Stein and Stoodley, 2006, pp 412-426). Once a particular connection has been made across a synapse, various processes increase the likelihood of the connection happening again: deliberate recall at spaced intervals, associations, rehearsal and reflection.

At the physiological level, the current view is that if the 2 neurons on either side of the synapse fire together they cause changes in the proteins in the synapse and that these enhance their likelihood of firing together in the future – 'neurons that fire together wire together' (Stein and Stoodley, 2006, p 415).

These changes are more permanent than the chemical and electrical signals of working and short-term memory.

From conversations with dyslexic/ SpLD people, it seems clear that some memories are very much shorter than the equivalent ones of non-dyslexic/ SpLD people and that others are very much more enduring.

PSYCHOLOGY:
§4. p 103
RELEVANCE:
§5.10 p 131
Stein and Stoodley
(2006, pp 412-426)

Stein and Stoodley
(2006, p 415)

> **Insight: Short- or long-lived thoughts**
>
> When writing down instructions from someone else's dictation, a dyslexic/ SpLD person will often have to ask for words to be repeated one at a time: there is no memory for retaining a few words together.
>
> With no memory for temporarily storing words, anything that is heard or read has to be understood immediately. As a result, more effort is put into initial understanding. The memories created will last longer than those of non-dyslexic/ SpLD people who do not need to pay so much attention.

Exercise: How long do your thoughts last?

Use *TEMPLATE: B3 - COMPARE EXPECTATION AND REALITY* to capture details and help observation.

TEMPLATES:

Template columns	Example reflection
Event: Write down what's happening	Having a conversation with my aunt.
Expectation: Write what you and others expect to happen.	We're discussing arrangements; everyone will remember details.
Reality: Write details that strike you as unexpected.	I needed to ask questions (I wasn't remembering in short-term memory). My aunt was patient while I wrote details down.
Reflection: Write any observations on the results of the conversation.	Later, others checked the plans with me because I had written down the details (they hadn't remembered in long-term memory).

3.3.2 Learning

Hebb put forward the theory that 'Neurons that fire together, wire together' (Stein and Stoodley, 2006, p 415), i.e. that learning comes about through structural changes in synapses. The changes result from frequent use of the synapses and the neurons. If a group of neurons frequently fire together, there is an increased likelihood that they will continue to fire together in the future. The brain structure changes and learning takes place.

Stein and Stoodley (2006, p 415)

One strong theme in my work with dyslexic/ SpLD students has been to do with getting their minds to hold information together so that it can be remembered and used: it is about enabling 'firing together' in order for learning to happen. Links are made between pieces of information so that they become a unit, they have 'wired together'. It is by paying attention to the characteristics of the thinking preferences and using mind techniques that the 'wiring together' becomes effective.

3.4 Arousal system

PSYCHOLOGY:
§4.2.3 p 115

RELEVANCE:
§5.12 p 133

Being alert is important if you want to stay able to think. Many students have told me that they fight sleep and drowsiness while working with words.

In 1992, at a conference, I heard a scientist discuss the arousal system and anaesthesia (going to sleep). His talk made me think about the way reading without understanding makes me struggle with drowsiness and sleep. I experience the same effects while writing, if I haven't got my ideas clear in my head.

The sleep-wake cycle is controlled by the hypothalamus and reticular activation system. It is a complex system of several parts of the nervous system and five diffuse networks. The networks infiltrate the whole of the rest of the brain and release neuromodulators which control the excitability of neurons; i.e. the ability to arouse them into activity (Stein and Stoodley, 2006, pp 366-368). The reticular system also deals with challenges; and one of the persistent challenges of everyday life for dyslexic/ SpLD people is dealing with words.

Stein and Stoodley (2006, pp 366-368)

So the same system that controls the sleep-wake cycle is also controlling the dyslexic/ SpLD challenge of words.

Stein and Stoodley (2006, pp 371-372) say that sleep must have benefits for humans since we spend a third of our lives asleep. They say that these benefits are not really understood yet; that there is a large number of processes that are repaired or consolidated during sleep; and among these processes is the growth of synapses that underlies learning.

Stein and Stoodley (2006, pp 371-372)

One finding by Finn et al. (2014) is that, by comparison with non-impaired readers' brains, dyslexic readers' brains use alternative neural networks and don't readily integrate the visual signals of the text. The research highlighted the need for synchronicity across different brain regions.

Finn et al. (2014)

My work with dyslexic/ SpLD students indicates the importance of keeping the reticular system in its awake state. *USING THE MIND, THINKING PREFERENCES* and *THINKING CLEARLY* all contain material that helps you to stay alert while working with words [5].

USING THE MIND:
p 138

THINKING PREFERENCES:
p 188

THINKING CLEARLY:
p 254

4   A little psychology

My main sources for this section are two books by Alan Baddeley (1982, 2007). Baddeley has been working in the field of psychology since the late 1950s and he is a well respected researcher. He became Professor of Psychology at University of York in 2003. His interests are listed on the York website as 'human memory, neuroscience and the practical application of cognitive psychology'.

Baddeley (1982, 2007)

The terms working memory, short-term memory and long-term memory are used in this section. They come from various models of memory that have evolved in response to experimental evidence; the following is a very brief sketch of models of memory that came before Baddeley's.

A two-component model of memory had been proposed in 1890 and it was revived in 1949 by Donald Hebb. The two components were a short-term memory and a long-term memory. The short-term memory depended on electrical activity in the brain and was short-lived. The long-term memory involved changes in the brain that were more durable.

---

[5] The brain changes as it works and there are processes, collectively called allostasis, which bring the brain back to its normal state, homeostasis. When the brain has to deal too often with stressful changes, there is 'wear and tear' on the brain and body, which is called 'allostatic load' (McEwen and Gianaros, 2010). As part of their conclusion, McEwen and Gianaros state:
> 'Interventions should focus on top-down strategies intended to alter brain function in ways that will improve allostasis and minimize allostatic load. Instilling optimism, a sense of control and self-esteem, and finding a meaning and purpose in life should be among the chief goals of such interventions. Indeed, virtually all policies of the public and private sector are, in fact, health policies.'

In the modal model of memory put forward by Atkinson and Shiffron (1968), there is a single short-term store which holds information for a while and allows it to be processed, see *FIGURE 2.5*. The sequence for the model is: input from the environment > sensory registers > a single short-term store > response output; with exchange of information, backwards and forwards, between short-term store and long-term memory.

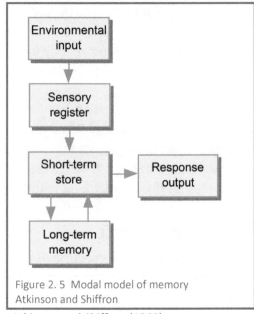

Figure 2. 5 Modal model of memory Atkinson and Shiffron

Atkinson and Shiffron (1968)

In Baddeley's multiple component working-memory model, see *FIGURE 2.6*, the single short-term store has been replaced by several components, some of which have short-term storage capacity.

Baddeley defines working memory as 'a temporary storage system under attentional control that underpins our capacity for complex thought'. (2007, p 1)

Short-term memory doesn't feature as a component of Baddeley's model, though short-term storage is a function of several of the components. Where the term 'short-term memory' is used in this book, it refers to all temporary storage of memories.

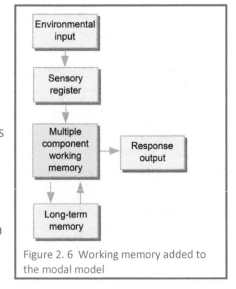

Figure 2. 6 Working memory added to the modal model

Temporary memories last for anything up to a few minutes and storage of the memory is not a main feature of the processes involved. According to the earlier book by Baddeley (1982), memories stored in long-term memory have the same characteristics whether

Baddeley (2007, p 1)

Baddeley (1982)

they are tested a few minutes later or years later; one feature of interest is how they become more or less accessible rather than how they change. Therefore, long-term memory refers to the storage of information that is durable and accessible over a period of time longer than a few minutes.

In discussing how the mind is used to process thoughts[6], I'm going to use Baddeley's multiple model for working memory. He wanted to understand how we think using memory, and to pull together all the different work that has been carried out: the result was the model he proposed in the book, with the different components evolving as understanding progressed. Working with ideas from Baddeley's model has made sense of work with dyslexic/ SpLD students.

Baddeley (2007)

The model evolved in close connection with experimental and medical data and it provides a structure and language for discussion about thinking and memory. Initial work on memory often comes from working with patients who have a disability or have had a major trauma, then experiments are devised to test certain ideas suggested by the medical data.

One method used in experimental work often relies on trying to restrict the mind to a single type of process and then seeing how that process can be disrupted by other processes[7]. Considerable care is needed to make sure interpretations are as accurate as possible. By comparison with the richness of thinking that people are capable of, the experimenters are restricted in how much they can deal with in one set of experiments. Researchers must be careful not to over-generalise their findings. As neurological imaging improves, more precise data may become available that can tell us much more precisely how the mind is thinking.

---

[6] The flow of brain signals can be disrupted by *EMOTIONAL HI-JACKING*, p 260. Under the influence of emotional hi-jack, your responses and subsequent actions don't benefit from the more measured processing of your mind.

[7] For example in the task to remember words seen in a sequence:
The single process is using sight only; verbal repetition has to be switched off which is done.by repeating the word 'the'.
Disruption comes from the words to be remembered being surrounded by other words which are similar in sound or meaning.

2   About the Mind

Overview of subsections

WORKING MEMORY and its components are discussed in *§4.1*.

§4.1: p 106

FURTHER COMMENTS, §4.2, has four comments about mind processes that I have found to be important with respect to dyslexia/ SpLD:

§4.2: p 113

> forgetting
> efficiency of processing
> being alert
> automaticity.

Forgetting can be due to something inherent in the memory trace or it can be caused by a memory trace not being accessible; in either case the knowledge or skill in the memory is no longer available to the processes of thinking and using the mind.

The theory about efficiency is interesting; it suggests to me that most people's minds naturally seek strategies without conscious attention, whereas dyslexic/ SpLD people have to be very deliberate in the way they keep their minds efficient.

Staying alert is a problem for many dyslexic people.

Not being able to use automatic processes creates extra mental effort for them.

LONG-TERM MEMORY, §4.3, is about the store which holds information in different ways and then lets it be available to the processes of thinking.

§4.3: p 116

§5: p 120

The ways in which I find these ideas relate to dyslexia/ SpLD are spelt out in *§5, RELEVANCE TO DYSLEXIA/ SPLD.*

4.1   Working memory

Baddeley's requirements of working memory are that:

- it processes stored information
- it uses material from various sources, including long-term memory
- it depends on a 'limited capacity, attentional control system'
- it is a flexible system that allows us to think about the real world.

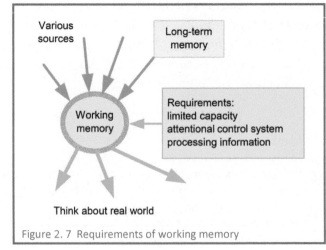

Figure 2. 7 Requirements of working memory

These requirements are shown in *FIGURE 2.7.*

Currently the components are: phonological loop, visuo-spatial sketch pad, central executive, episodic buffer and hedonic detector. The different components became defined as research and experience showed that different functions of working memory can be destroyed or dysfunctional in isolation from other functions and that clusters of functions belong together. No doubt other components will be delineated as we understand more about the workings of the mind in years to come.

There doesn't seem to be a neat, linear flow of processing from one element of working memory to another. The mind works by using parallel processing: many different functions operating simultaneously. Thus, each component of working memory has certain functions and capabilities which are used in conjunction with the other components and with parts of the mind that are not included in working memory. Depending on the situation, they will be used in different combinations. For the sake of clarity, the functions of the components of working memory are outlined separately.

Examples: Situations that challenge working memory

1 holding more information than you've got capacity for:
- taking down an address on the phone
- taking notes in lectures

2 holding information and manipulating it
- long multiplication and division

3 holding onto new answers and still retaining original information
- comparing different travel options.

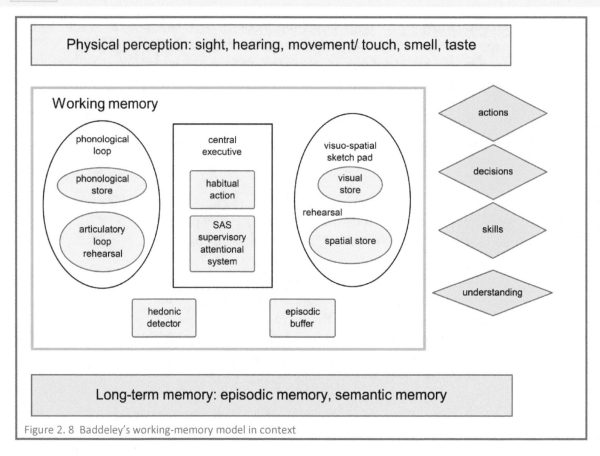

Figure 2. 8 Baddeley's working-memory model in context

FIGURE 2.8 shows the components of working memory and its context. Physical perception in this diagram includes the environmental input and the sensory register of Atkinson and Shiffron's modal model *FIGURE 2.5*.

Working memory uses the input information from physical perception and information from long-term memory to produce output, including: actions, decisions, skills and understanding.

In the rest of the discussion in *A LITTLE PSYCHOLOGY*, the components of working memory are in italics.

4.1.1 Perception

We take in information through our senses: sight, sound, touch and movement, smell and taste. How the different senses are used by different people is discussed in *THINKING PREFERENCES;* for the moment I'm dealing with the flow of mental processing. Perception in the early stages of processing is not seen as part of working memory, but it is worth noting that processing stimuli[8] starts before working memory is involved and that the core difficulties of dyslexia and dyspraxia are thought to be in the perception processes that feed into working memory, for example the phonological deficit theory of dyslexia. In *FIGURE 2.6*, the perception processes are in the *SENSORY REGISTER* and in *FIGURE 2.8*, they are in the *PHYSICAL PERCEPTION*.

4.1.2 Phonological loop and visuo-spatial sketch pad

The *phonological loop* and the *visuo-spatial sketch pad* are the two recognised temporary stores for receiving perceived information (stimuli). The *phonological loop* encodes verbal information; the *visuo-spatial sketch pad* encodes both visual and spatial information, and the two can be shown to be separate sets of information.

Insight: Verbal and visual information

Directions can be displayed as a map or written as a list of instructions; the first is visual information, the second verbal. Whichever is given first can be translated into the other form.

The *phonological loop* comprises two sections: the *phonological store* and the *articulatory loop*. Signals are stored for 30 seconds when there is no rehearsal. Rehearsal is carried out by the *articulatory loop*. Even then the storage time is of the order of minutes only. The storage time can be shortened by interference or replacement, as well as by decay, see *FORGETTING*.

RELEVANCE:
§5.1 p 121

THINKING PREFERENCES:
p 188

FIGURE 2.6: p 104

FIGURE 2.8: p 108

RELEVANCE:
§5.2 p 123

Ⓖ p 353: rehearsal

FORGETTING: p 113

---

[8] stimuli: plural of stimulus: anything that provokes a reaction, for example, light falling on the eyes, sound entering the ears, a movement happening

The *visuo-spatial sketch pad* was included when it was found the model for the *phonological loop* could not explain certain observations. It is harder to do experimental work with visual stimuli than with verbal ones, so rehearsal in the *visuo-spatial sketch pad* is not as well understood as that in the *articulatory loop* but it is thought to take place. Spatial and visual stimuli are stored separately; visual information doesn't show short-term forgetting, whereas spatial information does.

Insight: Visual and spatial information

If you recognise a friend's house <u>when</u> you see it, you are using visual information.
If you remember <u>where</u> it is, you are using spatial information.

Visual and spatial information can be translated by verbal encoding into verbal information and stored in the *phonological store*; similarly, verbal information can be translated and stored in the *sketch pad*. There is an extra process of translating the information from one way of coding to the other.

The sequence of stimuli (the serial order of them) can be retained in both the *phonological loop* and the *visuo-spatial sketch pad*. How it is retained still seems to be under discussion, but it is important to mention the ability, as order and sequence are often an issue for dyslexic/ SpLD people.

4.1.3 Central executive

The *central executive* component of working memory has no storage capacity; it is purely concerned with processing. It has two components that have different ways of contributing to decision-making processes: the *habitual action* component and the *supervisory attentional system, SAS*.

RELEVANCE:
§5.3 p 125
§5.4 p 125
§5.5 p 126

The processes that are fundamental to the *central executive* are:

> 'the capacity to focus attention
>
> the capacity to divide attention between two concurrent tasks
>
> the capacity to switch attention from one task to another
>
> the capacity to integrate working memory and long-term memory' (Baddeley 2007, pp 124-133).

These processes 'should operate across modalities[9] and be applicable to a range of situations and tasks' (ibid).

Baddeley (2007, pp 124-133).

Present understanding is that the central executive depends on brain activity in the frontal lobes of the brain. The importance of frontal lobe activity is discussed further in BREATHING.

BREATHING: p 266

When the *habitual action* component operates, decisions follow previously established patterns that depend on automatic schema, such as coming downstairs, or following a known route to work. *Habitual action* demands very little attention. It can operate when it should be switched off: if you've just moved house but you go home to the old one instead, *habitual action* is operating when it shouldn't be.

The *supervisory attentional system, SAS*, overrides habitual actions; it looks for new solutions to situations for which no *habitual action* exists. A 'situation with no *habitual action*' includes those situations for which you want to replace an old habit with a new one, for example, you want to put your keys on a new key rack as you enter the house whereas you used to leave them in your coat pocket.

Decisions about anything that is new will involve SAS. As the task or situation becomes familiar, memories relating to it will be stored in long-term memory and used by the *habitual actions* component to continue the decision-making.

---

[9] Modalities: The mind operates in several different ways at the same time: for example, you can 1) see and 2) hear at the same time as 3) react to the emotional content of a situation, 3 different modes. Thus, the mind can be said to operate in different modes and certain functions of the mind will operate across 'modalities'.

4.1.4 Episodic buffer (capacity and chunking)

The *episodic buffer* is one of the more recent components of the working-memory model. It stores information from several different systems, including long-term memory. It allows for integration of the information. It has limited capacity, or span, currently put at 4 chunks, where a chunk is 'a package of information bound by strong associative links within a chunk, and relatively weak links between chunks' (Baddeley, 2007, p 148). It can manipulate the information and is involved in conscious awareness. The time scale for retaining information hasn't been thoroughly investigated, but it will be somewhere between the short time, seconds to a few minutes, of the *phonological loop* and *the visuo-spatial sketch pad* and the days to decades of long-term memory.

RELEVANCE:
§5.6 p 128

Ⓖ p 353: chunk

Baddeley (2007, p 148)

Originally memory span was thought to be 7 ± 2 (Russell, 1979 pp 91-95)

Although the span of the *episodic buffer* is small, the amount of information that can be contained can be considerably enhanced by CHUNKING.

Ⓖ p 353: chunking
CHUNKING: p 154

The *episodic buffer* hasn't been researched to the same extent as other components of the working-memory model, but the functions ascribed to it (as given above) occur in our minds. Some of the important differences between dyslexia/ SpLD and non-dyslexia/ SpLD involve these functions. When the model is refined further, we may have to change the way we talk about the differences; it is even possible that the discussion about the differences will contribute to new understanding of the components of working memory.

4.1.5 Hedonic detector

The *hedonic detector* is the final component of the working memory in Baddeley's book. It was proposed to accommodate emotions within the working-memory model. As with *episodic buffer*, research is needed to establish its functions, features and applications, but, again, the area of thinking covered is an important one within the dyslexia/ SpLD field.

RELEVANCE:
§5.7 p 128

Baddeley (2007)

The *hedonic detector* is expected to collect the positive and negative emotional associations of tasks, situations and objects from the *episodic buffer* and weigh different levels of response against each other. It will need to be able to define a neutral point at which negative turns to positive and vice versa; it needs to be sensitive to changes in the emotional elements of situations etc.; it should be able to store judgements for future use; it should be able to discriminate between different assessments; and it should be stable in the values given to different assessments.

4.1.6 Development of the model for working memory

Working memory is not yet fully understood. As more becomes known, the model will change and that may alter the language used to discuss dyslexia/ SpLD but the experiences being discussed don't depend on the model. The discussion about dyslexia/ SpLD in terms of the working-memory model may well contribute to the next phase of understanding working memory.

4.2 Further comments

These four sections contain comments about mind processes which are very relevant to dyslexia/ SpLD: forgetting, efficiency of mind, alertness and automaticity.

4.2.1 Forgetting

Forgetting can happen 1) when a memory trace has changed or 2) when recall of a memory doesn't happen.

  There are two main theories of forgetting in which a change to a memory has occurred:

- a memory trace can fade, or decay, over a certain length of time
- a memory trace is disturbed in some way, i.e. interference has occurred.

Interference contributions to forgetting:
  Retroactive interference occurs when old memories are disturbed by new information and then are no longer available for recall: they are forgotten.
  Proactive interference acts in the opposite way when old memories interfere with the recall of newer information.

RELEVANCE:
§5.8 p 129

FURTHER READING:
Baddeley (1982, pp 47-73)

With lack of recall, a memory may persist in the mind but not be accessible for some reason, for example:

- the cue to recall a specific memory may not be available, and so the whole memory is unavailable although it can still be in long-term memory.
- the brain can get damaged or deteriorate and prevent recall of memories.

The forgetting process was investigated by Ebbinghaus[10] (Baddeley, 1982). He found that memories decay following an exponential curve in which the decay is greatest at the beginning and gradually levels off. Buzan (2010, p 55) and Russell (1979) show that with recall repeated over time, the memory strength can be increased so that a high percentage of information is retained over a long period of time, which agrees with the long-term changes to proteins of neurons, as discussed in *DURATION OF THOUGHTS*. Repeated recall is built into the processes for *MEMORY CONSOLIDATION*.

Baddeley (1982)

Buzan (2010, p 55)
Russell (1979)

DURATION OF THOUGHTS:
p 98
MEMORY
CONSOLIDATION: p 160

Baddeley (1982) also discusses Jost's Law which states that if two memory traces have the same strength at a particular time, the older one will be recalled instead of the newer one. It would seem that once the decay of a memory has levelled off, it becomes resistant to further decay and is more durable and less easily forgotten than a memory created at a later time.

4.2.2 Eysenck's theory of processing efficiency

Baddeley also discusses Eysenck's theory of processing efficiency (2007, p 263): when thinking isn't effective, the mind will put more effort into working memory; when the effort reaches the limitations of working memory but thinking is still not effective, the mind finds other ways to perform the task.

RELEVANCE:
§5.9 p 130

Baddeley (2007,
p 263)

---

[10] Ebbinghaus was one of the first pioneers of experimental psychology; his work on memory was published in 1885.

Example: A girl with brain injury doing a reading task

The injury had damaged a considerable part of the reading skills of the girl. She was re-establishing her reading slowly by matching words on cards with the same words on a page. When she got to the last card, she knew there was only one place it could go, so she used the knowledge of space, which was not affected by the injury, to put the card down.

In a situation like that, it is very hard to make the mind go through the slow reading process when it has already realised there's another way to perform the task.

4.2.3 Being alert

RELEVANCE:
§5.12 p 133

The state of alertness ranges from deep sleep to being highly aroused, with various levels in between. The rhythm of the different levels is different for different people: some are more alert in the morning and some in the afternoon, and some late at night and into the early hours of the morning; yet others are affected by the seasons. Some people are affected by the environment, as well as by the time of day or season.

Story: Being alert

One student found she was more alert when there was a lot of yellow around her.

Another needed a bluish tinge to the light in his room.

The food we eat also affects our level of alertness and our ability to concentrate. Brookis (2016) recommends 'good food for stamina ... a positive mood ... for better cognition'. It is important to recognise those conditions that help you to be alert.

Brookis (2016)

4.2.4 Automaticity

RELEVANCE:
§5.13 p 136

Since automaticity is one of the lines of research into dyslexia, it is useful to bring together the comments about automaticity made in other sections of this chapter. Neuronal pruning should lead to the establishment of a single efficient network to accomplish tasks that are often repeated. The *habitual action* component of the *central executive* of working memory depends on automatic schema to make the decisions. The *supervisory attentional system* will be active when *habitual action* thinks a situation is new.

The presence or lack of automatic neural networks will considerably affect the efficiency of the working memory.

4.3 Long-term memory

PHYSIOLOGY:
§3.3.1 p 100
RELEVANCE:
§5.10 p 131

Long-term memory includes those memories that are stored for more than a few days; they can persist for many decades or the rest of your life. They contribute to working memory through the *episodic buffer*, so they are part of thinking processes. They can influence the way incoming stimuli are perceived, for example, the number of brown coats you see increases when you buy a brown coat.

Long-term memories are classified as procedural[11] or declarative, with episodic or semantic memories being subcategories of declarative memory (Stein and Stoodley, 2006, p 413).

Stein and Stoodley
(2006, p 413)

- Procedural, or implicit, memories cover the acquisition of automatic skills such as the use of objects or the movement of the body, such as how to use a spoon or ride a bike.

- Declarative, explicit, memories include all those that are accessed by consciousness. In the episodic subcategory, memories each relate to a specific event, whereas in the semantic subcategory, memories relate to the context of external or internal world. Episodic memories are whole events; semantic memories are more like pieces of information, see *FIGURES 2.9* and *2.10*.

---

[11] procedural: to know <u>how</u> to do something
declarative: to know <u>that</u> something is the case

Figure 2. 9 Flowers in an episode

Figure 2. 10 Flowers in semantic contexts

There are other ways of grouping memories. Russell (1979, p 82) lists the characteristics of memories as:

episodic	factual	semantic	sensory
skills-related	instinctive	collective	past-life.

Russell (1979, p 82)

Many of these categories are implied in the discussion of *THINKING PREFERENCES*; episodic is discussed below. Instinctive and collective are respectively: memories that are instinctive in nature, such as anyone knowing how to breathe; and collective in nature in that they belong to a whole race of people (after the work of Jung). The list is given here because it is important to remember the wide range of memories that people's minds store.

THINKING PREFERENCES: p 188

4.3.1   Episodic memory

RELEVANCE:
§5.6 p 128

 Episodic memory retains a whole event from start to finish; a journey from one place to another and the alphabet are both good examples of episodes. This type of memory seems to present a difficulty for dyslexic/ SpLD people; the memory can't be used in small sections around particular pieces of information, as explained in EXAMPLE: ROTE LEARNING UNHELPFUL.

---

e.g.

Example: Rote learning unhelpful

Many dyslexic people have managed to learn the alphabet as a list from a to z, but they don't know where any particular letter belongs, they have to either start at the beginning and recite until they find the letter, or they start several letters in advance and chant until the required letter turns up.

No amount of practice in a systematic way helps; which is one way rote learning can be unhelpful.

Other learning that can be hindered by rote learning includes:

- Times tables
- Touch-typing when practice is by rote.
- Months and seasons of the year

One solution for such problems is to randomise the learning, probably from the start. For example, don't learn the three times table from 1 to 12, but have the multiplications on flash cards and present them in different orders.

Touch-typing courses that present keys in patterns don't help because the patterns are recognised and become fast while the letters involved get ignored.

Example: Main task not learnt

In a touch-typing course, keying 'fjfj dkdk slsl' becomes a pattern of finger movements: alternating first fingers, then second fingers, then third. You go faster and faster and very quickly there is no knowledge of which letters are being typed. When you need to use the letters, you still don't know where they are.

This happens even when the learner is aware of the dangers and is trying to avoid them.

Tip: Antidote to rote learning

The solution is to use a typing course that works with random presentation of letters, words and sentences.

4.3.2 Semantic memory

In using semantic memories, the mind is able to associate a given memory to a wider context rather than keep it solely remembered in terms of a single episode. You go out to buy a new mobile and the salesman shows you how to use it; that is an episode. If the mobile is to be any use to you, you have to be able to use it in many different situations; you don't want to go back to the shop and get the instructions again every time you want to send a text. When the mind uses the instructions as independent memories it is using them as semantic memories.

RELEVANCE:
§5.10 p 131

5   Relevance of ideas to dyslexia/ SpLD

One model of SpLD is shown in *Figure 2.11.* It is based on work by Morton and Frith (1995). Similar models have been widely used in the field.

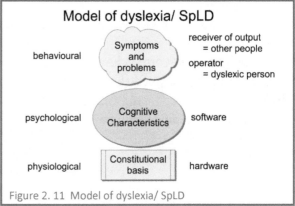

Figure 2. 11 Model of dyslexia/ SpLD

Morton and Frith (1995)

The model has 3 levels.

- The constitutional level is the physiology that underpins the dyslexia/ SpLD.

- The psychological level is the processing part of dyslexia/ SpLD[12].

- The behavioural level is the observed behaviour patterns that don't fit the expectations of society.

Figure 2.11 contains an analogy with computers and electronic equipment: you need hardware of some description; the software, the packages and apps allow you, the operator, to use the hardware to produce outcomes, which often are sent to another person, the receiver. Your brain structures allow you to use your working memory, your mind and your psyche to achieve the various behaviours of your life.

The constitutional level is outside the remit of this book. The physiological section of this chapter has discussed just a few processes that seem to be relevant to the experience of dyslexic/ SpLD people. It is not dealing with any constitutional causes of dyslexia/ SpLD.

A Little Psychology has discussed some theoretical concepts which I want to use to discuss some experiences of dyslexia/ SpLD. Work with students helped me refine and develop the ideas. This section is not about the processing part of dyslexia/ SpLD as usually discussed, though it does make sense of some of the experiences that dyslexic/ SpLD people talk about.

A Little Psychology: p 103

---

[12] Working memory is part of the psychological level, as are the mind and psyche of the discussion in *Context*, p 89.

The whole section is recommended as demonstrating the contrast between dyslexia/ SpLD and non-dyslexia/ SpLD.

This section may make sense of experiences you had as a child. It is relevant to work with children (Stacey, 2020b)

Stacey (2020b)

5.1 Perception

PSYCHOLOGY:
§4.1.1 p 109

Perception is the interpretation of information from the environment, by sight, sound, taste, smell, movement or touch. It involves signals, stimuli, coming in from the world around being recognised by your mind. When a baby is born it hasn't got the experience to make sense of all these signals. There are several ways in which the experience of dyslexic/ SpLD people does not lead to trouble-free perception.

For a baby, what should happen is that gradually the baby's mind makes sense of all the information about the world around, the people, and how he feels and thinks.   A complex body of long-term memories is built up that are then continually used to help with new situations and tasks. In this way, long-term memory helps the interpretation of new information early in the perception stage.

 With dyslexia/ SpLD, when this pattern of long-term memories does not get constructed during the initial exposure it is not available to help the perception stages on subsequent occasions.

The lack of useful long-term memories also restricts the resources available to the episodic buffer and the processing that uses the content of the buffer.

The processes of working memory also develop as a child grows. Piaget's work showed that a child of about 7 begins using abstract thought, with the use of logic, classification, inferences, conservation of volume, and concrete operations (Ginsburg and Opper, 1988). These processes develop in relation to the society in which the child lives and there will be certain expectations about the normal way thinking is happening.

Ginsburg and Opper (1988)

It is assumed that all the modalities of sensing, visual, auditory, movement, smell and taste can work together; if that weren't the case, broadcasting would be only by radio or silent films.

Insight: Senses not working together

The senses may not work together for some dyslexic/ SpLD people.

I went to an outdoor concert of Handel's *Music for the Royal Fireworks* accompanied by a fireworks display. I found I could watch the fireworks, in which case I didn't hear the music, or I could watch the musicians in which case I heard the music but was unaware of the fireworks.

I have mentioned this in talks about dyslexia/ SpLD and found others experience the same thing. One person said:
"You mean you're supposed to be able to hear and see together?"

I have also discovered that closing my eyes changes the way sound comes to me: with eyes closed it is all around me, with eyes open watching a performer, the music is less in volume and restricted to the performer.

Others have reported similar reactions.

EXAMPLE: WHAT PEOPLE SAY IN WORKSHOPS:
p 199
is making the same point; it also includes reactions from other people.

Perception that relies on more than one sense working together may not have the result intended, for example diagrams that are used to explain complex ideas may be unhelpful to someone who doesn't easily process diagrammatic representations.

5.2 Phonological loop and visuo-spatial sketch pad
– input components (my term)

PSYCHOLOGY:
§4.1.2 p 109

Both these components could well be contributing to the problems of dyslexia/ SpLD: sequencing is a function of both, as is holding the information for long enough for other parts of working memory to be operational. Sequencing is frequently a problem for dyslexic/ SpLDs, as is immediate forgetting.

The functioning of these two components won't be helped when the signals coming from perception are not coherent, or when long-term memory is not providing good clues.

The visuo-spatial sketch pad may be more important for dyslexic/ SpLD people in reading.

Tip: The look of the printed page

The visual aspects of the printed page can make a difference in so many different ways:

- the colour of paper
- the colour and contrast of computer screens
- the font used
- italics may not be read as easily as normal
- full justification distorts the words or their relative position
- hyphens can help or hinder.

This list shows just a few of the possibilities; they are specific to individual people and some dyslexic/ SpLD people have no problems with the way print is presented.

I've repeatedly heard about the ways dyslexic/ SpLD people turn what they hear into a visual picture or a movement, or what they see into a verbal string. This transformation means that they are not processing thoughts with the most obvious working-memory input component. The result is likely to be slower processing times. Tests used to identify dyslexia/ SpLD are designed to measure specific types of responses; when dyslexic/ SpLD people don't use their senses in the expected way, the test results might be measuring responses due to processes other than the intended one.

 From my work with dyslexic/ SpLD students, I don't think these are the only two input components of working memory. Baddeley (1982) summarised an experiment to investigate the effect of place on recall and retrieval of information (situation learning).

Baddeley (1982, p 107)

Story: Place affects memory recall

The experimenters worked with deep-sea divers, giving them tasks on land and at considerable depth. They discovered that recall of information was better in the place where it had been learnt, but given a prompt and asked to recognise was not affected by the place of learning.

Story: Place important in learning

I had a student who was reading with me at his home. He half said the word 'do' and then looked at me saying, "I've done that at school, I haven't done it with you." We had to work through the fact that words had the same meaning and sound wherever they were encountered.

SENSES and RATIONALE OR FRAMEWORK discuss other ways that information needs to be held together in order for some people to be able to think about it. It seems to me that there should be other input components that are used in parallel with the two already defined.

SENSES: p 197

RATIONALE OR FRAMEWORK: p 216

5.3 Central executive

PSYCHOLOGY:
§4.1.3 p 110

The abilities of the central executive:

>   to focus attention

>   to observe how thinking is progressing

>   to be able to select and prioritise

are all skills that dyslexic/ SpLD people need to learn deliberately and separately. They can be acquired through the *EXERCISE: KNOW YOUR OWN MIND* and in the other ways discussed in this book.

EXERCISE: KNOW YOUR OWN MIND: p 57

5.4 Habitual action

PSYCHOLOGY:
§4.1.3 p 110

Habitual action (part of *CENTRAL EXECUTIVE*) uses habits from long-term memory to produce decisions. Without the development of habits to govern language (in dyslexia), movement (dyspraxia), attention (ADHD) and mathematics (dyscalculia), working memory has to be much more active than is expected. Neuro-imaging indicates that the frontal lobes (which are where the central executive activity is thought to take place) are used more by dyslexic people than others, which seems to support the previous statement that the working-memories of dyslexic/ SpLD people work harder than expected.

Habitual action can be established fruitfully for dyslexic/ SpLD people, which is the aim of much of the support work given.

 Nothing works the same for all dyslexic/ SpLD people. You have to take into account which types of mental processing lead to good habitual patterns and which are vulnerable to confusion.

Story: Time vs. space – authors' experience

For one of us, time processing is totally unreliable, if not non-existent, while space processing is so good, she can afford to get lost because she's confident of finding her way back.

For the other of us, time processing works without effort, but space requires care and attention.

For non-dyslexic/ SpLD people many of these habitual patterns are established without much attention; they develop alongside other processing and are available for use; this way of learning rarely seems to happen in dyslexia/ SpLD.

Habitual action can also be established in the wrong way, which can contribute to the different problems people experience.

Insight: Habitual action resistant to change

"Verbs are doing words" is an explanation given to children. It gets established, and it's not wrong, but it can be very, very difficult for dyslexic/ SpLD people to add to it and to expand the words covered by the concept of 'verb'.

"How can 'to sleep' be a doing word?" is a frequent question.

5.5   Supervisory attentional system, SAS

PSYCHOLOGY:
§4.1.3 p 110

SAS (part of the *CENTRAL EXECUTIVE*) will be the decision-making component when habitual action is not able to make decisions because long-term memory can't provide the necessary stable patterns. For example, if long-term memory is not providing word recognition, SAS will be used to decode and interpret words. A lot of information that is treated as new by dyslexic/ SpLD adults should be well known. Processing times will be slow because automaticity has not been established.

Even when a person has good management of dyslexia/ SpLD, any old patterns in long-term memory are not erased therefore SAS has the continual task of monitoring thinking to make sure that dormant dyslexic/ SpLD neural networks[13] have not been activated, see *LEARNED CONFUSION* and *DEGREES OF SEVERITY*.

LEARNED CONFUSION:
p 342

DEGREES OF SEVERITY:
p 344

---

[13]Dormant neural networks are discussed in *THE PHILOSOPHY OF THIS SERIES*, p 4.

Insight: Mental energy reserved for monitoring

Some part of the mental capacity has to be alert for problems, especially in meetings or exams and similar situations.

FIGURE 1.6: MENTAL ENERGY TO MONITOR: p 72

 Converting memories from short-term to long-term involves: deliberate recall at spaced intervals, associations, rehearsal or reflection (Russell, 1979, pp 144-149); all of these could involve some kind of attention from SAS. Learning material that is difficult requires attention.

Russell (1979, pp 144-149)

Insight: Straight to long-term memory

As a dyslexic/ SpLD, you have to pay so much attention to 'get hold' of something that it probably goes straight into long-term memory, instead of remaining within working memory and being more temporary in nature.

Once the information is in long-term memory, it is harder to alter later.

It is important to pay attention to the difference between the temporary storage of working memory and the permanent storage of long-term memory and to have suitable expectations, e.g. if you know that what people say to you rarely gets beyond temporary storage, you have to write down even trivial things that need remembering for a short time.

The management of concentration and taking breaks will involve decision making and therefore attention from SAS. For example, taking short breaks is often deemed to be good for the learning process (Buzan, 2010, p 55); however, the level of concentration and preparation to get going needed by dyslexic/ SpLDs means that breaks can be counterproductive, see *CONCENTRATION* for further discussion. Careful decision making is required to achieve the best balance.

Buzan (2010, p 55)

CONCENTRATION: p 173

5.6   Episodic buffer

The amount of information that working memory can process is determined by the way information can be chunked together in the episodic buffer (Baddeley, 2007, p 148). The number of chunks is thought to be 4 (Baddeley, 2007, p 145) but no limit has been discussed as to how much can be bound into a single chunk. *CHUNKING* is discussed further as a technique to use to enhance memory. The limited number of chunks and the lack of effective chunking have a considerable impact for dyslexic people (Stacey, 2020b). There will be extra demands on working memory to deal with dyslexia/ SpLD, by comparison with demands on the working-memories of non-dyslexic/ SpLD people. One of the most common indications of dyslexia/ SpLD is poor working memory; further research might turn that into overloaded working memory with no spare processing power.

PSYCHOLOGY:
§4.1.4 p 112

Baddeley (2007, p 148 and p 145)

CHUNKING: p 154

Stacey (2020b)

5.7   Hedonic detector

Two serious side effects of dyslexia/ SpLD are a low level of confidence and a low self-esteem. *THINKING CLEARLY* deals briefly with the way these low levels can be triggered and concentrates on methods to establish and maintain high levels. All the functions expected of the hedonic detector are relevant to healthy self-appraisal.

PSYCHOLOGY:
§4.1.5 p 112

THINKING CLEARLY:
p 254

The processing by the working memory is also disrupted by depression, anxiety and cravings. Depression is assumed to cause increased negative thoughts because the hedonic detector has a low neutral point. Anxiety and cravings lead to patterns of thought cued by emotional stimuli. The extra processing by working memory caused by these three states of mind means there is less working memory available for any other task to be done.   The effects of dyslexia/ SpLD get worse when a person is under some kind of emotional stress as a result of the disruption to working memory (Baddeley, 2007, p 300).

Baddeley (2007, p 300)

5.8   Forgetting

The different patterns of forgetting discussed above have counterparts in the experiences of dyslexic/ SpLDs.

PSYCHOLOGY:
§4.2.1 p 113

Story: The perfect sentence immediately lost

Countless numbers of times, discussing with a student how to express an idea, one of us says: "You mean ..." and produces the sentence that perfectly encapsulates the ideas. Immediately, neither can remember it at all; the memory trace has instantly decayed.

Many dyslexic/ SpLDs have note pads in a variety of places: beside the bed, in the bathroom, in the car, on every desk and eating table. They know that when a thought comes across the mind they have to capture it there and then; there is no time to go to fetch a note pad from somewhere else; the thought will have gone; the memory trace will have decayed.

Forgetting varies across modalities: for example, some have found that they forget what they see or say but when they sing the idea, it will stay. This is an example of the cue-for-recall not being available when the two modalities of seeing and saying are used but, it is available when the singing modality is used.

Singing in INSIGHT:
EXPERIENCES OF
LISTENING, SPEAKING AND
SINGING: p 203

Interference is important. Students have to be careful about working on several subjects simultaneously as the memories are not kept separate and so are not recalled properly. If new information clashes with something in long-term memory, it may be rejected. It seems to be blocked from even getting to working memory and properly assessed. Many reading or listening problems can occur from such interference.

MARGIN NOTE:
strategies for reading
and listening
problems are
discussed in Stacey
(2021)

Interference can occur from the surroundings too.   Many dyslexic/ SpLDs have difficulty shutting out noises, though some find that the right music helps them to concentrate.

Impact of the
environment is
discussed in Stacey
(2020a)

There are many other ways in which forgetting and not being able to recall are serious difficulties for dyslexic/ SpLD people. Some seem to have an obvious connection with the theories: the perfect sentence that is instantly forgotten fits the theory of decay and memory traces being of very short duration. Though interesting, fitting a theory is not the important issue.

Tip: An approach to forgetting

More important is to recognise that forgetting happens; to observe when and how; to find strategies to deal with the prospect of forgetting; and to openly own those times when you can't be relied on to recall something.

5.9 Eysenck's theory of processing efficiency

PSYCHOLOGY:
§4.2.2 p 114

THINKING PREFERENCES:
p 188

The *THINKING PREFERENCES* discussed in this book are general ones that could be used by everyone, and probably are, without people
1) being aware of them[14] and
2) being aware that one thinking preference has been changed for
      another.
Most people have good language and organisation systems for dealing with information, much of which has a strong verbal component. Their working-memories will be reasonably good and the information can be held in working memory long enough for other ways of thinking to be used as and when necessary to increase efficiency without conscious awareness.

 Dyslexic/ SpLDs either don't have good systems or the systems are not entirely dependable so that the information is often not held together long enough for the mind to bring in other thinking methods.

---

[14] In the story *It's as simple as one, two, three*, Feynman (1988) describes how he and a colleague compared counting for 60 seconds. They discovered they did it by different thinking processes. Feynman counted verbally in his head. His colleague visualised a tape with numbers going by. Feynman also investigated what he could and couldn't do while counting.

Tip: Conscious attention

Conscious attention is needed to promote and maintain efficient processing.

5.10 Long-term memory

Long-term memory has been mentioned in several previous discussions of this section.
I think there are two other points to make:

- there is an important difference between the two types of declarative long-term memory, episodic and semantic
- how activating information in long-term memory can assist working memory.

Long-term memory: episodic and semantic

When children learn the alphabet they are usually taught to recite it from beginning to end, which would involve episodic memory. The idea is that they can then use the letters and their order as pieces of information, in a semantic way.
They are expected to realise:

- the letters have sounds attached to them in different ways
- they appear visually in words
- they are used for labels in many different situations
- they appear all over the world
- they are the same set of symbols which were learnt in the string from a-z.

Thus episodic memory, by use, converts to semantic memory, and rote learning has been useful.

There are many situations where the transformation from episodic memory to semantic memory doesn't happen. Many adult dyslexic/ SpLDs experience the same effect when they have to start a journey at an unusual place: they can't break a known journey into sections and start part-way through. Rote learning is almost always a waste of time for dyslexic/ SpLDs. The transformation just

PHYSIOLOGY:
§3.3.1 p 100

PSYCHOLOGY:
§4.3 p 116

LONG-TERM MEMORY
ASSISTING WORKING
MEMORY: p 132

MARGIN NOTE:
episodic memory relates to a specific event,
FIGURE 2.9: p 117;

semantic memory relates to context,
FIGURE 2.10: p 117

EXAMPLE: ROTE LEARNING
UNHELPFUL: p 118

doesn't happen. The lack of the process is not specific to dyslexia/ SpLD, but, because it happens in basic systems like the alphabet and times tables, it causes problems for dyslexic/ SpLD people.

**Tip: Deliberate attention
to thought processes during learning**

Pay deliberate attention to your thought processes during any learning. You should take your best thinking preferences into account. You need to assess the appropriateness of rote learning before it can contribute more confusion from your dyslexia/ SpLD.

Exercise: Rote learning in childhood

Are there pieces of information that you learnt by rote as a child?

Do any still cause problems for you?
Are they pitfalls for which you need to use strategies?
Are they obstacles for which you need accommodation?

Add anything significant to your *INDIVIDUAL, PERSONAL PROFILE OF DYSLEXIA/ SPLD* or your *REGIME FOR MANAGING DYSLEXIA/ SPLD*.

INDIVIDUAL, PERSONAL PROFILE OF DYSLEXIA/ SPLD: p 64

REGIME FOR MANAGING DYSLEXIA/ SPLD: p 71

5.11 Long-term memory assisting working memory

PSYCHOLOGY: §4.1.4 p 112

Long-term memories can contribute to the *EPISODIC BUFFER* and, probably, to the input components of working memory so that what is already known can be used to increase the capacity of the episodic buffer by allowing more information to be bound into the four chunks of the buffer. The use of long-term memory can be increased by deliberately using them in *MIND SET: MENTAL PREPARATION*.

MIND SET: MENTAL PREPARATION: p 152

5.12   Being alert

AROUSAL SYSTEM looks briefly at the need to be alert from a physiological perspective. *BEING ALERT* (in the *PSYCHOLOGY* section) accepts that different people are affected by different circumstances. *A MODEL OF LEARNING* discusses those times when it is important for dyslexic/ SpLD people to make deliberate choices to keep thinking effectively.

Often dyslexic/ SpLD people struggle with staying alert, especially when reading. People are then very sympathetic about the hard work of reading which they assume produces fatigue.

Insight: Going to sleep over reading

It is important to stress that this will happen when you have dealt with all the environmental influences correctly: enough sleep, good diet, enough air, good health, the right place, good motivation, etc.

You can still go to sleep over reading.

 I have learnt to recognise fighting sleep as a sign that I am not processing material effectively, while reading, listening or writing.

I need to pause and manage my dyslexia.

I think this is one of those situations when the internal experience of dyslexic/ SpLD people and the external observations need some case history investigation that includes changes in approaches to reading.

Going to sleep over reading is not exclusively a dyslexic/ SpLD experience: many people find reading late at night induces sleep, and they will read before going to sleep for that very purpose. (Sometimes it backfires in that the book is so interesting, the mind wakes up and starts being efficient again and you don't go to sleep.) There are also many factors involved that alter whether a non-dyslexic/ SpLD person will go to sleep or not.

PHYSIOLOGY:
§3.4 p 102

PSYCHOLOGY:
§4.2.3 p 115

A MODEL OF LEARNING:
p 178

2 About the Mind

For dyslexic/ SpLD people, it can be important:
1) to dispel the sense of isolation
2) to look for solutions that make reading and staying awake easier.

Once I recognise that I am fighting sleep, I try to re-establish alertness. Possible approaches that might help you include:

- standing to work
- specific movements that help from *BRAIN GYM*
- *MIND SET* and *CHUNKING* can be used to help your thinking processes
- changing the way you are using your *THINKING PREFERENCE*
- using the steps in *REGIME FOR MANAGING DYSLEXIA/ SPLD*
- changing what you are doing for a while.

BRAIN GYM: p 275
MIND SET: p 152
CHUNKING: p 154

THINKING PREFERENCES: p 188

REGIME FOR MANAGING DYSLEXIA/ SPLD: p 71

Tip: Changing activity to re-establish alertness

Possibilities:
baking, cooking

physical activity: walk the dog, do sport,
chop wood, dig potatoes, mow the lawn, polish shoes

at the same mental level: play a musical instrument
review material you are systematically getting into long-term memory

Not advised:
any activities that:

1) are too passive or repetitive

2) allow you to continue thinking about the subject you are taking a break from.

Make sure your break is of the right length for you to re-establish alertness but not to take you away from your task for too long.

It is also important to consider other influences that could be affecting your alertness, such as food, light, time of day and environment.

Exercise: Find your best conditions for staying alert

Experiment to find out the best conditions while being flexible enough to change them or to function reasonably well when you can't achieve the best conditions. The most important thing is to recognise that lack of progress is not always something about you; it can be caused by something outside you and something you can't change.

Use *TEMPLATE: B3 - COMPARE EXPECTATIONS AND REALITY*. Collect information whenever you are struggling against sleep or drowsiness.

I rarely find succumbing to sleep solves anything.

TEMPLATES:

Story: Standing and being alert

While researching for this book in a library, I observed that another reader frequently stood for long periods. When I asked why, she told me that standing affects the hormones and improves alertness.

You never know when a good idea will be given to you. I have changed my 'work' environment so that I can stand to work if I want to.

5.13   Automaticity

PSYCHOLOGY:
§4.2.4 p 116

In many situations, dyslexic/ SpLDs are continually starting from the beginning because their minds have not automatised basic processes, for example:

- reading: working memory will be used to sound out words
- writing: working memory will run through the mnemonic that supports the spelling of a particular word.

While engaged on these tasks, working memory is not available for comprehension and other more advanced processes.

The automatic networks for basic process such as reading or spelling words have not been established. It is important to deal with the basic processes in such a way that they do not hamper the higher order ones. For example, ignore spelling while writing the first draft of anything and keep the flow of ideas going.

References

Atkinson, R.C. and Shiffron, R.M., 1968, *Human Memory: A Proposed System and Its Control Processes*, in Spence, K.W. (ed.), 1968, *The Psychology of Learning and Motivation: Advances in Research and Theory*, Vol 2, 89-195, Academic Press, NY

Baddeley, Alan, 1982, *Your Memory: A User's Guide*, Penguin Books, London

Baddeley, Alan, 2007, *Working Memory, Thought, and Action*, Oxford University Press, Oxford

Brookis, Jenny, 2016, *Future Brain*, Wiley Australia, Melbourne, Australia

Buzan, Tony, 2010, *Use Your Head*, BBC Active, Harlow

Eagleman, David, 2015, *The Brain, the Story of You*, Canongate Books, Edinburgh

Feynman, Richard, 1988, *What Do You Care What Other People Think?*, Penguin Books, Canada

Finn, Emily, et al., 2014, *Disruption of Functional Networks* in *Dyslexia: A Whole-Brain, Data-Driven Analysis of Connectivity*, Biological Psychiatry, Vol 76, 397-404

Galaburda, Al, et al., 1985, *Developmental Dyslexia: Four Consecutive Patients with Cortical Anomalies*, Annals of Neurology, Vol 18, 222-233

Ginsburg, Herbert and Opper, Sylvia, 1988, *Piaget's Theory of Intellectual Development,* Prentice Hall, NJ, 3rd Ed.

Grant, David, 2005, *That's the way I think,* David Fulton, London

Jefferies, Sharon, 2008, Conference talk, BDA Conference 2008, Harrowgate, and private communication

McEwen, B.S. and Gianaros, P.J., 2010, *Central role of the brain in stress and adaptation: Links to socioeconomic status, health, and disease,* Annals of the New York Academy of Sciences, 1186(1), 190-222

Morton, John and Frith, Uta, 1995, *Causal Modelling: A Structural Approach to Developmental Psychopathology*, in *Developmental Psychopathology*, Ch 13, Vol 1, 357-390

Newby, Michael, 1995, *The Dyslexics Speak for Themselves,* in Miles, Tim and Varma, Ved (eds), *Dyslexia and Stress,* Whurr, London

Rattray Taylor, Gordon, 1979, *The Natural History of the Mind,* Secker & Warburg, London

Russell, Peter, 1979, *The Brain Book: Know Your Own Mind and How to Use It,* Routledge, London

Stacey, Ginny, 2020a, *Organisation and Everyday Life with Dyslexia and other SpLDs,* Routledge, London

Stacey, Ginny, 2020b, *Development of Dyslexia and other SpLDs,* Routledge, London

Stacey, Ginny, 2021, *Gaining Knowledge and Skills with Dyslexia and other SpLDs,* Routledge, London

Stein, John and Stoodley, Catherine, 2006, *Neuroscience, An Introduction,* Wiley, Chichester

West, Thomas, G, 1991, *In The Mind's Eye,* Prometheus Books, Buffalo, NY

Wolf, Maryanne, 2008, *Proust and the Squid,* Icon Books, Cambridge

Website information

Alan Baddeley
https://www.york.ac.uk/psychology/staff/emeritusfaculty/ab50/ Accessed 12 February 2021

Series website: www.routledge.com/cw/stacey

3 Using the Mind

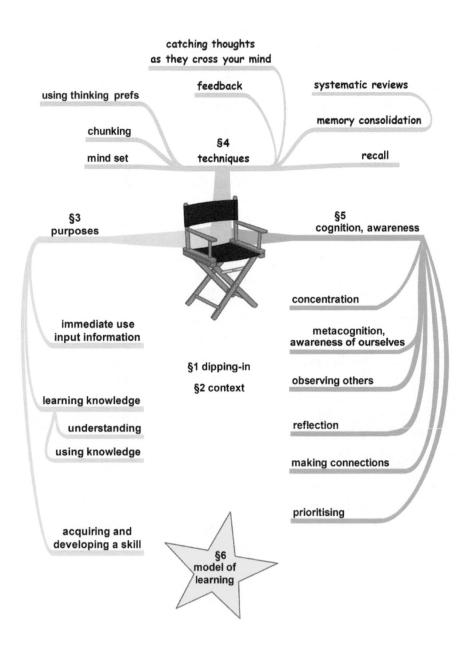

catching thoughts
as they cross your mind

feedback

systematic reviews

using thinking prefs

memory consolidation

chunking

§4
techniques

mind set

recall

§3
purposes

§5
cognition, awareness

concentration

immediate use
input information

metacognition,
awareness of ourselves

§1 dipping-in

§2 context

observing others

learning knowledge

understanding

reflection

using knowledge

making connections

acquiring and
developing a skill

prioritising

§6
model of
learning

Contents

Vital for dyslexic/ SpLDs, good practice for all

The mind skills in this chapter will be valuable to anyone. As a dyslexic/ SpLD person you need to pay attention to learning them and applying them. The mind skills are in *Techniques to Assist Using Your Mind* and *Cognition, Awareness*.

Other people will probably gain the skills as they work on other tasks, i.e. they will learn them subliminally. They are also likely to apply them without paying too much attention.

Dyslexic/ SpLD people also need to be aware of the context when applying these skills. *Purposes of Thinking* and *A Model of Learning* are 2 ways of discussing the context.

There is no section that applies only to dyslexic/ SpLD people.

Techniques to Assist Using Your Mind:
p 151
Cognition, Awareness:
p 172

Ⓖ p 353: subliminal learning

Purposes of Thinking:
p 142
A Model of Learning:
p 178

Working with the chapter

You can apply the ideas and skills in this chapter to any task or situation.

Use the *Template: A2 - Bookmark – Purpose* as a check-list. You can highlight those skills and ideas that you have tried, and how they worked for you.

Templates:

You can gain insights into your *Thinking Preferences* and many other aspects of the way you think or deal with life. Build the insights into your *Individual, Personal Profile of Dyslexia/ SpLD* and your *Regime for Managing Dyslexia/ SpLD*, see *Appendix 2*.

Thinking Preferences:
p 188

Appendix 2: p 314

Templates on the website

Templates:

A1   *Jotting Down as You Scan*
A2   *Bookmark – Purpose*
A4   *Jotting Down as You Read*
B1   *Collecting Ideas That Relate to You*
B3   *Compare Expectations and Reality*
B4   *Actions, Results, Next Step*

Appendix 1 Resources

Three sections could be helpful as you work with this chapter:

Surveying
Recording as You Scan
Monitoring Progress

Surveying: p 309
Recording as You Scan:
p 310
Monitoring Progress:
p 311

Appendix 2 Individual, Personal Profile of Dyslexia/ SpLD and Regime for Managing Dyslexia/ SpLD

Build any relevant insights into your Personal, Individual Profile of Dyslexia/ SpLD or your Regime for Managing Dyslexia/ SpLD.

Appendix 2: p 314

Appendix 3 Key Concepts

Appendix 3: p 328

This appendix has a summary of the key ideas I cover when doing an audit of skills and knowledge with a dyslexic/ SpLD student. It shows which of the 4 books in the series covers each idea in full.

1   Dipping-in to try out ideas

Scan *A Model of Learning,* either the table or the diagram or both.
   Particularly, note the stages that are underlined in the
   diagram.
Look at the mind map, or use the contents of the chapter, to find the
   key ideas in the chapter.
Read the *Context*.
Scan *Techniques to Assist Using Your Mind* and *Cognition, Awareness*
Decide which sections of the chapter are most relevant to you
   immediately. Read them and follow any cross-references that
   are suitable for you.
Skim any sections you don't read now, so that you know what's in
   them, and can come back to them when they are relevant to
   you.

A Model of Learning:
p 178

Context: p 142

Techniques to Assist
Using Your Mind:
p 151
Cognition, Awareness:
p 172.

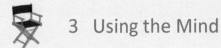

2   Context

One of the most exciting skills is to be able to use your mind well.
The Director's chair is a good icon for this chapter:
> you can consciously choose how you use your mind
>> when you have practised the techniques you need
>> and become aware of your thinking and your state of being.

Figure 3. 1 Directing the mind

The upshot can be that you

- think and take-action at the level of your best abilities
- minimise the effects of your dyslexia/ SpLD.

Ⓖ p 353: taking-action

You will probably find you use the ideas in this chapter in ways that are different from those used by others, even from other dyslexic/ SpLD people. The more you gain insights into how you use your mind well, the more you will find that the differences from others will become a point of interest rather than a point of difficulty.

PURPOSES OF THINKING considers whether your thinking is for the short
> term or long term, and the purpose of your thinking.

TECHNIQUES TO ASSIST USING YOUR MIND has many important ideas for
> using your mind more effectively.

COGNITION, AWARENESS is more about qualities and attributes than
> techniques. Awareness is a key aspect of managing dyslexia/ SpLD.

A MODEL OF LEARNING shows various stages when it can be necessary to
> make choices about the way you use your mind.

PURPOSES OF THINKING: p 142
TECHNIQUES TO ASSIST USING YOUR MIND: p 151

COGNITION, AWARENESS: p 172

A MODEL OF LEARNING: p 17

3   Purposes of thinking

The mind is engaged in almost everything we do:
> from eating, sleeping[1] and breathing
> to being idle, living and working.

---

[1] Even in sleep, brain waves can be detected, we don't have an off switch.

You use your mind to think:

> to process information
> to acquire knowledge
> to develop skills

to become expert in various ways.

The amount of mental effort involved varies, but your mind is still engaged.

If you look up 'information', 'knowledge' and 'skill' in the Oxford English Dictionary you will find there is overlap between the three, with information and knowledge being very similar, and skill arising from the other two. In the present context:

'information, n.',
'knowledge, n. 4b'
and 'skill, n.1.' OED
(2020)

- *information* is facts or ideas presented by someone or something outside you, or it could come as unprocessed facts or ideas from your memory

- *knowledge* is a deeper appreciation of information, whereby you have added some intelligent thought to the information and you are deliberately learning about some topic

- a *skill* is the ability to do something well; you acquire skills through practice and learning.

This section is looking at purposes of thinking depending on whether:

1   you are going to use the information or your thinking immediately

2   you are building knowledge

3   you are acquiring a skill.

IMMEDIATE USE:
p 182
LEARNING KNOWLEDGE:
p 149
*ACQUIRING AND
DEVELOPING A SKILL:*
p 150
WORKING MEMORY:
p 106

3.1   Immediate use and input information

Even for immediate use, you have to hold information in your mind while you think about it (process it), so you will be using your *WORKING MEMORY*. When your thinking is for immediate use your mind may also use long-term memory, but it may not do so[2].

*LONG-TERM MEMORY
ASSISTING WORKING
MEMORY:* p 132

---

[2] A psychologist friend commented that long-term memory is always involved, that your mind searches for past experience to apply to a new task. The lack of automaticity in reading and spelling, the difficulty of building on past experience make me wonder whether this is another area of difference for dyslexic/ SpLDs.

3 Using the Mind

From working with dyslexic/ SpLD students, I recognise several different stages of immediate use that need careful attention:

Stage 1 The way in which information is given to you may make a significant difference as to how well you can remember it, even for a short time, see *FIGURE 3.2*.

Stage 2 How you store information, even in the input components of *WORKING MEMORY* and the *EPISODIC BUFFER (CAPACITY AND CHUNKING)*, can affect your effectiveness.

Stage 3 How you recall anything you already know is likely to be important

Stage 4 The way you set about processing all the information can mean your thinking is more or less effective.

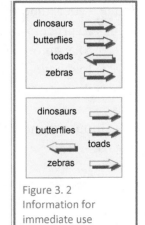

Figure 3. 2
Information for immediate use

WORKING MEMORY: p 106

EPISODIC BUFFER (CAPACITY AND CHUNKING): p 112

These 4 stages are discussed below. The numbering is only a label to separate one stage from another; it doesn't indicate a sequence.

All these facets of using your mind for immediate use can be affected by whether:

> your best ways of thinking are used
> you are motivated or mentally active
> you have a clear sense of your goal.

Stage 1: Information being given

Examples: Different ways of giving information

- A person says, "The project will last three years," and draws a line on a piece of paper. The line drawn can tap into the visual memory of a visual thinker who has poor auditory processing. The information will be retained because of the line.

- Information is often given in a story format which is dynamic in some way and catches attention. The story allows the information to be remembered.

Stage 2: Remembering information for a short time

Tip: Be active about remembering

Even if an interesting style is used to present information, it may not be the right one for you.

You need to be aware of what you can do to make the information stay in your mind.

Some of the more commonly used methods are:

- You create an internal picture to hold the information together.
- You deliberately think about people or situations you already know that make the information come alive for you.
- You know what activity you are about to take part in, and that having everything you need will help you enjoy it more; you listen to instructions with your enjoyment in mind.

Examples: Three ways to retain information

You are being given information about the next football match:

- As you listen, you create a picture in your mind of yourself collecting the equipment that is being listed; you see yourself following the directions to get to the coach (vehicle).

- You think about the last few matches, about which of your mates had good equipment, what's going to be the same or different about the coach waiting for you (still vehicle).

- You remember the pleasure of being ready and the extra time to kick the ball around, the enjoyment of winning; the information about the next match becomes more memorable because past enjoyment lifts the effort of present preparation.

In short, you use your *THINKING PREFERENCES* in a deliberate way to retain the information while you use it. The technique of *CHUNKING* is relevant.

THINKING PREFERENCES:
p 188

CHUNKING: p 154

Stage 3: Recall from long-term memory

Many students I've worked with don't easily build on past experience[3]; it is as if nothing they have done before has any relationship to the task they are embarking on now. They do not remember that they already know quite a lot!

You need to question your long-term memory to find useful past experience:

> Have I done this before? If yes, what happened?
> Who is around now? Have I been with them before? What was going on before?
> What interest do I have that relates to the current situation?
> Does that bring to mind anything that would be helpful?

Tip: Questioning long-term memory

It's impossible to list all the questions that will be helpful in different circumstances

> You can use your best ways of thinking, your motivation and your goal to formulate the questions.

Fundamentally, you need to give yourself time to be in the present situation and to allow your memory to contribute; *MIND SET* is one way to a achieve this aim.

Ⓖ p 353: mind set

MIND SET: p 152

Gradually as you become more familiar with working this way, you will probably find more information is recalled from your memory. You can take some tension out of a situation, if you acknowledge that your memory doesn't always produce what you need. Often, the release of tension allows you to remember more anyway.

---

[3] Wry aside: What I find difficult is to remember that I forget!
So I don't take any action to make sure I remember ...

Stage 4: Processing the information in working memory

In many learning situations, you are given information and expected to do something with it immediately. For example, if you ring up a help desk to sort out a computer problem, you will often be told different processes to test, and you are expected to carry out the steps exactly as instructed.

First you need to know you've got everything and that you understand what you want to do with the information or what you are being asked to do with it. You may need to use your *Thinking Preferences* to capture the information.

Thinking Preferences: p 188

Example: Working memory and different thinking preferences

You have been asked to go to 3 shops to buy several items.

The items to buy are the information that you are going to use soon.

Your immediate goal is to capture the information.

Thinking preferences	Possible application
As a visual thinker, you might see the information being used and you run through the complete sequence of its use before enacting it; then as you put it into action, you mentally tick off the actions.	You use a mental movie to see yourself going into the first shop, finding the items and paying. You continue the movie at the second & third shops.
As a linear thinker, you would possibly make a list of steps to be carried out, with secondary lists of what is necessary at each stage.	You write the items in the order you will go to the shops.
As an analytical (linear) thinker, you might use a process of weighing up the pros and cons of actions involved.	You plan the logistics of your route; you relate the items to the reasons for buying them.

Thinking preferences	Possible application
As a kinaesthetic, experiential person[4], you might imagine through your body the actions or processes involved in achieving the desired outcome. As you imagine it, you would be thinking about the feasibility of the project or the difficulties involved.	You feel yourself entering the warmth (or coolness) of the first shop, you feel the weight of the items as you pick them up, you feel your card as you put it in the card machine, you feel yourself standing while the transaction goes through, etc.

Exercise: To improve immediate use of information:

As you deal with an immediate situation, use one of *Templates: B6 or B8 - Recording Templates - 2 or - 4* to observe what happens.
Column headings:
A = event and date   B = stage of *Immediate Use*
C = what happened   D = comment
E = anything to try next time (5th column in B8, if used)

Templates:

Example: A dead phone and immediate use of information

One person's phone went dead and he had to contact the service provider. He was questioned about the fault and given instructions to carry out tests.

- Stage 1: As the conversation progressed, he checked the words used and asked for the meaning of some technical ones.

- Stage 2: He made sure he was linking the information together into a framework.

---

[4]'Person' replaces 'thinker' in the other options because the whole body is involved and not just the brain.

- Stage 3: He checked that it made sense in the context of the fault.
- Stage 4: He visualised himself following the instructions he was being given.

Gradually as you accumulate insights, you will know which stages you need to pay attention to and how you might think effectively for immediate situations. You may also realise what you need to ask other people to do or say in order to help you.

3.2   Learning knowledge

LEARNING KNOWLEDGE builds on using the mind for IMMEDIATE USE. The added process is making sure the knowledge is stored in long-term memory, as discussed in MEMORY CONSOLIDATION. While 'knowledge' indicates that a deeper level of thinking is involved, learning pure facts is also a useful part of building memories in long-term memory.

IMMEDIATE USE: p 182

MEMORY CONSOLIDATION: p 160

3.2.1   Understanding

It is important to realise that remembering something is not the same as understanding it. In remembering, you are creating facts-type memory traces that can be re-activated at a later date. In understanding you are finding out the relationships between different pieces of information, their relative importance or significance; you are seeking to understand a bigger picture. You then need to remember the results of the understanding. So the memory traces will have values assigned to them, in a way similar to the values discussed in relation to the HEDONIC DETECTOR.

HEDONIC DETECTOR: p 112

3.2.2.   Using knowledge

Once facts and knowledge have been stored in long-term memory, they can be recalled and used in new ways that are relevant to a new situation or task. The information or knowledge will be re-processed in working memory, see A MODEL OF LEARNING.

A MODEL OF LEARNING: p 178

3.3 Acquiring and developing a skill

Skills relate to 'doing something' rather than 'knowing something'. You can 'know' about art and artistic techniques; the 'skills' of art are being able to use the techniques to create something.

Acquiring and developing a skill both build on *IMMEDIATE USE*. All practice to develop the skill is a moment of *IMMEDIATE USE*, the goal being to improve the skill.

IMMEDIATE USE: p 182

Some skills are acquired subliminally by practising them without being aware of the skill. For example, the majority of people use their native language to communicate without deliberately learning most of the rules. It is assumed that the mind makes sense of the rules through the use, and there are only a few rules that need to be learnt deliberately.

Ⓖ p 353: Subliminal

SUBLIMINAL LEARNING: p 186

Other skills must be learnt with attention or awareness, but after practice they become automatic. Learning to drive is a good example. Initially, an instructor is needed who will give the right instructions to the learner driver. Through practice, the learner's mind constructs the right habitual patterns and driving becomes automatic. The development of driving skills happens when the basic skills are adapted for use in the many situations encountered during driving.

Many jobs and hobbies require a certain set of skills, but they may not be used in fixed ways every time; the skills need adapting to suit new situations. For example, you can learn the functions of spreadsheets for one job and then adapt them to suit another, quite different job. You would probably extend your spreadsheet expertise in doing so.

Skills can be adapted from quite different tasks. You can learn to focus your attention on the game when playing football and then transfer that ability to focus on reading; if you do so, you probably find your reading improves quite considerably.

Example: Transferring skills from one task to another

On the football pitch, you learn to focus your mind where it is going to help you play, on:

> your position, where opponents are, where the ball is, where your team mates are, how you are playing.

You try to ignore:

> comments from the crowd, photographers near the pitch, aggravation from opponents or crowd.

Once you have the skill to focus your mind on football, you can transfer the skill to help with reading; you focus on:

> what you want to know, what the author thinks are the key points.

You ignore: information that is not important to you, any thoughts that take you away from the ideas you want to get from the reading.

METACOGNITION, the awareness of what you are doing, is a skill. For example, being aware of how you are thinking while writing is a skill, and one which can be developed and used to good effect, especially by dyslexic/ SpLD people.

METACOGNITION:
p 174

4   Techniques to assist using your mind

There are many techniques for improving the way you use your mind. CHUNKING, RECALL and MEMORY CONSOLIDATION are particularly useful for exploring and refining the use of your THINKING PREFERENCES.

THINKING PREFERENCES:
p 188

Tip: These techniques are all tips

When used well, these techniques improve the performance of working memory and the storage of memories in long-term memory.

People have said: "It's as if I've got mental capacity to think, now that I'm not trying so hard to work out what's what, or to remember something."

4.1 Mind set: mental preparation

Mind set, or mental set (Russell, 1979), is a process whereby you switch on your mind for the coming task, such as listening to a lecture, going to a meeting or reading a train timetable.

Russell (1979)

Insight: Analogy for mind set

Imagine going into a dark cottage, in the country, on a moonless night with the light switch the other side of the room: you will bump into furniture and anything else, you may fall over, you will move slowly and carefully across the room feeling for the light switch when you get to the other side.

But if you switch on a torch, you can walk confidently over to the light switch.

This analogy shows the difference between starting a new task with your mind switched off and with it switched on.

In mind set, you are using about 5 minutes to energise your mind in thinking about the new task. By deliberately thinking about it, you stimulate the neural networks that need to be closely involved in the process; and you prepare the brain-mind for the task; thus mental hooks are alert, waiting to catch your new thinking (Russell, 1979). Many dyslexic/ SpLDs have the experience that information 'comes in one ear and out the other', with little impact on the way. Mind set enables you to capture the information.

Russell (1979)

Story: Mind set before lectures

One student found mind set useful on many occasions, especially just before lectures. One day he got the title of a lecture wrong and so applied mind set to the wrong part of his syllabus; but he said he was still able to follow the lecture and take notes because he was thinking about chemistry and not the next meal.

Mind set can be used before any task: research, lectures, meetings, organising a family trip, exams ...

Tip: Using mind set

Mind set can be done by any method that gets you actively thinking about the task, or subject, that you are about to engage with:

- brainstorm: get down on paper everything you know about it, or dictate to a recording device
- make a mind map
- create a drawing or diagram that contains what you know or are interested in
- recap the last meeting, lecture, event or whatever is closest to the task in hand
- look up technical, or jargon, words used; get correct pronunciation.

Ⓖ p 353: brainstorm, mind map

Explore some useful questions:

- Why am I involved with this event/ studying this subject?
- What ideas are being discussed?
- What does anyone think is important?
- What is the scheme of the event/ framework of the subject?

Mind set extras for reading a book: pick up key ideas by looking at
contents, glossary, index, preface, covers,
chapter headings, summaries, tables, pictures, diagrams.

Passive thinking is unlikely to work as a mind set process because you
are doing nothing to stimulate the networks in your brain that would
be most useful for the task you are about to do.

4.2   Chunking

As discussed earlier, the *Episodic Buffer (Capacity and Chunking)* span is
four chunks of information; the span can't be increased in number,
but the chunks can be expanded by making sure information is linked
together, chunked together.

*Episodic Buffer
(Capacity and
Chunking)*:
p 112
Ⓖ p 353:
chunks
chunking

Tip: Chunking

Chunking is the process of creating links between different pieces
of information so that they can be bound into the same chunk.
Chunking increases the amount of information that can be stored
in the *Episodic Buffer (Capacity and Chunking)* of working memory.

*Episodic Buffer
(Capacity and
Chunking)*:
p 112

Chunking seems to happen in two ways:

- you learn to play with information and find specific, though sometimes random, ways to make associations that suit your ways of thinking

- you understand the information in a way that is meaningful to you and that produces the necessary chunking.

In the first way the chunking mechanism can be unrelated to the information, in the second it is part of the information.

Examples: Chunking

To remember how to tie a bowline knot, the novice is told to think of "a rabbit coming up from its hole, going round the tree and back down the hole". In this chunking, the rabbit and tree have nothing to do with the knot.

One person had a number that had to be inserted into forms: 04340 354 221
    The patterns 04340 and 221 were remembered.
    354 didn't have an obvious pattern and the 5 got lost.
    Solution: 5 was linked to the last group as 5 = 2+2+1.
Here the solution relates to the information being remembered.

Following directions: the information can be chunked in different ways:

- some people use verbal rehearsal and repeat the instructions as they are given (verbal)

- some keep hold of left and right by moving their hands as appropriate (kinaesthetic)

- some draw a map (visual, kinaesthetic)

- some write out road numbers, and it is the process of writing that is chunking the information together (kinaesthetic).

4.3   Using *THINKING PREFERENCES*

THINKING PREFERENCES:
p 188

Once you know what your thinking preferences are, or you have started to find out about them, you can deliberately choose to think in the most suitable way for the task in hand.

Insight: Thinking preferences and 5 objects to remember

You have been asked to take a collection of objects to a meeting and for other people to use, say a tape measure, a pair of scissors, a camera, tea bags and cake.
You could:

1)	make a list	verbal thinking or kinaesthetic thinking, if making the list is all you need to do
2)	picture all the items	visual thinking
3)	know there are 5 in the list	'other': it works, but I don't know where to put it!
4)	run a video in your mind	visualisation
5)	weave a story of the items being used	interpersonal (MI)
6)	remember the reason for the items	rationale

These are just a few of the ways that you could use. The skill is to know the style that works for you, and to develop it to be really good. Be confident in your chosen style.

When your best way of thinking is involved, remembering is not such hard work; you will probably find that your mind has made progress when you aren't even thinking about that particular subject; see the examples in the next section, *RECALL*.

4.4 Recall

Being able to recall information when you want it is a common problem for all sorts of people. It is probably particularly challenging for you as a dyslexic/ SpLD person because the information is often not stored in your memory in a coherent way. Strengthening the process of recall by frequently using it is a very useful habit to get into. The steps for the process are set out in *EXERCISE: RECALL AND CHECK*.

EXERCISE: RECALL AND CHECK: p 62

Tip: Memory recall used to explore thinking preferences

As you recall anything, you can look at what you recall easily and decide which *THINKING PREFERENCES* are helping you to remember and recall.

THINKING PREFERENCES: p 188

Having seen what you recall easily and why, you can then think about the information you don't recall and you can alter the way you think about it so that there is some trigger associated with it that will bring it back to your conscious mind.

By repeating this process at different times, you strengthen your memory and you learn more about which thinking preferences suit you and which tasks they help you with.

The following comments and stories are all about the ways different people have responded to recall in different situations.

Story: Memory recall triggered by movement

One successful company executive could never remember whether she had put the milk back in the fridge at the end of the day; the question would surface in her mind just as she was dropping off to sleep and then, whether she got up to check or not, going to sleep became difficult. She was a kinaesthetic thinker; she found that if she made some bizarre movement as she put the milk away, a different one every night, she could think of the movement, remember the milk going into the fridge, and go to sleep.

Story: Memory recall aided by intrapersonal motivation

One student was a highly motivated scientist who was very conscious of his position in the field and only interested in showing his originality. He could not remember steps in the development of his field that were later shown to be inaccurate. As part of exam preparation, he needed to be able to recall the earlier work. He could remember an invalidated theory by remembering the arguments against it, and by 'going for the jugular' in the way he demolished the theory. His process fitted his motivation to show his originality.

The way you make notes, or display anything you want to remember, can improve recall.

Story: Memory recall and linking information

One architecture student found she liked mind maps. She could remember the whole of her third year work by putting up mind maps of the various topics and then finding one key item for each mind map. When that key was brought to mind, the rest of the mind map followed easily.

The words or thinking that you use for recall can have an impact.

Story: Memory recall and words used to check spelling

My spelling improves when I think "How have I seen this word?" rather than "How do I spell this word?" My seeing memory for words is much better than my writing memory.

By contrast, Sally has to ask herself "How do I say this word?"

Tip: Remembering and positive concept

To use the positive concept of remembering rather than the negative one of forgetting can be an important shift. Try thinking "I must remember ..." rather than "I mustn't forget ..." and even "I won't remember that!" is more useful than "I'll forget that!"

You can mentally 'hang' information and ideas on different physical places. Roman orators had a process of mentally putting their speeches on different features round an auditorium; from this habit we still use phrases like: 'in the first place...; in the second...'.

Insight: Recall aided by walking

People go for walks while revising and 'hang' parts of their syllabus or topic on lamp posts, trees, gates, or whatever they find on the walk; then when they need to recall the information, they mentally go for the walk again and retrieve it.

Story: Recall aided by visual and kinaesthetic thinking

One visual, kinaesthetic thinker saw that the house plants needed watering as she left the house in a hurry, with no time to write herself a note. She thought, "When I come home, I will see the flowers in the front, I'll remember the house plants need water; I'll cross my fingers until I get inside and can write a note or put the watering can in a place where I can't avoid it."

Recalling appropriate memories can be useful in so many situations. Having fun finding out what works best for you is a constructive approach to improving your recall. The resources to draw on are:

- observing what works well and what lets you down

- seeing how you can use your THINKING PREFERENCES or other memory systems (Buzan, 2010; Russell, 1979).

THINKING PREFERENCES: p 188

Buzan (2010)

Russell (1979)

4.5   Memory consolidation

Repeated review can be used to consolidate long-term memories of information and knowledge. Many people revise by re-reading material, which involves re-using input processes. It is much better to set up a steady review pattern that creates long-term memory patterns as you study, and that deliberately uses recall processes.

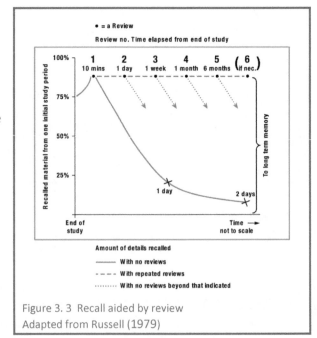

Figure 3. 3 Recall aided by review
Adapted from Russell (1979)

Tip: Use recall

You want to be able to recall information and skills. Revision should start with using and strengthening recall processes. Only after you have recalled all you can, should you start re-reading material or listening to recordings again.

Russell (1979) shows curves of decay of memory and retention of memory by repeated review. He sets out the programme listed below. He makes the point that a month's period of studying for 6 hours a day can be made significantly more productive if 1 hour a day is spent in reviewing previous work in a systematic way.

Russell (1979)

Tip: The value of repeated review

The 'improvement of long-term memory is from 10% to 90%, the overall gain in efficiency is about 750%. *Thus a few minutes devoted to review makes the hours spent studying effective and worthwhile*'. (his italics) (Russell, 1979, p 149)

Russell (1979, p149)

Buzan (2010, p 54) discusses the review processes. After you have been studying for about an hour, if you leave about 10 minutes before making a good set of notes, you will find that your mind has made more sense of the material; it needed time to 'let it sink in'. Your notes made after the pause will be more comprehensive. This set of notes becomes the blueprint for subsequent recall; it's not final, as subsequent recall may show changes you need to make. Your work and the creation of the blueprint are effectively the beginning of the process described in EXERCISE: RECALL AND CHECK[5].

Buzan (2010, p 54)

Ⓖ p 353: blueprint

EXERCISE: RECALL AND CHECK: p 62

---

[5] In EXERCISE: RECALL AND CHECK, p 62, these processes are discussed from the perspective of building an individual, personal profile. Here they are used to improve memory. The processes are the same, even though the aims are different.

Subsequent reviews:

- You jot down on a piece of paper everything you can remember about the topic and you organise it to show your growing understanding.
    - You can make a mind map, or
    - write a linear set of keywords.
    - You can use any form of brain storming that suits you, providing you have a record that you can check against your blueprint.
- When you can't remember any more (only allow a few minutes),
    - you check with the blueprint to see what you are remembering and what you are missing out; this is the 4th step of *EXERCISE: RECALL AND CHECK*.

EXERCISE: RECALL AND CHECK: p 62

- The 5th and 6th steps of *EXERCISE: RECALL AND CHECK* set out ways to use what you remember well to help you remember what you are currently forgetting. You then change how you think about anything missing and add any necessary notes to the blueprint.

The reviews of work done on previous days can be used as *MIND SET* when they relate to the study of the day, that way they enhance the work about to be done and you don't feel they are holding up your immediate study.

MIND SET: p 152

Tip: Blueprint notes

In many situations, a set of notes about a topic or a system is useful.

- Students learning and expecting to take exams.
- Book keepers who need to follow a monthly system for pay roll.
- Heating engineers who install and repair many different models of boiler.

You don't want to re-read any book or manual; you eventually want brief notes which allow you to recall what you need.

This is the blueprint set of notes.

As you initially learn the topic or develop the system, you are likely to make changes to the blueprint.

When you use it as a check in the *RECALL AND CHECK* process it should have no errors. You want the recall and check process to be guiding you to the best possible outcome.

EXERCISE: RECALL AND CHECK: p 62

Consolidation of memory to produce automatic skills also requires repeated review, namely practice. Baddeley (1989, p 27) discusses an experiment carried out when postal workers sorting letters had to learn to touch-type.   It was found that little-and-often practice was more effective than long periods of practice.

Baddeley (1989, p 27)

Tip: Little-and-often for skills

Practising a skill in small, frequent sessions is more effective than long periods of practice.

The following story illustrates the value of little-and-often practice, the mind using time to 'let it sink in' and the benefit of using one's own thinking preferences.

Story: Memory consolidation aided by framework

When I learn a new piece of music, I have to approach it in the best way for me. Fairly quickly, I need to understand its patterns, rhythms and phrases; I hardly hear the music until I've understood it. Then, I can play it for 10 minutes or so, go away for several hours, come back to it again and find I'm playing it better than I was when I stopped.

If I don't take the time to understand the structure (framework) of the piece, playing it never progresses, it stays at the beginning stage.

4.5.1   Systematic reviews

The following 2 schemes for systematic review evolved after seeing a student develop her own scheme to help her with an undergraduate degree in physics.

One involves index cards organised by days of the month. The other is an equivalent electronic scheme.   Both are based on the review patterns proposed by Russell (1979) and Buzan (2010). Both are flexible enough to be adapted to individual need.

Figure 3. 4 Index card system

Russell (1979)

Buzan (2010)

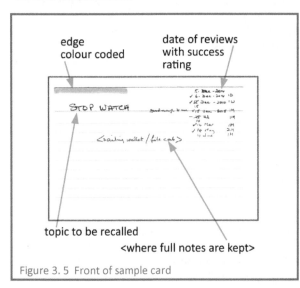

edge colour coded

date of reviews with success rating

topic to be recalled

<where full notes are kept>

Figure 3. 5 Front of sample card

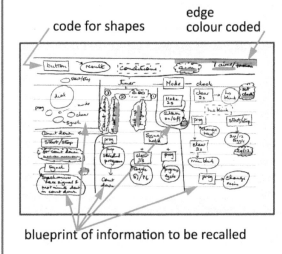

code for shapes

edge colour coded

blueprint of information to be recalled

Figure 3. 6 Back of sample card

The *Index Card Review Scheme* is set out in full. The instructions for the *Electronic Review Scheme* are written as an adaptation of the *Index Card Review Scheme*. *FIGURES 3.4, 3.5* and *3.6* are samples of a scheme. The scheme is much easier than the word description sounds.

Index Card Review Scheme	Electronic Adaptations
<u>What you need</u> Index cards. Choose the size of cards that will work for you. A box with a lid that will hold them. 31 dividers, numbered 1 – 31 for the days of the month, 'day-of-the-month' dividers. Some spare card that will stand proud of the cards but still allow the box to close.	<u>What to get</u> A reminder app with tag facilities.

Index Card Review Scheme	Electronic Adaptations
Setting up the cards On the front 1) put the title or a few key words of something you want to memorise, just enough to identify the topic. 2) if appropriate, record where you keep any notes you might want to use for further details. 3) write the date of the next review, probably in a column on the right-hand side.	Setting up the reminders (1) goes on the subject line. (2) first line of the body of the reminder. (3) the date of the reminder is the date of the next review. Record the review dates and the success of each review after (2).
On the back 4) write or draw the information you want to remember, in whatever style suits you. On the top edge of the cards, you can use highlighter pens to mark the edges and use colour coding to separate out different subject areas.	In the main body of the reminder write (4) below the review date list (3); (4) will gradually get lower as you record the review dates and success ratings. Using different tags separate different subject areas
Organising the box At the front: any cards relating to skills, or knowledge, that need reviewing every day. Day-of-the-month dividers and cards for review, with today's date always at the front. Behind each day-of-the-month divider, you will have cards to be reviewed in different months. A card to mark the end of the review cards. Any templates you have of the way you've decided you want to organise the information on the cards. Spare cards, some with their top edges already marked, as above 'On the top'.	Organising the electronic scheme Use the tag system to filter your reminders so that you are working only with the review scheme. Have a daily master reminder to use the review scheme. In the body of this reminder you could either record your organisation of the scheme or where you keep any notes about your scheme.

Index Card Review Scheme	Electronic Adaptations
Using the scheme These are initial suggestions which you can modify to suit you: Open the box at the beginning of a day. Keep it open until you've finished for the day. There is satisfaction in closing it when all the reviews are done for that day. If there are skills to be learnt (see below) that need little-and-often rehearsal, keep them at the front so that they get attention every day.	Using the electronic scheme The master reminder will trigger using the review scheme. You could set an alarm to go off until you have finished for the day. Arrange a tag system that keeps skills together, and to be done first each day. If there are any reviews you want to repeat first each day, tag them to come up with the skills.
<ul><li>Keep the day-of-the-month divider and the review cards relating to today's date always at the front.</li><li>Each day, work through the cards for that day in an order that suits you.</li><li>On the cards, mark the date when you've done the review:<ul><li>✓ means the review was good;</li><li>- means the material is not being remembered as well as you want;</li><li>x means the material is not being remembered at all well.</li></ul></li><li>Decide when you will do the next review for each topic.</li><li>Write the date on the front of the topic card, and the interval from the current review.</li><li>Put the cards behind the day-of-the-month of the next review and in month order.</li><li>Put today's divider, and any relevant cards, at the back of the pack.</li></ul>	Work through the reminders in an order to suit you. Change the date of a review reminder to that of the next review. Record the date and success of the review, as at (3) in setting up the reminders above.

Index Card Review Scheme	*Electronic Adaptations*
Including skills Subjects with a strong skills basis can be divided into knowledge and practical skills, e.g. maths procedures, process for lab work, playing music, operating a digger, manoeuvring a lifeboat. For most tasks there is some knowledge that supports the practical skills and it can be learnt using the review sequence 1 day, 1 week, 1 month, 6 months.	Including skills You could use the tag system to separate skills and knowledge reminders.

Learning the practical skills will be much better done more regularly. You don't have to be on site to do it though.

Story: Playing a cardboard keyboard

I've known one dedicated person who learnt to play the piano by practising on a cardboard keyboard that made no sound. This way, she enjoyed playing whenever she could use a piano. She wasn't using valuable time at the piano to gain the movements in her fingers.

Flexibility
By reviewing what you recall, you can easily monitor how well you are developing the scheme to make it work well for you. You choose the repetition rate to make good progress. If something needs reviewing every week for a while, give yourself permission to do the recall that often. Adapt the scheme so that it works well for you.

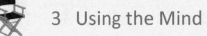

Examples: Review scheme modifications

1) A-Z cards

A set of A-Z cards was used by one person instead of dates. There are 24 (21 individual letters, PQ, XYZ and Mc). He used the cards as a 3-week system, with some built-in flexibility.

The box is opened at the beginning of the day and closed when the day's cards are completed. Missing a day happens naturally. There is no relentless pressure from the dates. The pleasure of progress keeps the system in use.

2) Review periods of more than a month

A separate box is used for any topics that are sufficiently well known for the interval for recall to be more than a month.

3) The blueprint is kept elsewhere

Some blueprints don't fit well on a single card. The card has the topic on the front and where to find the blueprint. The cards are used to maintain the review programme, while the blueprint is used to check the recall.

4) Voice recording

People who don't want to write down their recall use the voice recording on their phone. It's important to capture the recall so that you know it is accurate.

5) At odd moments

One person used odd moments for the review. The box was kept where she would come across it during the day. As she passed the box, she would pause and use a few of the recall cards for the day.

Recall doesn't work

Some things may well still be difficult to remember. Think about the way you remember well and explore different ways of making links between different parts of a topic. *EXERCISE: RECALL AND CHECK* uses the

EXERCISE: RECALL AND CHECK: p 62

reviewing process to develop your knowledge of your *Thinking Preferences*. The insights gained should help you use *Chunking* to improve recall. As you gain in general confidence, you may find that the things you can't recall don't matter so much.

Thinking Preferences: p 188

Chunking: p 154

4.6   Feedback

Feedback is information received 'about the result of an experiment, a performance, etc.' (OED, 1993). The purpose of feedback is to use the result to make the next cycle of the process better in some way.

Example: A process with feedback

Process: You try out a new recipe
Feedback: the eaters tell you their reactions

Next cycle: you use the recipe again, adapting it in the light of the comments.

reading a book → take notes → information stored in memory → information recalled → essay written

feedback loop

improve notes and information in memory

check with notes from book

Figure 3. 7 Example feedback loop

In *Figure 3.7, Example Feedback Loop*, the quality of recall from memory is improved by the use of feedback. The essay-writing is then improved too.

The feedback loop applies to gaining skills as well as remembering ideas, facts, decisions, processes, etc.

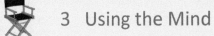

Tip: Quality feedback

Feedback is generally the most significant factor for improving performance for learners. The feedback has to suit the person learning, to be positive and constructive.

To use long-term memory well, the correct neural pathways need to be established as soon as possible and reinforced, see pruning in BRAIN GROWTH. A suitable feedback loop is part of these processes.

BRAIN GROWTH: p 92

- The steps outlined in EXERCISE: RECALL AND CHECK are one way of providing a suitable feedback loop.

EXERCISE: RECALL AND CHECK: p 62

- How your THINKING PREFERENCES are used in the feedback loop can be important.

THINKING PREFERENCES: p 188

- Any situation or task can be an opportunity to find out what feedback will be most useful.

Other people will often be involved in providing feedback. It is very important that they do so in a way that makes sense to you and that your mind can process well. You may need to negotiate in order that the processes used suit you well.

Example: Feedback that works for you

If your mind retains information that you understand but doesn't retain information that you've merely heard, the feedback needs to concentrate on the reasons behind the information; just repeating the information verbally is likely to be a waste of time and frustrating.

You may need to be the one searching for the reasons and linking them to the feedback that you are being given by someone else.

Sometimes it is important that the person giving feedback understands the issues of dyslexia/ SpLD. Support specialists often are not experts in the subject or task you are tackling. They will often need to question you to check that your work makes sense. In doing so, they can uncover gaps in your knowledge. The subject teacher, or manager, automatically uses his/her own knowledge to fill in the gaps and so misses the opportunity to help you complete your understanding.

One issue that can get overlooked is the difficulties some dyslexic/ SpLD students have with the relationships between facts, arguments and evaluations. To make a sound evaluation of an issue, you need to know what all the arguments are. The arguments should be based on sound facts.

Insight: Feedback should help you develop

I could see one student focusing on clever angles. He was not showing the facts behind his ideas. His tutors were recognising his cleverness and assuming his background knowledge was as clear as their own. They were not rigorously checking what he understood.

If he didn't become aware of the gaps in his work, he would produce poorer quality work than his true potential allowed.

He needed feedback that checked his understanding of the relationships between facts, arguments and evaluations. Without this perceptive feedback, the student would miss developing very useful skills for employment.

4.7   Catching thoughts as they cross your mind

Random thoughts can appear in the mind at any time, especially at times when you are not thinking very hard about anything: in the shower, just as you go to sleep, at a meal.

Many dyslexic/ SpLD people know they are unlikely to recall the thoughts, even important ones. They need strategies to catch these thoughts. Some have notepads beside their bed or the shower; some put a message on their answerphone; some keep a notebook in their bag. Several of the techniques discussed in *RECALL* can be used to capture a thought, e.g. attaching a thought to an object or place.

RECALL: p 157

Story: Catching thoughts as they come by

One colleague said, "Oh look! Here's this thought again, I'd better capture it this time!" She experiences thoughts randomly surfacing in her mind; she will recognise that they are important; she knows they are unlikely to surface at an appropriate time; so when she is able to, she writes them down.

5   Cognition, awareness

Previous sections of this chapter have looked at what we use our minds for, and how we can improve the way we use them. This section looks at cognition, the faculty of knowing, and processes related to it.

Cognition is the act or faculty of knowing. It includes perceiving and conceiving:

    perceiving is the ability to collect facts or ideas, to understand their meaning;

    conceiving is the ability to take ideas into the mind, to have an open mind, and also the ability to devise plans and ideas (OED, 1993).

OED (1993)

Cognition seems to be another area of processing that is restricted by the problems of dyslexia/ SpLD. When working memory is inefficiently used, there isn't the mental capacity to be aware of the cognitive levels of thinking. Therefore, they constitute an area of processing that has to be deliberately learnt by dyslexic/ SpLD people.

5.1 Concentration

To concentrate is to be able to focus the mind for a considerable length of time and to pay attention to something without being distracted by thoughts or the external environment. The *EXERCISE: KNOW YOUR OWN MIND* strengthens the ability to concentrate. Concentration can be poor for each of the 4 SpLDs, but for different reasons (Stacey, 2020b).

Discussing concentration with many dyslexic/ SpLDs, one can again see a variety of patterns.

* Some people are easily distracted and have to be very careful about the environment in which they work; see *THE IMPACT OF THE ENVIRONMENT* (Stacey, 2020a).
* People with AD(H)D often need breaks for physical activity.
* Some find taking breaks unhelpful and they need to take very few or none at all.

Fatigue will set in at some point; it is useful to recognise a genuine need for food or rest (genuine physical need as opposed to restlessness because a task is difficult) and to take a satisfying break to meet the need.

EXERCISE: KNOW YOUR OWN MIND:
p 57

Stacey (2020b)

(G) p 351: descriptions of the 4 SpLDs covered by this series

(Stacey, 2020a)

Tips: Aids for concentration

* Some find their concentration is improved by having music on.
* Some find breaks, going for a walk or run, are useful ways to refocus when concentration has been broken.
* For others, the break needs to engage the mind at the same intellectual level, e.g. by playing the violin, so that the mind is diverted, given a break but still intellectually active.

However, breaks can be a hazard, even if they are potentially useful. You can forget that you are *'taking a break in the middle of studying'* and find that you have been happily occupied elsewhere for a couple of hours or more. Breaks involving physical movement can be kept short by using *BRAIN GYM*.

Ⓖ p 353: hazard

BRAIN GYM: p 275

Some dyslexic/ SpLD people find their concentration has to be built up over a period of time. It then reaches a level at which good work is done and care has to be taken not to let it drop below that level. The level of concentration can be quite intense. If it does drop below, more time is then needed deliberately to build it up again, see *FIGURE 3.8*. People with this pattern of working find breaks unhelpful.

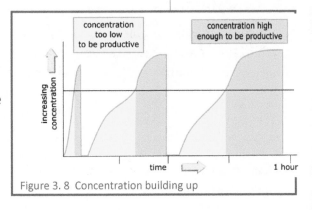

Figure 3. 8 Concentration building up

Some have the feeling that they process the information at a deeper level in the first instance and that the material gets to long-term memory storage faster for them than for their peers.

With the problems of short working memories, breaks can result in loss of information. If the information is only partly digested, taking a break can mean it gets lost completely.

Your ability to concentrate, or to remain alert, may also depend on how well you are processing the material you are studying or reading.

5.2 Metacognition, awareness of ourselves

The mind *EXERCISE: KNOW YOUR OWN MIND* shows that we have the ability to observe ourselves as we are thinking. This is the skill of being aware of ourselves, sometimes called mindfulness or metacognition.

EXERCISE: KNOW YOUR OWN MIND: p 57

'Meta' at the beginning of a word denotes something of a second-order or more fundamental kind (OED, 2020).

Metacognition is a more fundamental level of knowing; knowing about yourself in the present moment; knowing how you are thinking[6] and feeling as the thoughts and feelings occur; being aware of yourself as the thinker and feeler.

For example, this level of knowing is necessary to take action against going to sleep, as discussed in *BEING ALERT*. If you do the *EXERCISE: KNOW YOUR OWN MIND* frequently, you will develop metacognition.

Insight: Not knowing you are asking questions

The absence of metacognition is shown by a comment from one dyslexic colleague: "You are so busy asking the questions that you don't realise that you are asking questions."

The lack of awareness of how we are thinking, what we are doing, could mean that the *CENTRAL EXECUTIVE* doesn't have the right information to guide working memory effectively.

Much of the management of dyslexia/ SpLD relies on accurate metacognition.   It enables you to:
- keep on task
- avoid distractions
- make choices, especially to choose the most appropriate techniques
- avoid pitfalls from dyslexia/ SpLD
- see when a pitfall has occurred and take action to minimise its effects.

Margin notes:

'meta-, prefix 2.b'
OED (2020)

BEING ALERT: p 133

EXERCISE: KNOW YOUR OWN MIND:
p 57

CENTRAL EXECUTIVE:
p 110

See also *REGIME FOR MANAGING DYSLEXIA/ SPLD*:
p 71

Ⓖ p 353:
pitfall

---

[6] The *EXERCISE: KEYWORDS* in *Gaining Knowledge and Skills with Dyslexia and other SpLDs* (Stacey, 2021) allows you to develop metacognition of how you are thinking.

Metacognition is a skill that anyone can develop and use. Most people don't do so on a day-to-day basis; they haven't got the chaotic networks of dyslexia/ SpLD to guard against.

5.3   Observing others

It is very useful to observe others, especially others with the same set of problems. It is worth asking them to be specific about the way they think through tasks or carry them out. Ask them whether they are solving a particular dyslexic/ SpLD problem in doing so.

Tip: Be selective of ideas from others

However, don't expect other dyslexic/ SpLDs' solutions to become yours; don't adopt them without testing whether they will work for you. Other people's strengths could be quite different from yours, and their strategies may not work at all for you.

As you question what people are doing, you become more aware of the different processes used, in study, in the workplace and in life. You become aware of the patterns of communication that good teachers or managers use. You know when facts are being given, and whether the arguments are sound. You become aware of missing information and are able to ask pertinent questions.

5.4   Reflection

Having observed yourself or others, you then need to make something of the observations: you need to reflect on them.

You may need to interpret the observations in terms of:

   how you think

   what your *Thinking Preferences* are

   what you are feeling.

Thinking Preferences:
p 188

You may need to assess

> how you are processing a course you are on
>
> the way you are doing a job
>
> the way you are relating to those around you.

Monitoring Progress will help you use templates on the *Series Website* for your reflections.

Monitoring Progress: p 311

Work on disruptive feelings is beyond the scope of this book, but *Emotional Hi-jacking* discusses the way emotions have an immediate impact and *Neuro-Linguistic Programming* (*NLP*) has some suggestions for making changes to feelings.

Emotional Hi-jacking: p 260

NLP: p 279

5.5 Making connections

One of the benefits of metacognition and reflection is to see how various ideas (objects, events, people) fit together. You see the relationships; you see patterns repeating themselves between different groups of ideas (objects, events, people).

Chunking: p 154

The ability to see connections then allows you to use the capacity of working memory better as you use the technique of *Chunking* to hold more information in the *Episodic Buffer (Capacity and Chunking)*.

Episodic Buffer (Capacity and Chunking): p 112

5.6 Prioritising

As a result of increased skills in cognition:

> you can see the relationships between different parts of a situation
>
> you can then weigh up one aspect against another
>
> you can think about the outcomes of different actions
>
> you can prioritise and set appropriate goals.

These are, again, skills that many dyslexic/ SpLD people often find very difficult to acquire without deliberate, steady development at a level not needed by those without these syndromes.

One way to develop *Prioritising* is set out in *Appendix 1 Resources*.

Prioritising: p 304

6   A model of learning

>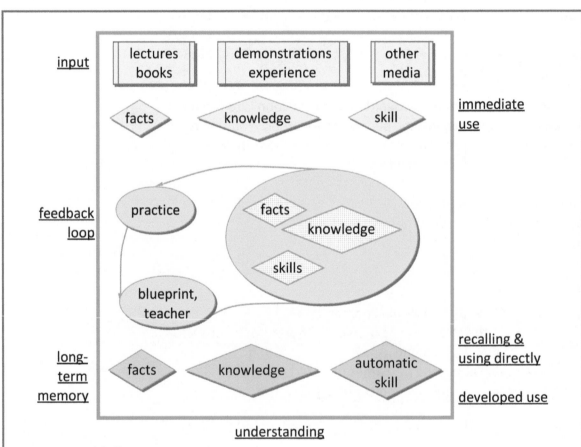
>
> **Tip: Stages of learning and managing dyslexia/ SpLD**
>
> *FIGURE 3.9 A MODEL OF LEARNING*, is a diagram showing the various stages of learning at which dyslexic/ SpLD management is important. The stages are underlined.

Figure 3. 9 A model of learning

Knowledge and understanding can mean the same thing. In this diagram, 'knowledge' is part of learning processes and 'understanding' is part of using what has been learnt.

Having a skill means you can carry out some process in a competent way.

*   Ⓖ p 353: blueprint

Table: Stages of the Model of Learning	
Stage of Model	*Outline of stage*
Input	includes • perceiving information • understanding information and • the initial phase of memorising it
Immediate use	represents facts, knowledge and skills used immediately for some purpose
Feedback loop	is the process of checking that • facts and knowledge are being accurately memorised and getting into long-term memory • or a skill is being developed in the right way
Long-term memory	facts, knowledge and skills stored for recall and later use
Recalling and using directly	represents facts, knowledge or skills used as intended, without much development
Developed use	can extend beyond mere recall • knowledge can be used for a different purpose or with extra knowledge • a skill can be adapted to a new (but similar) or different situation
Understanding	can grow at any stage; it is different from memorising plain facts

Essentially, you can use
        the skills from COGNITION, AWARENESS
the TECHNIQUES TO ASSIST USING YOUR MIND and apply them to
        the purposes set out in PURPOSES OF THINKING.
You can incorporate
        your THINKING PREFERENCES
and maintain good thinking by using
        THINKING CLEARLY

COGNITION, AWARENESS: p 172

TECHNIQUES TO ASSIST USING YOUR MIND: p 151
PURPOSES OF THINKING: p 142

THINKING PREFERENCES: p 188

THINKING CLEARLY: p 254

Putting all these ideas together should result in your using your mind well for all stages of the *MODEL OF LEARNING*. Equally, the stages of the *MODEL OF LEARNING* are opportunities to develop these different aspects of thinking well.

At each stage, I have found it is necessary to look at the way dyslexic/ SpLD people are thinking and to make sure the most effective methods are being used. It is possible that different thinking preferences will be used at the different stages.

Example: Variations in *THINKING PREFERENCES*

One person could

- perceive information from experience
- understand it by using a mind map
- start memorising it through the logical connections on the mind map.

While another person could

- perceive information visually
- understand it by making a list of keywords
- start memorising it through the rehearsal of the keywords.

FIGURE 3.9, A MODEL OF LEARNING, applies to
> formal situations, such as education and employment

> everyday living, such as shopping or dealing with text messages,
>> you may not be learning much that is new
>> you will be using what you have learnt.

6.1 Input information

Information can be presented to you in many different ways; some you will find easier to relate to than others.

- 'Lectures and books' rely heavily on words.

- 'Demonstrations' (someone showing you what to do) have a practical element.

- Your own 'experience' means the practical aspect is done by you.

- Examples of 'other media' are film and music.

- Notices (also 'other media') are a mixture of words and visual elements.

You may be able to absorb the information (perceive it) straight away or you may have to adapt it by using your particular thinking preferences, see *EXAMPLE: MBPT MOTIVATION AND MEMORY RECALL*. Your motivation or interest is likely to help you either understand or remember the information. To use the information you have to retain it, sometimes for a very short length of time, sometimes for a long time.

EXAMPLE: MBPT MOTIVATION AND MEMORY RECALL: p 49

New information from external sources will be retained more easily if it is related to something you already know or are interested in, which means that recalling memories from your long-term memory should also help you with receiving input information, see *MIND SET*.

MIND SET: p 152

Many dyslexic/ SpLD people find it very hard to retain information for even a short time. A few suggestions to try:

- you may have to use the right sense to perceive it (i.e. you may have to switch between seeing, hearing or doing)

- you may have to understand it immediately

- you may need some kind of holding framework for it

- you may have to add memory tags immediately in some way.

These adaptations are part of the input process and without them, there may be no information registered by the mind in any way that gives you access to it, see also *IMMEDIATE USE*.

IMMEDIATE USE: p 182

6.2 Immediate use

Once you have dealt with the way information is presented to your working memory, you can think about how long you need to retain it for.

Some information you will only need for a very short time for an immediate task. For example, you could be in a group which is being given the option to do one of four different activities. While you decide which activity to join, you need to use the information you have been given about them all.

You will need to understand enough about all the activities to make the choice, but you won't need to gain long-term knowledge or skills. Once you have made your choice, you only need its details and instructions; you can forget the rest since it is not useful beyond the immediate task of making the decision.

You need to be free to alter the way you think about something for different stages. You may find you use different processes for:

- capturing the information at the input stage
- understanding and thinking about it without remembering it long term
- getting it stored in your long-term memory.

Example: Vary how you think

You may spatially separate and colour-code ideas needed to make a decision for a course project, or a job, or shopping expedition.

To make the decision, you then visualise stories depending on the different possible decisions.

6.3 Feedback loop

The way you practise needs to produce the required neural networks in a straightforward manner.

Example: Learning to spell 'schizophrenia'

A nursing student from a group of dyslexic students wanted to know how to learn to spell 'schizophrenia'. He needed useful thoughts to assist his practice of the word until motor memory could be relied on. We looked at the other two related words, 'schizophrene' and 'schizophrenic' at the same time.

We used colour and space in the way we analysed the word. It was useful to know that 'schizo' comes from a Greek word meaning 'to split' and 'phren' comes from a Greek word meaning 'mind'. It was also useful to know that the look of 'phren' is kept the same even when the sound of it changes for 'schizophrenic'.

There were 3 problematic sounds which were dealt with as follows:

Sch-: like sch in school; this thought made the word more friendly for one student

-iz: 'sounds like its' (not helpful, see below*); not the standard English sound for z, but like the z in Mozart;

-ph-: in Greek that's the single letter φ; we often use 'ph' for φ in translation.

The rest of the letters didn't present a problem.

Most of this information helped him practise spelling the word until it was securely in motor memory and could be written without undue thought.

*However, the information '-iz sounds like its' was not useful for a dyslexic person practising the word: it produced a hiccup in the practice. As you practise the word, you have to discard this information every time; anything you have to negate should be left out. You do not want the sequence: sch its ~~its~~ iz ophrenia,

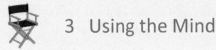

which is what happened as a result of the unproductive information. With this sequence, the motor memory doesn't easily settle to the required pattern. Keeping to 'un-English z: like Mozart' would have been better.

Everything that is helping your practice needs to be positive and useful. You need to avoid useless information that doesn't assist the recall of what you are learning.

Short-cuts or whacky methods may also produce nothing useful.

Story: Ineffective spelling practice

One girl I knew had 20 spellings to write out 3 times each. She wrote every first letter down the page, then every 2nd and so on until all the words were finished. This method produced 60 words that looked right, it satisfied the teacher, it seemed less boring to the girl but it didn't help her spelling at all.

Tip: Error-free practice

Practice should not contain errors. It can be very difficult to modify errors. You need to check against a correct blueprint or get someone to check what you are doing.

The style of the blueprint has to be right for you; any person making comments should encourage you as well as put you right when necessary.

Ⓖ p 353: blueprint

6.4 Long-term memory

Some dyslexic/ SpLD people's use of working memory seems sufficiently inefficient that long-term memory has to be used: people comment that they are not as quick initially as others, but they understand in greater depth once they get hold of something.

Examples: Examples of using long-term memory

One student of Fine Art had found lectures difficult until she started using *Mind Set* regularly. Without mind set, her working memory didn't store the information of the lecture long enough for her to understand. With mind set, she was using long-term memory to give her working memory the help it needed to be efficient; she was able to ask questions and felt that her questions were being answered with respect for their content.

Mind Set: p 152

A scientist found he would never retain information when reading, but that if he worked slowly and carefully, the information went into long-term memory and could be recalled.

You can work really hard and seem to make no progress learning something. I would suggest you explore how you are trying to learn; many times, working the wrong way will produce no results.

6.5   Recalling and using directly

For this stage to work well, you need to keep your long-term memory as accurate as possible; you need to recall information when you need it and then you have to process it in working memory, so *Recalling and Using Directly* builds on all the previous stages of the *Model of Learning*.

Recall is a particular problem for dyslexic/ SpLD people. Finding the recall triggers that work for you can make a significant difference.   You may need to find out how to maintain your *Self-Esteem* while asking questions. Sometimes you find others don't know either but they are better at pretending they know, then the questions you ask may often help others in your group; see *Example: Detailed Information That Is Likely To Be Useful, Event 2.*

Self-Esteem: p 265

Example: Detailed Information That Is Likely To Be Useful: p 66

Revision is a particular time when recall and use of information is important. Many people do revision by repeating the input stages and they pay no attention to being able to recall what they have learnt. You need to make sure that recall schemes are being strengthened, see *MEMORY CONSOLIDATION*.

MEMORY CONSOLIDATION: p 160

6.6   Developed use

Often what has been learnt needs to be adapted. Skills learnt on one set of equipment need to be altered to work for another. Material learnt during a previous term or training needs to be put together in new ways for an exam or another situation at work. You need to know your strengths and weaknesses when it comes to developing what you know or how you do something to meet a different challenge.

6.7   Subliminal learning

Subliminal learning is learning that takes place 'below the threshold for conscious perception' (OED, 2020). So your mind still goes on learning about a topic when you are not consciously working on it. Buzan (2010) suggests you wait 10 minutes after a period of study before you make a good set of notes. This allows for a period of subliminal learning. My experience in *STORY: MEMORY CONSOLIDATION AIDED BY FRAMEWORK* is an example of how subliminal learning becomes possible after I have paid attention to how my mind needs to think.

There are several common experiences of subliminal processing. People often can't remember a word, or phrase or someone's name. They stop thinking about it and then it surfaces in the consciousness. The mind has gone on looking for the missing information subliminally.

Another example is working on a problem and not finding the solution. You 'sleep on it' and in the morning the solution often occurs to you. Subliminal processes have been at work to produce the solution.

In my experience of working with dyslexic/ SpLD people, subliminal processes have been important 1) in preparation for a period of study and 2) for learning material.

Ⓖ p 353:
subliminal learning

'subliminal, adj.' OED (2020)

Buzan (2010)

STORY: MEMORY CONSOLIDATION AIDED BY FRAMEWORK: p 163

1) In preparation for a period of study, one very useful routine at the end one day's work is to:

    decide what you will cover tomorrow

    MIND SET, in a way that suits you, about the topic for 10 minutes or so. *MIND SET*: p 152

The next day, subliminal processing will mean you make more progress with the topic.

2) For learning material, students have often gone over their revision notes with me. I get them to recall the notes before they show them to me. We then discuss what has been recalled and what is missing. Frequently, what has been recalled has drawn on their thinking preferences and been remembered with no effort on their part.

A key factor in allowing subliminal learning to work is that each student's own thinking preferences have been involved. Without using your own thinking preferences, there is little subliminal learning and progress is hard work, slow or non-existent.

References

Buzan, Tony, 2010, *Use Your Head,* BBC Active, Harlow

OED[7], Brown, Lesley Ed in Chief, 1993, *The New Shorter Oxford English Dictionary on Historical Principles*, Clarendon Press, Oxford

Russell, Peter, 1979, *The Brain Book: Know Your Own Mind and How to Use It*, Routledge, London

Stacey, Ginny, 2020a, *Organisation and Everyday Life with Dyslexia and other SpLDs,* Routledge, London

Stacey, Ginny, 2020b, *Development of Dyslexia and other SpLDs,* Routledge, London

Stacey, Ginny, 2021, *Gaining Knowledge and Skills with Dyslexia and other SpLDs,* Routledge, London

Website information

OED Online, December 2020, Oxford University Press. Accessed 15 February 2021.

Series website: www.routledge.com/cw/stacey

---

[7] The online OED has been consulted every time, and the meanings are consistent. Sometimes the words used in the hard copy of OED (1993) are clearer, or more to the point in the context of this book, in which case, the reference is to the hard-copy edition.

4 Thinking Preferences

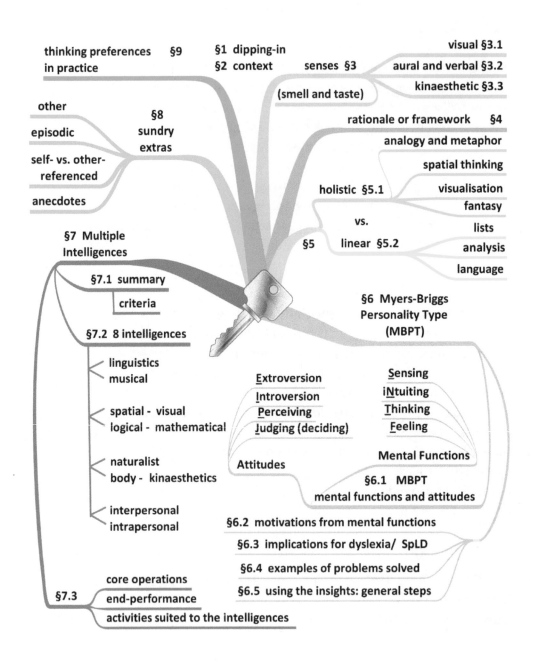

thinking preferences §9
in practice

§1 dipping-in
§2 context

senses §3

visual §3.1

aural and verbal §3.2

kinaesthetic §3.3

(smell and taste)

other

§8
sundry
extras

episodic

self- vs. other-
referenced

anecdotes

rationale or framework §4

analogy and metaphor

spatial thinking

holistic §5.1

visualisation

fantasy

vs.

lists

§5

linear §5.2

analysis

language

§7 Multiple
Intelligences

§7.1 summary

criteria

§6 Myers-Briggs
Personality Type
(MBPT)

§7.2 8 intelligences

linguistics
musical

spatial - visual
logical - mathematical

naturalist
body - kinaesthetics

interpersonal
intrapersonal

Extroversion

Introversion

Perceiving

Judging (deciding)

Sensing

iNtuiting

Thinking

Feeling

Attitudes

Mental Functions

§6.1 MBPT
mental functions and attitudes

§6.2 motivations from mental functions

§6.3 implications for dyslexia/ SpLD

§6.4 examples of problems solved

core operations

§7.3 end-performance

§6.5 using the insights: general steps

activities suited to the intelligences

Contents

Vital for dyslexic/ SpLDs, good practice for all

All of this chapter can play a vital role in your management of dyslexia/ SpLD. *THINKING PREFERENCES IN PRACTICE* sums up why thinking preferences can be so vital for so many dyslexic/ SpLD people.

For people in general,

- it is useful to know a wide range of options

- it can aid communication if you are aware of the many different ways of thinking that are used unconsciously by other people.

THINKING PREFERENCES IN PRACTICE: p 251

4   Thinking Preferences

Working with this chapter

You can use this chapter to explore the way you think best. Use the templates listed below to record what you discover.

BUILDING UP INSIGHTS has some suggestions for gathering your stories as you work.

When you have some clear ideas about the way you think, you can add them to your INDIVIDUAL, PERSONAL PROFILE OF DYSLEXIA/ SPLD and your REGIME FOR MANAGING DYSLEXIA/ SPLD

BUILDING UP INSIGHTS:
p 316
AN INDIVIDUAL,
PERSONAL PROFILE OF
DYSLEXIA/ SPLD:
p 64
REGIME FOR MANAGING
DYSLEXIA/ SPLD:
p 71

Templates on the website

TEMPLATES

In the initial stages of working with this chapter, use:

A1   JOTTING DOWN AS YOU SCAN
A4   JOTTING DOWN AS YOU READ
B1   COLLECTING IDEAS THAT RELATE TO YOU

As you explore different styles of thinking, use:

B2   KNOW YOUR OWN MIND
B3   COMPARE EXPECTATIONS AND REALITY
B4   ACTIONS, RESULTS, NEXT STEP
B5   RECORDING TEMPLATE - 1
B7   RECORDING TEMPLATE - 3
B11   MONITORING PROGRESS

Use the templates for THINKING PREFERENCES to gather together the insights about the ways you think best:

E1   LIST OF OPTIONS FOR THINKING PREFERENCE
E2   TABLE OF THINKING PREFERENCES (SPATIAL)
E3   EXAMPLE: TABLE OF THINKING PREFERENCES (SPATIAL)
E4   THINKING PREFERENCES (SPATIAL)
E5   THINKING PREFERENCES (LINEAR)
E6   VISUAL, AURAL, KINAESTHETIC QUESTIONNAIRE
E7   THE BOX 'OTHER'

Add your THINKING PREFERENCES to your INDIVIDUAL, PERSONAL PROFILE OF DYSLEXIA/ SPLD:

C1   INDIVIDUAL, PERSONAL PROFILE OF DYSLEXIA/ SPLD (SPATIAL)
C3   INDIVIDUAL, PERSONAL PROFILE OF DYSLEXIA/ SPLD(LINEAR)

Examples of INDIVIDUAL, PERSONAL PROFILES are shown in templates:

C2   EXAMPLE: INDIVIDUAL, PERSONAL PROFILE OF DYSLEXIA/ SPLD
C4   2 EXAMPLES OF AN INDIVIDUAL, PERSONAL PROFILE OF DYSLEXIA/ SPLD

Add your *Thinking Preferences* to your *Regime for Managing Dyslexia/ SpLD*:

D3   *Managing Dyslexia/ SpLD (spatial)*

D4   *Managing Dyslexia/ SpLD (linear)*

See the example of *Thinking Preferences* in:

D5   *Experiences for Managing Dyslexia/ SpLD (example)*

All the *Templates* suggested in this chapter are shown in the *List of Templates*.

List of Templates: p 362

Appendix 1 Resources

Appendix 1: p 300

This appendix will help you collect information together, decide on priorities and monitor progress.

Appendix 2 Individual, Personal Profile of Dyslexia/ SpLD

Appendix 2: p 314

Use this appendix to add the insights about your thinking preferences to both your profile and your regime.

Appendix 3 Key Concepts

Appendix 3: p 328

This appendix has a summary of the key ideas I cover when doing an audit of skills and knowledge with a dyslexic/ SpLD student. It shows which of the 4 books in the series covers each idea in full.

1 Dipping-in to try out ideas

In the *Context* notice the example results of the *Exercise: Know Your Own Mind*.

Context: p 192
Exercise: Know Your Own Mind: p 57

Scan the chapter. Use *Exercise: Initial Purpose for Reading* to collect
    the ideas relevant to you. Replace the subsections in step 2
    with the suggestions here:
    What do you recognise as relating to you?
    What catches your attention as being interesting to try?
    Look for:
        stories that are similar to your experience
        strategies you use or
        ways in which you are hampered.
    Scan the bullet points as well as the coloured boxes.
    Explore the sections that tally with your experience.
    If you are a kinaesthetic thinker, read *Kinaesthetic Thinking* in
        detail.

Exercise: Initial Purpose for Reading: p 14

Kinaesthetic Thinking: p 206

4 Thinking Preferences

Skim the other sections so that you are aware of possibilities that might be useful in the future.

2 Context

This chapter is about many different ways of thinking that are helpful to bear in mind when trying to identify the best thinking preferences of a particular person.

A common view of dyslexia/ SpLD has three levels:

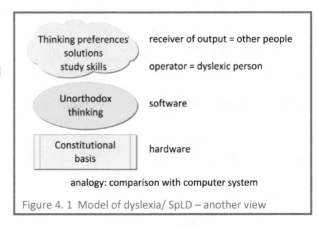

Figure 4. 1 Model of dyslexia/ SpLD – another view

- the constitutional basis
- cognitive characteristics
- symptoms and problems (Morton and Frith, 1995).

Morton and Frith (1995)

FIGURE 4. 1 MODEL OF DYSLEXIA/ SPLD – ANOTHER VIEW has basically the same levels from a positive view point:

- constitutional basis
- unorthodox thinking
- solutions and study skills coming from thinking preferences.

The figure contains a comparison with a computer system, which is a good way of understanding how these levels interact.

Finding your thinking preferences is not a fixed once-for-all process. Any task in the future may require you to find new thinking processes to help with that task.

The range of thinking preferences[1] that I bear in mind has grown over the years as I have helped other dyslexic people find what works best for them, see *TEMPLATE: E1 - LIST OF OPTIONS FOR THINKING PREFERENCES*.

TEMPLATES

The selection of preferences varies from person to person. I use *TEMPLATE: E4 - THINKING PREFERENCES (SPATIAL)* to collect my observations about my students. The linear version is *TEMPLATE: E5 - THINKING PREFERENCES (LINEAR)*. Use the one that suits you. Ultimately, it is useful

---

[1] See *CAVEAT ABOUT THE THEORIES USED IN THIS BOOK:* p 22

to know which of the various thinking preferences you use best and when, as in the *TEMPLATE: E2 - TABLE OF THINKING PREFERENCES* and the *TEMPLATE: E3 - EXAMPLE: TABLE FOR THINKING PREFERENCES*.

I always find it useful to have *TEMPLATE: E7 - THE BOX 'OTHER'* to hand, because I can never be sure that a new student will have the same thinking preferences as students who've gone before; I always want to have an open mind to look for patterns that are new.

TEMPLATES

THE BOX OTHER themes:
situation
intelligence shown by
practical abilities
unfamiliar patterns
interests
possibilities

Example: Checking spelling and thinking preferences

Examples of the ways people think differently can be seen in how they test whether a word is spelt correctly or not.

- Some pick up a pen and try the movement for writing the word, or they can imagine picking up a pen and writing the word

- others will think: how have I seen this word?

- others will think of the sound of the word and test it out by listening to the syllables

- others will check using conscious or subconscious knowledge of spelling patterns.

All of these indicate different types of memory being accessed.

Insight: Switching between thinking preferences

The thinking preferences discussed in this chapter are not particular to dyslexic/ SpLD people; they are available to everyone. Eysenck's theory of processing efficiency says that the mind switches the way it performs a task when its current way is not working.

EYSENCK'S THEORY OF PROCESSING EFFICIENCY:
p 130

For most people when the brain becomes overloaded and cannot be effective, the mind probably uses other thinking strategies without the thinker being aware of swopping to another system.

When there is some difficulty because of dyslexia/ SpLD, the mind is probably struggling too much for this automatic switching to different thinking processes to take place. Therefore the switching has to be consciously done.

Even people without any form of dyslexia/ SpLD can find it helpful to know their thinking preferences. There are often challenges in life that need new thought patterns. It can be more satisfying to switch deliberately and earlier than the mind would because it was being inefficient.

The *EXERCISE: KNOW YOUR OWN MIND* is one way that can be used to find out how people think. I have used the exercise many times since 1991 when running workshops about dyslexia/ SpLD, as well as using it with individual students.

EXERCISE: KNOW YOUR OWN MIND:
p 57
Re-cap: people are given 1 ½ minutes to gather ideas relating to their own choice of colour or shape.

In the discussion after the exercise, I ask several participants to say what has come into their minds. As they are talking I listen to the type of comments and the way they are telling me what they thought about. When several people have given their list, we go back and think about the thinking processes involved in their choices. One reaction that participants frequently have is to be surprised at the variations in ways people think.

Example: Mind exercise from a workshop

Contributions from 7 people were as follows:

RED: sun, Barcelona, car, fruit, wine, warm, happy, cotton rep
GREEN: grass, apple, algae, Mum, feeling sick, traffic lights, hospital walls, unripe, fields
STAR: Christmas, money, family, wine, tree, presents, music

'cotton rep' is a type of fabric.

RED: ketchup, blood, Santa Claus, tomato, sea, pen, pepper
STAR: starry night, twinkle twinkle, starfish, brittle star, Southern
         Cross, star-crossed lovers, star student
BLUE: favourite colour, sad, jazz, rude movies, Scottish flag,
         smelly cheese, hair (blue rinse), blue tit, sapphire, flowers,
         ink, Mum, sea, water, sky, paint box, eyes
TRIANGLE: cheese, tortilla, pyramids, C in band, arrow,
         child's play block, roof, tent

'C in band' was how this person recalled the triangle instrument in an orchestra.

The first RED came from a person who was seeing one particular
         holiday; the implication was that she was using the visual
         memory and episodic memory.
The person centring on GREEN was smelling some of her list; the
         strongest memory was lived experience. She only used
         vision when seeing the fields; the implication was that she
         had a strong kinaesthetic memory, with smell and vision also
         aiding her recall.
The person centring on STAR visualised herself in a scenario; she
         was remembering the situation in a way which showed a
         tendency for visualisation with kinaesthetic memory.
The second RED collection of ideas came from a person who was
         using visualisation, with taste where food was concerned.
The second STAR collection of ideas was triggered by songs, or
         verbal association with the word 'star'.
The BLUE collection was remembered by linguistic connections, or
         personal association.
The TRIANGLE collection was recalled visually, with personal
         associations, and with auditory memory.

You need to probe carefully to decide what is indicated. The exercise
gives a good starting point which can then be tested by using relevant
strategies and seeing what works well in practice.

As said elsewhere, anything that doesn't work well is equally
important because it is also telling more about the ways you think: it
is as important to know what doesn't work as to know what does.

*TASKS NOT GOING TO
PLAN ARE USEFUL:*
p 48

4 Thinking Preferences

Research has been carried out to look for a common learning style for dyslexic people. Nothing has been found that can be used in a 'one size suits all' way.

MARGIN NOTE:
'/ SpLD' is deliberately left out of this paragraph, because the research focused on dyslexia.

Insight: No one size suits all

There are stories of the response, "You're dyslexic, you must like mind maps," to the deep irritation of those dyslexics for whom mind maps are anathema.

Insight: Use all the thinking preferences that work for you

EXAMPLE: PROGRESS USING THINKING PREFERENCES is just one story showing that a range of different styles is useful to any given individual. What you want to use may depend on the task or situation. Have fun experimenting.

EXAMPLE: PROGRESS USING THINKING PREFERENCES: p 50

From my work with students, what is common are the stages of the *MODEL OF LEARNING* at which it is important to be using thinking preferences. Possibly, the most important stage is the initial perception, when the processes that suit a dyslexic/ SpLD person need investigating: whether the right senses are being used or whether knowing the rationale/ framework is important. Subliminal learning is more likely to happen when the right thinking preferences have been used.

A MODEL OF LEARNING: p 178

Ⓖ p 353: subliminal learning

One benefit of knowing what your thinking preferences are is that you are able to direct your thoughts in a way that keeps them together and coherent.

Story: A spanner in the notes

One student came to me, for the first time, just before he had to do a presentation. We discussed his thinking preferences and how he was making his notes. He stopped making verbal notes for his presentation, because we had decided he was a visual thinker, and he drew his notes. A week later he came back with a grin on his face; he said that his conclusion was a drawing of a spanner. He looked at the spanner, knew what it meant; he looked his audience in the eye, and he "socked it to them".

This chapter sets out the different thinking preferences that I have found useful in working with dyslexic/ SpLD students, with examples to illustrate various points made.

3 Senses

The senses that we use to communicate with the world around us are:
  visual: sight
  aural: hearing
  physical: touch, body movement and position
  smell
  taste.

FURTHER READING:
Bell (2007)
Vitalle (1982)
Williams (1983)

There is some discussion as to whether the physical senses – of touch, movement and knowledge of the physical position of our bodies – are separate or part of the same system. For the purposes of this book, the term 'kinaesthetic sense' is used to cover all of them.

(G) p 353:
kinaesthetic

The way we process the signals from the senses is beyond the scope of this book. This section is about some impacts of the senses, including using the various ways they can influence our thinking.

VISUAL THINKING and *AURAL AND VERBAL THINKING* are based on the senses of sight and hearing, respectively. They are the thinking ways most commonly used in communication and general education.

VISUAL THINKING: p 200
AURAL AND VERBAL THINKING: p 201

KINAESTHETIC THINKING is based on the kinaesthetic sense. It is not given as much attention in general education as visual and verbal thinking.

KINAESTHETIC THINKING: p 206

Using our senses, we build collections of memories. Some memories will have strong associations with the different senses. These memories can assist visual, verbal and kinaesthetic thinking.

For some people smell and taste are very strong senses, and there is a smell or taste association with many of their memories. However, most of the time communication does not include deliberate use of smell and taste. I haven't considered them further in this book, but if I were working with someone for whom they were important we would explore how they could be useful. I would be using the processes described in METHODS FOR OBSERVING, which are at the heart of everything that has been learnt and presented in this book.

METHODS FOR OBSERVING: p 55

When I taught groups of dyslexic/ SpLD students, I used a questionnaire that was designed to see whether people's thinking was based on their visual, aural or kinaesthetic sense. We found that the preferences could vary:

- from one sense being stronger than the other two which were nearly equal, A

- one sense being much weaker than the other two, and again these being nearly equal, B

- one sense being the strongest, another being a second choice, with the third sense being the weakest of all, C .

The patterns are shown in FIGURE 4.2.

Figure 4. 2 Variations in use of senses

It was quite rare for there to be no preference among the senses. The scores could show considerable difference between the way the senses were used, or just a minor degree of difference. The questionnaire was a self-reporting task and the insights gained from it would need to be explored by trying out the different strategies that depend on the different senses. It had the important purpose of making students consider how they thought, and it made them aware of other senses that they didn't use deliberately. The questionnaire gave some students permission to use their preferred sense and made them realise that they had been suppressing its use for many years.

TEMPLATES:

E6 - VISUAL, AURAL, KINAESTHETIC QUESTIONNAIRE

Amongst the dyslexic/ SpLD groups that used this questionnaire, there was no strong indication that any of the senses was more prevalent in their thinking preferences, or less prevalent.

It has been interesting to discuss using the senses with students and participants at workshops. I have come to realise that:

- the senses don't work with equal strength for everyone
- whether one sense dominates another can be a help or a hindrance
- it is useful to be aware of the interplay between the senses.

Examples: What people say in workshops

I start with: "I can't listen to Handel's *Fireworks* and watch a fireworks display. I can do one or the other but not both."

This statement often prompted the reply:
"Do you mean people CAN listen and see at the same time?"

Others:
"I need my glasses to hear you properly"
"I understand what you say better when I don't look at you."
"What I've done myself, I remember."
"I can't repeat what a lecturer has just said, but when I need it for an essay, I know I will remember it."

Interplay of the senses, see *PERCEPTION:* p 121

The language that people use may indicate preferred senses (O'Connor, 1987). Among many possible phrases are:

O'Connor (1987)

> I see what you mean.
> I hear you.
> You've put your finger on it.

O'Connor also gives details about the direction of eye movement during recall and construction of, say, an image that hasn't been seen before. He says the most usual pattern is:

- up and right to construct an image
- up and left to recall an image
- sideways and right to construct a sound
- sideways and left to recall a sound
- down and right to imagine a feeling or physical sensation
- down and left relates to internal dialogue.

O'Connor reports that

- the pattern is consistent for each individual
- it indicates which senses are being used
- you can learn which is your most reliable sense.

The point is to explore using the senses and not to squash one because no-one else seems to be using it. The best outcome is to find out what is useful to a particular individual in a particular situation.

3.1   Visual thinking

Visual thinking uses what we see as a major component of learning, understanding and communicating. Some people have a natural preference for visual thinking. It is not necessary to have internal vision for someone to use visual thinking. As with many other ways of thinking, we tend not to discuss whether we use internal vision. I was 30 years old before I even discovered that anybody had internal vision. Yet I use a great many visual techniques for understanding and memorising. I've met others who also have no internal vision.

There is a variety of ways of using visual techniques to help you process information.

Visual techniques

a wide variety of uses of colour	cartoons	pictures
mind maps tables flow charts	graphs	timelines
drawings diagrams charts	mandalas	
reading text		

Examples: Visual techniques used in the book

mind maps	line drawings	coloured boxes
coloured text	photos	art work
indenting text	bullet points and similar layout	

VISUALISATION: p 272
It is also included in *HOLISTIC THINKING:* p 224

mandala: a circle from the Buddhist tradition which contains reflections on information about a particular topic.

Visual distractions or slowness of words

There are various ways in which dyslexic/ SpLD people are distracted, or misled, by what they see.

Insight: Visual distractions

Nothing lines up

Visually pleasing

That's better

Figure 4. 3 Visually pleasing

- Going into a new place and needing to become familiar with it before paying attention to anything else.

- Making what you are looking at pleasing to you: see *FIGURE 4.3*.

- 'Reading' a computer layout and taking-action before the words can give you another meaning.

- 'The door is alarmed' prompted the question, "What's it alarmed about?" The alternative meaning dawned on my colleague as she went through the door and set off the alarm system for an educational building at a weekend.

In the first two, it is as if visual processing takes over working memory and there is no capacity to think about anything else, especially what is said to you; you then miss part of the situation you are in and have no internal resources to rectify your position. In the second two, the time taken to process words is too slow to prevent inappropriate action.

Non-dyslexic/ SpLD people could also be affected in the same ways, but their minds will be more practised at chunking anything they should pay attention to and making it available to working memory.

CHUNKING: p 154

3.2   Aural and verbal thinking

The aural sense receives sounds whether you pay attention to them or not – you are hearing. You are listening when you pay attention to what you are hearing. You may be hearing words, or music, or sounds of some other nature.

Aural processing and thinking involve anything related to using sounds as the basis of the processing and thinking. In general communication and education, aural thinking is absorbed into verbal thinking.

Language evolved from the sounds early humans made. It is now a major element in the way humans learn and communicate. Verbal thinking encompasses all the thinking processes that use words to communicate; verbal thinking includes both listening and speaking. Some people prefer to process ideas in verbal ways, that is to say, they have a verbal thinking preference.

Most of the time listening and speaking go together; however, there are some situations when they don't.

Example: Listening or speaking , but not both together

- When you are at a lecture or listening to somebody on the radio or the TV, you have no opportunity to engage in conversation with the speaker; in such situations you may be listening and not speaking.

- If you are concentrating very hard when you are speaking you may not hear what you say; for example, if you are trying to work out the words when you're reading out loud, you may not hear what you actually say; if you are focusing on your ideas while delivering a speech, again you may not hear what you actually say.

There are many options for using listening and speaking to help you process information:

Verbal techniques

Listening:

reader	lecturer	recording device
TV	radio	discussions
music	mnemonics	voices (in your head)

verbal rehearsal (repetition cycles of what you have heard)

EXAMPLES: MNEMONICS:
p 205

Ⓖ p 353:
rehearsal, verbal

Speaking:

> explaining to others   singing information
>
> telling anecdotes
>
> speaking or singing to a recording device or yourself

To explore different ways of listening:

- you can just listen

- you may find it helpful to shut your eyes

- if text is involved you can listen and follow the text

- you can try listening with visual aids

- try listening and taking notes, or doodling.

If you shut your eyes, you are stopping any interference from the eyes. If you use the text or visual aids, sight is helping listening. If you write notes or doodle, the kinaesthetic sense is helping.

Insights: Experiences of listening, speaking and singing

- Some people find that they need to be kinaesthetically engaged with the listening, therefore taking notes at the same time is a very important part of listening.

- Some people find that they get distracted by what they see and they need either to shut their eyes or to look away from the speaker. One student never used to look at her parents when they were giving her important information and she was told off many times, "Look at me while I speak to you". She had instinctively discovered that looking at people interfered with the quality of her listening but as a child she didn't know how to explain that to the adults around her.

- Some people find explaining their ideas to another person is very helpful. The other person doesn't have to understand the ideas, it is enough for them to listen to the dyslexic/SpLD person. For other people, the discussion with another person is a major part of understanding ideas.

- Some people find that what they have spoken or produced by voice makes a strong impact on their mind, either to help them understand something or to sort out their ideas or simply to memorise information.

- Some people use a recording system and then listen to themselves.

- Some people have found that singing instead of saying makes a difference. One person sang her school revision notes (out of boredom initially) and then found that singing them once through fixed them in her memory. When playing a new piece of music that has a complicated rhythm, I find I have to sing the beats rather than say them: when I am playing I can hear myself singing, I can't hear myself speaking.

- Some people find they need to read out loud in order to understand text; some read out loud to a recording device without trying to understand the first time round, and then find they understand the material when they play back the recording.

- For some people listening to lectures is better than reading, because the person speaking adds understanding to the words by the way they use their voice.

- Some people use different voices in their head to add sense to information. Some people repeat the main points over and over; or repeat a list of things that has to be remembered; both of these are verbal rehearsal.

- Some people play a particular piece of music as they are studying a given topic; they find remembering the music brings back the ideas and understanding of that topic.

Mnemonics are a system of using an easy to remember sound, phrase or sentence to hold some information that you are trying to remember.

Examples: Mnemonics

"HONC" is the four main chemicals in organic chemistry: Hydrogen, Oxygen, Nitrogen and Carbon.

"No plan like yours to study history wisely" has the houses of the kings of England: Norman, Plantagenet, Lancaster, York, Tudor, Stuart, Hanover, Windsor.

North East South West can be remembered by: "Never Eat Shredded Wheat" or "Naughty Elephants Squirt Water".

"See My Very Easy Method Just Set Up Nine Planets": for Sun Mercury Venus Earth Mars Jupiter Saturn Uranus Neptune Pluto.

Insight: Difficulties arising from words and sound

- Some people read 'situations' rather than listen to any words. In fast-developing situations, their reading of what is happening can be faster than their use of language. The reading could be kinaesthetic, visual, 'sixth sense' or emotional or 'other'. Those who read like this need to be aware that it happens, and work out ways to keep communication clear with other people in certain situations.

- Word retrieval is a frequent difficulty for dyslexic/ SpLD people. You know what is happening and what you need to say but the words to say it just don't come readily to your mind. Often, the nouns are missed out: "Put that over there and pass me the other". You need to be in tune with the speaker to interpret.

- Sometimes there are nouns; not the right ones but something quite close: "Pour out the milk" for "Pour out the water".

3.3 Kinaesthetic thinking

Ⓖ p 353:
kinaesthetic

Kinaesthetic thinking is done through the body in some way, using processing based on kinaesthetic information, including from:

> the kinaesthetic sense – touch, body movement and position
>
> the memories of physical experience
>
> the physical element of any topic or skill being learnt.

Kinaesthetic thinking can play an important part in the way we use our minds and our memories. In many forms of communication and education, kinaesthetic methods can be less used than visual and verbal ones; one of my colleagues (Todd[2], private communication) working in employment support says that the kinaesthetic thinkers often have more problems than visual or verbal thinkers.

MARGIN NOTE: proprioception: the reception of information by sensors which receive signals relating to position and movement. ('proprioception, n.' OED Online, 2021)

Insight: Physical energy used to sort out thinking

Todd wrote:
Some highly intelligent, kinaesthetic thinkers find their thought processes are sabotaged by sitting at a desk. They need to think by doing something quite physical and feel their thoughts through their bodies; it is as if their learning percolates by doing.

One client, who is extraordinarily gifted, goes on his bike when he wants to crystallise complex ideas and decide how he will convey them to others. He says his "gut gets it, understands it, but only by doing can I formulate and execute – I don't have a picture or the words, but I know it's there. It needs to grow, – and it can't; sitting at my desk or in my office just does my head in".

---

[2] Jo Todd has been Managing Director of Key 4 Learning for many years, supporting employees, running workshops and developing materials.

Therefore, this section will discuss in some detail what is involved in kinaesthetic thinking, and what can interfere with it.

We know where our body is and what is happening to it through the sensations of touch and through the information from all the muscles and joints in our body. The touch sensations are transitory; most of the time, you are not aware of the clothes on your body. We do know where our bodies are, therefore our joints are giving signals to our brain all the time; you can stop whatever you're doing and know whether you're standing or sitting or lying down and whether you've been in that position for a long or short while.

For kinaesthetic thinkers, the information about your body, whether by touch or from the joints in your body, is an important part of your memory system, and the kinaesthetic component will give you access to a significant number of your memories. These kinaesthetic memories can play an important part in taking-action and experience.

Ⓖ p 353: taking-action

Example: Kinaesthetic thinking in action

In "I need to move there in order to …" the thought of the place comes before the reason for which it is of interest (also discussed in *OTHER KINAESTHETIC EXPERIENCES*).

OTHER KINAESTHETIC EXPERIENCES: p 213

Using kinaesthetic memory, people learn easily through concrete (real) objects and practical experience rather than learning through abstract concepts. It is useful to observe those tasks for which the kinaesthetic sense is the most important element, those for which it is supporting another sense, and when it is really insignificant.

Ⓖ p 353: concrete

Kinaesthetic thinking can be used at all stages of processing information: understanding, memorising, recalling from memory, demonstrating to others. For some kinaesthetic thinkers, practice or doing is the only way they can understand and learn; they probably need to attach practical concepts to abstract ones; for them, some ideas won't make sense until they have been experienced in some way or until an experience is attached to the ideas, as in the example below, in LEARNING AND RECALLING THROUGH MOVEMENT, when handstands and cartwheels provide the kinaesthetic element.

4th bullet point in
LEARNING AND RECALLING
THROUGH MOVEMENT:
p 210

Some methods of learning through experience:
The box lists different ways of learning using kinaesthetic memory.

Kinaesthetic techniques

A   Touch and Movement, in which the physical reaction is part of the learning:
>   writing (notes or prose)
>   drawing, doodling, making things, including anything listed under seeing
>   walking, running, athletic movements
>   using hands or body for expression
>   adding a physical movement, possibly unrelated

B   Real situations, in which learning is through participation in events:
>   direct experience
>   laboratory experiments
>   experimenting in general living
>   field trips
>   hands-on work, doing for oneself

C   Concrete objects, learning through the physical presence of objects:
>   manipulating real objects
>   seeing real objects   demonstrations
>   working with original sources: artefacts, original documents

D   Make-believe, learning about a topic through activities:
>   role-play
>   simulations

If kinaesthetic thinking is an important thinking preference for you, devise ways that you can use it to enhance your learning:

- deliberately switch your mind to give attention to touch and movement

- give concrete associations or practical applications to abstract ideas

- change the language you use to evoke physical memory (O'Connor, 1987)

- attach physical tags: gym exercises, places on a walk

- feel music as a movement

- use any of the options in *KINAESTHETIC TECHNIQUES,* previous page, making sure the kinaesthetic component is fully recognised.

Ⓖ p 353: concrete

O'Connor (1987)

Learning and recalling through movement

Once you know that kinaesthetic thinking is a strong preference of yours, you can deliberately pay attention to what your body is doing and feeling. The awareness that you can learn from the *EXERCISE: KNOW YOUR OWN MIND* is useful in this process. You learn to pay attention to your physical self and observe how that is helping your learning, memory recall, or the way you carry out any task.

EXERCISE: KNOW YOUR OWN MIND:
p 57

Insight: Kinaesthetic techniques A

- You can walk out a shape or a problem on the floor and think about it while you're doing it. If you need to know what the shape of a diamond is, for instance, draw it on the floor and then walk round the shape.

- You may be able to sort out left and right by making an L-shape with thumb and finger of the left hand.

- When learning a new physical skill, e.g. touch-typing, think through the body and avoid using the eyes (for touch-typing, cover the keyboard and your hands so that you really can't use your eyes): this can help you to learn the movements with knowledge of the fingers and it can make the learning more effective.

MARGIN NOTE: 'Beating the Bounds' was a medieval custom to teach young lads where the parish boundaries were. It was originally highly kinaesthetic in that boys were beaten at certain points on a procession circling the boundary.

- One student used physical exercises to help her learning: she discovered that if she used handstands for one part of her subject, cartwheels for another part, head-over-heels for another, etc., she could recall the topics by thinking about the physical movement that had gone with the original learning.

- People who store the movement in their fingers sometimes need to trust their fingers and forget what their eyes, or their reasoning mind, are telling them. One dyslexic friend was on her third attempt to put her pin number into an ATM machine; she stopped thinking about the numbers and just let her fingers tap in their motion and she got the right number.

- Some people use their hands to express their thoughts while talking. The movement of their hands and arms is part of keeping their ideas clear in their head. For people who use their hands while talking, not doing so may mean the way they express their ideas will be very muddled.

Insight: Kinaesthetic techniques B

- You can keep your ideas together and clear in your mind if you think about a real experience and keep your attention focused on that experience while you are talking or while you are writing; you let the words follow your thoughts and you let go of trying to find the right word.

- Imagining a real situation even helps when listening to lectures. Many kinaesthetic students have found that they can make sense of theoretical lectures by thinking of relevant situations or people.

- Learning to use the computer, or other machinery and devices: some people can learn from a demonstration, others can only learn if they make the actions themselves.

MARGIN NOTE: kinaesthetic students often choose practical subjects, such as social work and healthcare or one of the sciences.

- Discussion with others can be important as part of the learning process:
  one nursing student knew he revised better through discussion with others and organised his year group to have joint revision sessions, to the benefit of all concerned.

Insight: Kinaesthetic techniques C

- In schools, many teaching aids are objects:
  in maths, Cuisinaire rods, Dienes squares;
  in geography, a globe, atlas or map

- One person learnt when to use capital letters by changing pens: all capitals were in a different colour and the pause to pick up the right pen gave time to think whether the letter should be a capital or not.

- Museums use kinaesthetic techniques to engage both adults and children in their exhibits.

- Ancient Roman narrators couldn't use notes or visual prompts; they hung different concepts on different places in a room. When we say "In the first place…, in the second…" we are harking back to their practice. Kinaesthetic thinkers can still use a similar technique by hanging ideas around a room or on objects on a familiar walk.

- Watching an experienced sailor managing the sails showed me what to do in a couple of minutes. Reading the same instructions in a book would not have made such a complete impact on my learning.

Insight: Kinaesthetic techniques D

- Role-play or semi-acting while talking can be used to assist learning and comprehension. The dramatic element in *EXAMPLE: MBPT MOTIVATION AND MEMORY RECALL* was role-play.

- Role-play and simulation are used to teach safety procedures such as life-saving.

- Many activities put on for families during holidays use role-play.

EXAMPLE: MBPT MOTIVATION AND MEMORY RECALL: p 49

Learning new movements

When you are learning a set of movements from another person it can be very useful to feel those movements on your own body as you watch them. Your relative position to the other person may be important; if you're both right-handed (or both left-handed) you probably need to face the same way; if one of you is right-handed and the other left-handed it may help to be opposite each other while you follow their movement.

To get a sequence of moves, it may be necessary to think about the timing of your thoughts and to choose when to give your body the instructions to move.

Insight: Folk dance calling

In English folk dancing, you learn to do certain manoeuvres, e.g. 'circle left' means a group of dancers join hands and all move in a circle going to the left. Most people don't learn complete dances, they rely on a caller to give the sequence as the dance progresses.

Skilled callers give the instruction for move B at the end of move A. If they wait until the beginning of move B, the dancers cannot process the information in time for the dance.

You may need to chunk a set of movements together and give that group of movements a name that makes sense to you and allows you to mentally record them easily.

CHUNKING: p 154

You may need to find a quiet corner on your own to sort out the way you are thinking through the new set of movements.

If music accompanies the new movements, observe whether it helps you or not, and how you listen to the music. You may be able to listen at the same time as watching; you may get confused by watching and just have to listen; you may find you get to a stage when you listen but don't need to watch any longer.

It may help to do the movements very slowly at first so that you can think your way carefully through them and know exactly what you are doing; later you will be able to speed them up with accuracy. Other movements lend themselves to the opposite approach: you just do them and they seem to sort themselves out.

3.3.1   Other kinaesthetic experiences

There are ways in which kinaesthetic processing can help or hinder learning or experience. Some are given below. The important approach is to recognise what is happening and to make objective observations, then use the beneficial experiences and avoid the unhelpful ones when you can.

Positive use of kinaesthetic processing:

- In any form of exercise, enjoyment and benefit can be increased by being aware of the balance and flow of energy through the body.

- Learning touch-typing without using the eyes: you can prevent your eyes from seeing the keyboard and your hands while you learn to touch-type. You are forced to think through your fingers, which is the desired end of the process. Cutting out the eyes and vision can lead to a much more reliable and stable kinaesthetic skill.

MARGIN NOTE:
the same approach can be used for children learning to write (Stacey, 2020)

Examples of place being important:

- Sometimes the place of a task or an object is the most immediate memory. One thinks "I need to move there to do ..." and the memory that you are moving to a particular place reminds you that there is something you have remembered you need to do; the place is a stronger memory than the memory of what you need to do.

- A similar, but different, experience is going from one place to another in response to a thought; finding you've forgotten the thought when you get to the second place and having to go back to the first place to remember what the thought was.

Possible problems:

- One important issue for several groups of people with dyslexia/ SpLD is the size of finger grip for any writing implement. If the grip is too small or too slippery then writing can be much more difficult than it need be.

- It is possible to lose track of where different parts of the body are and what they are doing while you are concentrating on a single part of an activity. For example, while playing music and concentrating on the score, it is possible to lose knowledge of where the hands are, and therefore not easily build the neural networks of movements of playing.

neural networks: see *BRAIN GROWTH:* p 92

- Do you know where different parts of your body are? Do you know your right side from your left? If not, consciously think about your body and where it is. One nine-year-old boy I was teaching could distinguish between his left and right side, once his mother allowed him to wear a single earring.

- When your head is twisted in relation to the rest of your body, certain tasks may be difficult. It may be difficult to follow a teacher during physical exercise when your head is not in line with your body because you have to turn your head to watch her.

- It may be difficult to read a screen, a notice-board, or a blackboard at an angle and retain that information when you bring your head back in line with your body. Many dyslexic/ SpLD people find using information difficult if they have to move their heads, for example looking straight ahead at a screen or board to read and then down at a desk to write.

Insight: Tying a bow tie using the internet

One man needed to use the internet to remember how to tie a bowtie. He couldn't work out the instructions because he could not mentally rotate what he saw and so understand what he had to do. We discussed standing beside the screen and turning his head, but that didn't work. Putting a mirror in front of the screen and standing behind the screen did work, after some effort, because then the demonstration was exactly in line with what he had to do.

- Some people feel split in space when signals are coming from too many different directions. For one class, I was working from a desk with information on both sides: on one side, a screen and on the other, a flip-chart. One particular student could not pay attention because the two visual aids were on either side of me as I spoke; I had to rearrange the furniture so that the two visual aids were on the same side. It is important to know how you are affected by details like this, so that you can either ask the teacher to rearrange things, or you can arrive early for a meeting in order to select the best possible position for yourself.

- It is important to think about which hand you use for different tasks. You may be right- or left-handed; some people are ambidextrous which means they can use either hand for a great many tasks; some people are mixed-handed which means there are certain tasks which they do with the right hand and other tasks which they do with the left hand. Even if you are right-handed for many things there may be some tasks for which the left hand is more suitable. For example, I've known some right-handed people say that they are left-moused.

In summary:

If you are a kinaesthetic thinker, deliberately using this sense to assist thinking is very satisfying; it gives you more control over the way your mind is learning. Even material with no apparent kinaesthetic component can be easier for you when given a kinaesthetic tag.

4 Rationale or framework

Ⓖ p 353: rationale, framework, schema

Some dyslexic/ SpLD students cannot retain information or remember what they have done, if they can't understand the reasons behind the information. If they are not retaining information in short-term or working memory they will not be able to process it further and build their own understanding of it, so they do not create their own schemas in a natural way. It is as if they need to know the rationale for information before or while they are being given it.

Insight: Rote learning not working

For people who learn by understanding, rote learning doesn't work.

Sometimes a framework is more suitable than rationale. The framework gives a structure that can be used for information, but it may not contain any reasons or underlying principles.

Example: Contrast between rationale and framework

Preparation for going out

Rationale (used in random order)	*Framework:* standard check-list
Weather constraints for clothes and objects to take	1: clothes
What's the bank balance? Can we spend without thought?	2: money

What are we doing and why? → what to take	3: list of things to take
How pressed for time are we? Who's going to run out of energy?	4: priorities

For the framework, an individual just wants a certain number of clear steps which remain uncluttered by any extra considerations; for the rationale, the reasons for the steps are the most memorable aspects and the steps on their own have no impact. A schema is a complete system of framework and rationale.

This need for rationale or framework is part of the input process of dealing with information. It needs to be taken into account in parallel with a person's preferences for the different senses. Changing the way the senses are used will make little difference for you if you are a person who needs an initial framework, or the rationale, to understand what is going on.

It may be that some minor detail is not linking properly to the rest of the information. You can then be unsettled by a piece of information that you don't know how to process properly, with the result that your thinking processes are hampered by interference.

It may be that the complete schema needs to be understood before any information can be retained and worked with.

Examples: Using rationale

- The *EXAMPLE: REVERTING BACK TO NOT MANAGING* relates a situation in which one student's need for a framework or rationale was not met and the lack nearly caused failure.

  EXAMPLE: REVERTING BACK TO NOT MANAGING: p 52

- In a sequence for using a computer program, the rationale behind the sequence is needed with indications of what could go wrong if you get out of sequence. Without knowing the rationale for some of the actions you don't remember what the actions are, even from one screen to another, and so you do the wrong thing. The results can range from mild irritation to a major crash.

- When using a mechanical engine and needing to know a sequence of actions to get it to operate correctly, it may be necessary to know what each stage of the sequence does and the implications for the engine in order to use the sequence correctly.

- When going to a meeting of some organisation, or protest group, you can create a rationale for yourself by thinking through the issues that are important to you, why they are important to you, what you want the outcome to be. You can add to the rationale by thinking about the concerns of other people. This way you have created a *MIND SET* that allows you to process the information in the meeting in a coherent way. You are then able to engage with the meeting much more effectively.

MIND SET: p 152

Example: Framework acquiring rationale
and becoming a schema

- When starting a new course, it is useful to turn the course syllabus into a framework. Then the whole course makes sense as you work through it, rather than it being a long experience of chaos and confusion. Using the framework as you work (including listening to lectures), you relate the course content to the framework, you see how it fits together (you add the rationale) and you develop the framework into a schema.

Examples: Using frameworks

- Setting up lighting for an amateur play, I couldn't remember which light was controlled by which slider, or what level of light the producer wanted. I made a chart which was pure framework, no rationale to it at all.

- Some people mentally hang items on their fingers. They remember how many fingers have been used at any time; that is enough for recall when necessary.

5 Holistic[3] vs. linear styles of thinking

Holistic thinking is happening when a large area of a topic is held in the mind and processed simultaneously. An example is when you look at a scene in front of you, you see that scene as a whole. This type of thinking doesn't involve words, but you are definitely thinking. When you have an art class concentrating on accurate representational still life, there is no chat in the room. The class is focused on the non-verbal, holistic thought processes and verbal processing is switched off.

Linear thinking involves analysing and breaking topics into their component parts. Linear thinking is thought to be localised to definite areas for specific tasks, whereas holistic thinking is diffused over larger areas.

---

[3] Holistic thinking is sometimes known as right-brain thinking and linear thinking as left-brain. It used to be thought that holistic thinking takes place on the right side of the brain and linear thinking on the left side of the brain. More recent research suggests that the two types of thinking can happen on either side of the brain. Edwards (2008) uses the terms R-mode and L-mode.

FIGURES 4.4 and *4.5* show the difference between holistic thinking (right hemisphere) and linear thinking (left hemisphere). There is an exercise in *THE NEW DRAWING ON THE RIGHT SIDE OF THE BRAIN* (Edwards, 2008) that allows you to see the difference between the silent, holistic way of thinking and the verbal, linear way.

Edwards (2008)

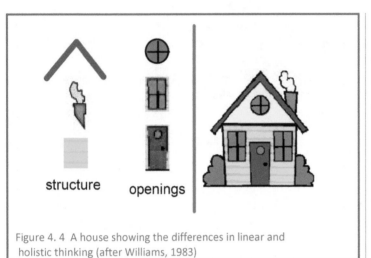

structure   openings

Figure 4. 4 A house showing the differences in linear and holistic thinking (after Williams, 1983)

'We possess a single brain, but it is made up of two hemispheres which process information in very different ways. [...]
[FIGURE 4.4] presents [the differences] in the form of an image [...] take a moment to study the image and consider the differences it suggests.' (Williams, 1983)

	Linear	Holistic	
5	numbers	patterns	○ ○ ○ ○ ○
HORSE	words	picture	🐎
	directions	map	
go to the roundabout *3rd exit* *2nd left* *3rd right and you're there*			

Figure 4. 5 Differences between the processing styles of linear and holistic thinking (after Williams, 1983)

You will sometimes see maps of the brain showing places in the two hemispheres where different types of thinking are thought to take place (Russell, 1979, p 54).

Russell (1979, p 54)

The types of thinking include:

mathematical, reason and logic
language, reading, writing
linear processing
analysis
recognition of faces, of patterns
rhythm

visual processing, images, depth
of field
creativity
parallel processing
synthesis

It can be very useful to recognise what type of thinking you are using and what type of thinking would be most useful for a particular task or situation. It is not so important to know where the thinking is happening in your brain.

A comparison of left-mode [linear] and right-mode [holistic] characteristics (Edwards 2008).

L-mode	ℛ-mode
Verbal: using words to name, describe, define.	Non-verbal: awareness of things, but minimal connection with words.
Analytic: figuring things out step-by-step and part-by-part.	Synthetic: putting things together to form wholes.
Symbolic: using a symbol to stand for something. For example, the drawn form 👁 stands for eye, the sign + stands for the process of addition.	Concrete: relating to things as they are, at the precise moment.
Abstract: taking out a small piece of information and using it to represent the whole thing.	Analogic: seeing likenesses between things, understanding metaphoric relationships.
Temporal: keeping track of time, sequencing one thing after another: doing first things first, second things second, etc.	Non-temporal: without a sense of time.
Rational: drawing conclusions based on reason and facts.	Non-rational: not requiring a basis of reason or facts; willingness to suspend judgement.

L-mode *cont.*	ℛ-mode *cont.*
Digital: using numbers as in counting.	Spatial: seeing where things are in relation to other things, and how parts go together to form a whole.
Logical: drawing conclusions based on logic: one thing following another in logical order – for example, a mathematical theorem or a well-stated argument.	Intuitive: making leaps of insight, often based on incomplete patterns, hunches, feelings, or visual images.
Linear: thinking in terms of linked ideas, one thought directly following another, often leading to a convergent conclusion.	Holistic: seeing whole things all at once; perceiving the overall patterns and structures, often leading to divergent conclusions.

'Going off at a tangent', wandering from the point

One important characteristic of holistic thinkers is the way they go off at a tangent when speaking or writing.

In *FIGURE 4.6*, re-drawn from *THE BRAIN BOOK* (Russell, 1979, Figure 18, p 54), the boxes represent an idea. The top set of boxes shows linear processing: one idea is processed by the mind and completed; it triggers the next idea which is processed and completed; that second idea then triggers the third, which is completed; it triggers the

Figure 4. 6 Distinction between linear and simultaneous processing[4]

fourth which then triggers the fifth and so on. This is the way linear processing happens. It is the type of thinking that you need for clarity when writing or speaking.

The lower part of the diagram shows spatial thinking: all the ideas relating to a particular subject, the circle, are held in the mind simultaneously; this is holistic processing. When you start by talking or writing about the idea in the middle box you are fully aware of the other ideas in your mind; you don't finish the idea of the middle box

---

[4] *FIGURE 4.6* is re-drawn from Russell (1979) and used with permission.

before you start writing or talking about the idea in the fourth box which connects very easily to the idea in the first box and so on. In this style of thinking, 'all the ideas relating to a particular subject' can be very wide-ranging indeed. Wandering from the point is easily done.

Insight: Managing holistic thinking

Many dyslexic/ SpLD people are told that they don't finish their sentences; that their speaking or writing is very confusing. It is very useful to explore whether simultaneous processing from holistic thinking is at the heart of the way you are thinking about ideas. Once you have decided that holistic thinking is being used, it is possible to translate the simultaneous thinking into linear thinking so that other people can follow your writing or speaking. The translation is part of good planning (Stacey, 2021).

Stacey (2021)

Insight: Speed of holistic thinking

Look at a scene in front of you. Imagine trying to put all the details you see into words. The words would take much longer than it takes you to see the scene. Dyslexic/ SpLD people who think primarily in holistic ways often find they are thinking and doing faster than they can speak to someone. There can be a breakdown in communication simply because the thoughts of a dyslexic/ SpLD person are going too fast.

5.1 Holistic thinking

Holistic thinking includes:

analogy, metaphor
visual-spatial thinking
visualisation
fantasy

Analogy, or metaphor, uses the ability to make connections between two unlike things by recognising that in some way they share a common trait or are examples of a common principle. For example, the key used in the mind map of this chapter: it is unlike thinking preferences, yet it represents the idea that thinking preferences have the power to unlock without specifying what is unlocked. Metaphors used in this way can be very powerful processes for understanding and working with ideas and thoughts.

Visual-spatial thinking can include any of the *VISUAL TECHNIQUES* listed above. It also includes paying attention to careful perception and being very aware of fine detail in the spatial-visual domain of *MULTIPLE INTELLIGENCES* theory.

VISUAL TECHNIQUES:
p 200

MULTIPLE INTELLIGENCES:
p 239

Visualisation includes thinking in pictures and letting those pictures tell a story rather than just being a static representation.

EXERCISES:
VISUALISATION OF A
HAPPY EVENT: p 273
and
BUILDING A GARDEN, A
HOUSE OR LANDSCAPE:
p 274

Some people use their internal vision and manipulate it in different ways. For example, there is a way of remembering and understanding information by mentally 'walking' through a room and posting ideas at different places in the room. When you want to access that information you mentally take yourself back through that room and recall all the understanding and ideas that you have put there.

You can manipulate the vision of your room by changing the time of day so that the lighting is different or by changing the way you've arranged the furniture. These changes are not necessarily done in the real world – they are done by changing your internal vision. As mentioned before, not everyone has internal vision, but you can still experiment with ideas like this and find them helpful.

Fantasy involves using make-believe. It can be done by imagining a situation as an observer, by seeing yourself in the fantasy, or by identifying yourself with a character in a fantasy.

- Observation fantasy: while learning about a medical procedure, a student nurse can create a fantasy of a patient being given that procedure; she could also create the fantasy of watching a trained professional doing the procedure as a demonstration.

- Experiencing fantasy: a boy going to play football could create a fantasy in which he sees himself in the changing room preparing to play, going onto the pitch and playing, and he checks what equipment he has in the fantasy; he can use this fantasy before he sets out to check that he has got everything necessary. As he is part of the fantasy as himself, he is experiencing the fantasy.

- Identification fantasy: a history student can make a scene from the past more real for herself by creating a fantasy from historical information and then identifying with one of the characters in the fantasy. Greater understanding of the scene can be gained through this identification.

5.2 Linear thinking

Linear thinking includes:

lists
analysis
use of language

- Lists are words or phrases or sentences that organise a group of ideas. Many people make shopping lists so that they remember to get what they want. Often lists are written vertically downwards, but they can be written in a single line. The contents at the beginning of each chapter are examples of lists; the mind maps are examples of spatial thinking that belongs to holistic thinking.

4 Thinking Preferences

- Analysis is often a linear process in which elements of a topic or a task are broken into component parts and those component parts are analysed in fine detail. In order to do any building project efficiently, you would probably look at the project and analyse the different stages of the project; you would analyse the materials needed; and you would plan the order in which you carried out the project. This analysis is most effective when carried out before you start the project. In many projects, the initial analysis forms the basis for analysing progress as the project is carried out.

EXAMPLE: FRAMEWORK ACQUIRING RATIONALE AND BECOMING A SCHEMA, p 218, is an example of analysis.

- Language has a linear structure. Words flow from one to another whether you're speaking, writing, listening or reading. The position of words within their sentences is a significant part of the meaning, as *FIGURES 4.7* and *4.8* show. Knowing how to recognise the components of language is a very useful skill for dyslexic/ SpLD people; it is beyond the scope of this book.

FURTHER READING:
Burchfield (1985)
Dukes (1992)
Gee (2004)
Truss (2005)

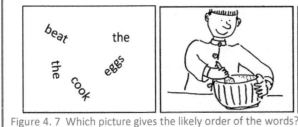

Figure 4. 7 Which picture gives the likely order of the words?

Experience gives the order of the words.

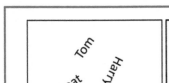

Figure 4. 8 Which picture gives the likely order of the words?

Without the order of the words, you don't know the result.

**Insight: An aside about language interpretation
by dyslexic/ SpLDs**

It was very interesting teaching a group of dyslexic/ SpLD people.
I knew that the way they interpreted what I said could be quite
different and you could hear the differences in how they spoke:

- some would almost repeat my words

- some would be describing a picture in their heads, as
  observers

- some would be relating the conversation to themselves

- some would come back with an analysis of the ideas

- some would go off at tangents prompted by what I had said.

It was quite possible that none of us would remember my exact
words, so any checking about the relationship between their
thinking and what I had actually said would not happen without
my visual teaching aids!

6   Myers-Briggs Personality Type (MBPT)

The Myers-Briggs system for personality types is one of many. It is the
one I have found most useful in helping dyslexic/ SpLD people to find
their best motivation in their studies and it has helped to explain
certain characteristics of the way they tackle the tasks in front of
them.

There have been many occasions when a student has been blocked in
their study because they have been working in a way that goes
against the grain of their personality. When you are using the
characteristics of your personality *CHUNKING* can enhance the amount
of information stored and manipulated in the episodic buffer. I think
this is more important for dyslexic/ SpLD people than for those
without a specific learning difficulty.

CHUNKING: p 154

Insight: Mental block from working with wrong type

I use an analogy to explain what I think is happening:
You want to send a message to someone in a different region; you
have your mobile phone and you can write a text message, but if
you are in a place where there is no signal from your mobile
provider, you can't send the text. The parallel is that you have
some ideas in your head, but you can't organise them in any way
to express them clearly, hence you can't communicate them to
somebody else.

A full discussion of the MBPT system is outside the scope of this book.
The ideas I have found most useful are discussed as follows:

FURTHER READING:
Briggs Myers (1989)
Lawrence (1993)
§6.1 p 228

§6.1   *MBPT MENTAL FUNCTIONS AND ATTITUDES* outlines the functions
and attitudes, giving a brief description of each in both a
theoretical and an experiential way

§6.2   *MOTIVATION*, outlines the motivations given by the mental
function that is developed first in a person's life.

§6.2 p 232

§6.3   *IMPLICATIONS FOR DYSLEXIA/ SPLD* explains some of the
impressions that caught my attention when first reading about
the Myers-Briggs Personality Types.

§6.3 p 233

§6.4   *EXAMPLES OF PROBLEMS SOLVED BY MYERS-BRIGGS PERSONALITY TYPES*
gives some of the stories of using Myers-Briggs insights to help
dyslexic/ SpLD students sort out problems they were
encountering.

§6.4 p 234

§6.5   *STEPS FOR USING MBPT INSIGHT TO HELP WITH DYSLEXIA/ SPLD* outlines
the way I use the insights from MBPT and has an exercise
based on the steps.

§6.5 p 238

6.1   MBPT mental functions and attitudes

The Myers-Briggs system is based on four mental functions and four
attitudes, shown in *FIGURE 4.9*. It is founded on work by Jung on his
observations, as a GP, of differences in the way patients
communicated with him.

The mental functions are: Sensing, iNtuiting, Thinking, and Feeling, represented by S, N, T and F respectively.

The attitudes are: Extroverted, Introverted, Perceiving and Judging[5] represented by E, I, P, J respectively.

The two mental functions, Sensing and iNtuiting, indicate how you prefer to gather information, i.e. to perceive.
The two mental functions, Thinking and Feeling, indicate how you prefer to make decisions, i.e. to judge.
The two attitudes Extroverted and Introverted indicate where you focus your attention.
The two attitudes Judging (deciding) and Perceiving indicate how you prefer to interact with the external world.

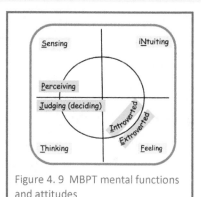

Figure 4. 9 MBPT mental functions and attitudes

Sensing - S
A person tends to collect factual information, to notice the details of here-and-now; usually practical and down-to-earth.

INtuiting - N
A person tends to collect information about ideas, meaning or future possibilities, to use 'sixth sense' to detect unspoken undercurrents.

Thinking - T
A person likes to make decisions based on logic, structure and efficiency.

Feeling - F
A person likes to make decisions based on personal relationships, making group dynamics work and on valuing individuals.

Extroverted - E
A person is energised by people, things and events in the external environment. Such a person is sociable and learns through interaction with others.

Introverted - I
A person is energised by the internal world of thoughts or personal understanding or personal needs. Such a person works well on his own or with just a few other people.

Perceiving - P
A person likes to observe the external world as it happens to be.

Judging (deciding) - J
A person likes to organise the external world and to make decisions on behalf of the external world.

---

[5] Judging in the context of Myers-Briggs Personality Type is the process of making decisions; it is not about judging success or failure, good or bad, etc. I think this distinction is so important that I have put 'deciding' in brackets whenever 'Judging' is mentioned.

The four mental functions can be used in either an extroverted or introverted direction. For example, you can use Sensing either to perceive the details of the external world or to be aware of how you yourself are.

Sensing vs. iNtuiting

We can perceive the world around us either by using the Sensing mental function or the iNtuiting one.

A sensing person will walk into a room and notice all the objects, the furniture and the people who are in the room; their thinking will stay in the room and be triggered by what they see, or hear, or register by any of their senses.

An intuiting person could walk into the same room, notice what is there and then start thinking about concepts and issues outside the room.

For example, a sensing person walking into a library will look at the books, the decor, the computer terminals and the people. They will look at the style of notices; they will look at the age range of the people there; they will watch what people are doing.

An intuiting person walking into the same library, seeing the same notices, furniture and people will then start thinking about the issues of the notices: any global policies that are displayed; any information about the economic situation or government policies; or the rules of the library. Their thinking is triggered by the same stimuli but very quickly they are thinking about concepts, models and issues that relate to what they see; their minds have left the room and have gone into abstract concepts.

Thinking vs. Feeling

Thinking and Feeling are the two ways in which we characteristically make judgements (decisions).

Thinking people will make their decisions based on logic, being efficient, using systems. They will speak the truth as they see it and not worry very much about the reactions of other people.

Feeling people will make their decisions based on considerations for people; they will want to make people, including themselves, feel

230

good about themselves; they will want to make group dynamics work. They have a tendency to speak in a way that deals with the emotional reactions of people; they will find it difficult to speak the truth if somebody else is going to be upset.

You can hear the difference between Thinking and Feeling judgements (decisions) when you listen to conversations at a staff meeting, around a dining room table, on the radio.

Perceiving vs. Judging (deciding)

Perceiving and Judging (deciding) indicate whether you prefer observing or deciding. Perceiving people prefer to observe and gather information; they will have Sensing or iNtuiting as their 'dominant' mental function (see 2nd paragraph below). Judging people want decisions made as soon as possible, if not sooner; Thinking or Feeling will be their 'dominant' mental function.

Extroverted vs. Introverted

The other dimension of attitudes is the extroverted-introverted polarity. An extroverted person wants to sort out their thinking in a dynamic way with the world around them, or with other people. An introverted person wants to sort out their own thinking and feeling by themselves before engaging in any dynamic way with the world around them.

You can see these two characteristics when you work in a group of people who are engaged in a task together. When they are given information or allowed to start on the task, some people immediately talk to their neighbours while others start working on their own. The same differences can be seen in children in a classroom situation. The topics talked about can be very much on task and the talking is necessary for those who do it.

Development of personality

The theory outlines a very distinctive way in which personalities develop. We can all use any of the functions or attitudes, but research shows that we have preferences for one or other of each pair S-N, T-F, E-I, and P-J. One implication of the preferences is to indicate the order in which the four mental functions, S, N, T and F, are developed from childhood to maturity.

The function developed between about the ages of 7-13 is called the 'dominant'; that developed between 13-18 is called the 'auxiliary'. The 'tertiary' function is developed between 18-35 and the 'inferior' one is developed between 35-50. The combination of preferences results in 16 different personality types. Your preferences indicate your characteristic mental habits which show strongest when dealing with unfamiliar situations, such as learning. *ACTIVITIES TO EXPLORE MBPT* are given in *APPENDIX 4*.

ACTIVITIES TO EXPLORE MBPT: p 346

6.2 Motivation

People have a characteristic approach[6] to learning, teaching and work arising from the mental function that is dominant. The approach can be a motivating drive, as indicated below.
NB: For each of the functions, how the person can become disengaged is also indicated.

S
respond to practical, functional tasks
"Can this teacher and subject show me something useful?"
"Will I learn skills I can master and put to good use?"
think best with their hands
get lost when steps are missed out

N
crave inspiration
find routines dull
want their imagination to be fired with intriguing ideas and plans
when bored they will seek out something to relieve the boredom

T
energised by logically organised material
thrive on things that can be analysed
resent material to be learnt, that fits no logical structure
resent and resist a teacher with non-logical organisation
when logical orderliness is absent, no way is open for them to use their best energies

---

[6] The characteristic approach is part of the innate interests that help interest-oriented readers, see p 10.

F
"Does this teacher care about me?"
"Can I give my heart to this subject?"
caring about the teacher carries them over boring tasks
caring about the teacher and subject brings out their best
when unable to care, lose their primary motivation and nothing is gained by
changing instructional procedures or physical conditions

A person will be highly motivated when their dominant mental function is fully engaged in the learning task (or any other activity). For a dyslexic/ SpLD when the dominant function is excluded from the learning task, that task becomes a near-impossible obstacle. Altering other details of the educational situation will not improve the learning ability.

6.3   Implications for dyslexia/ SpLD

- Dyslexic/ SpLD people have a range of different symptoms and problems; and for many problems you can find a person who excels at the skill required. However one common feature of dyslexic/ SpLD language problems is the Sensing/ iNtuiting divide. Dyslexic/ SpLD people can be struggling with the actual representation of language, the words, the letters, handwriting, word retrieval to such an extent that there is no mental capacity to appreciate the meaning of the words. So they are caught in the S mental function and N is nearly switched off. Or they can be so engaged with their own understanding that they don't see, or hear, that the words and letters do not match that meaning, i.e. they are caught in the N mental function.

- The S / N separation can have an impact on spelling and note-taking. In either situation, the dyslexic/ SpLD person can be struggling so much with the physical task of writing that there is no mental capacity to retain the meaning.

- The introverted part of thinking sometimes needs to be explored. It is possible that a spelling or an action is not as it should be, and you can work quite hard on trying to put it right; but success won't happen until an internal point of confusion has been identified and sorted out.

MARGIN NOTE: many of the exercises in the *DVD A TASTE OF DYSLEXIA* (Stacey, 2005) are based on the Sensing/ iNtuiting divide. They are designed to make it difficult for people to use the link between the physical reality of language and the meaning of it.

Story: The root of spelling errors

I could never spell 'development' and 'develop' until I realised there was confusion with 'envelope'; the letter pattern 'v-e-l-o-p' is common to all three words. It wasn't until I realised, aged 40+, that there was an overlap of letters with 'envelope' that I could stop putting an 'e' after the 'p' in 'development' and 'develop'.

- The teaching that has been found to be most appropriate for dyslexic/ SpLDs is multi-sensory and very systematic; this is the type of teaching that is suitable for Sensing people and Thinking people. It is the type of teaching that has been out of fashion for a while.

- Knowing your type can help with working-memory difficulties during communication. A dyslexic/ SpLD person can lose the thread of a conversation quite easily, especially when other people's point of view is quite different from their own. In preparation for an important conversation, you can think about the topic in the way that your least favourite mental function would think. You then are not so thrown by different aspects that other people bring to the conversation; this preparation can help you to keep your mind functioning when otherwise the problems of dyslexia/ SpLD would increase.

6.4 Examples of problems solved using Myers-Briggs Personality Types

Story: A feeling person trying to write a logical dissertation

One student was complaining about her dissertation. She couldn't feel comfortable with essay structure, with the discipline of literature reviews and methodology that are necessary for a dissertation.

Her dissertation research involved interviewing the pupils and staff at a particular school. The school was interesting because the pupils were part of the management system.

As my student talked you could hear her enthusiasm for the school's regime. It struck me that she was a Feeling person who was trying to write in a Thinking way.

We gave her the role of being an advocate for the school. She was writing her dissertation in order to present the ideas of the school to a wider public; she needed clarity so that her readership would appreciate the ideas of the school and be able to use them.

In this way the Thinking element was supporting her Feeling role. She was able to complete her dissertation.

Example: Practical people undertaking theoretical degrees

Many healthcare students are very practical people, with strong S qualities. The dyslexic/ SpLD ones often find it very difficult to realise how their practical experience fits the theoretical components of the degree, which will have strong N qualities.

One way to deal with this situation is to have a chronological list of their experiences on one side of a page and on the opposite side, a list of the elements of the degree. Then you have to draw linking lines to show which theoretical (N) elements each of the practical (S) experiences relates to, and it may be more than one.

The student then has to write her work using the elements of the degree for the structure and selecting parts of her experience when relevant.

Story: Report on a drugs trial

A practice nurse had done a drug trial for a Master's research project.

She found great difficulty in writing the dissertation. The way she spoke emphasised the practical skills (S) she had and her care (F) for her patients. Her way forward was to cut out pictures of people from magazines and to make a frieze to put in front of her while she was writing. The frieze reminded her of the people that she cared about and their need for the drug.

The frieze opened her ability to write; it tapped into her Feeling and Sensing mental functions, allowing her to cope with the N and T disciplines of her degree.

Example: Instructions 'written in stone'

One idea in *DEVELOPMENT OF DYSLEXIA AND OTHER SPLDS* (Stacey, 2020) is that the initial interpretation a dyslexic/ SpLD person makes of information becomes rigidly implanted in the memory.

Stacey (2020)

You can be mesmerised by the instructions you've been given; you can interpret these instructions in a particular way; it can be exceptionally difficult to help you to see that the instructions are open to a different interpretation which fits with module outcomes and is therefore probably right.

I have found it useful to discuss the Sensing/iNtuiting divide in order to help people appreciate different interpretations. It is sometimes necessary to help a student work out a series of questions to take back to the module leader in order to understand what the instructions really mean.

Example: Judging (deciding) people
wanting to get into action immediately

Some Judging (deciding) people want to make decisions immediately, get on with the task, start producing written work. They may have done no research work, nor investigated the task.

For a non-dyslexic/ SpLD person such a tendency might not be a difficulty (though as a perceiving person myself, I am sceptical).

For a dyslexic/ SpLD person, this tendency can produce difficulties. Often your mind unconsciously knows that you don't have the right information, and then your language becomes vulnerable and the dyslexic/ SpLD effects increase. It can be very difficult to go back and rewrite sections in the light of new information.

Once Judging (deciding) people recognise this characteristic, they can make decisions about the information to be gathered. In this way, Perceiving is organised by Judging.

Example: Perceiving people
reluctant to stop research, or exploring

Perceiving people have the opposite problem: they find it difficult to stop researching a topic, or exploring the environment around them, and get on with finalising the task or writing the essay.

Sometimes this can be resolved by seeing the end-product, or the conclusion of the essay, as the beginning of the next phase.

Having a pause in the gathering of information is seen as a way of really appreciating that information and assessing it so that future gathering of information builds in an exciting way on the present accumulation. In particular, the conclusion of an essay would be understood as 'indications of future work'.

Example: Extroverted or introverted learners

It is very useful to know whether you're an extroverted or introverted learner.

As an extroverted learner you immediately want to engage with other people, to make sure that you understand what's going on, to have revision sessions together, to work in groups together on projects.

For introverted learners, it is useful to recognise that you need to go to a quiet place to sort out your ideas; it's useful in a group to negotiate with others which bit you are going to do so that you can contribute effectively while working in an introverted way.

Neither is better than the other, it is more a question of recognising which works for you. Both can contribute to the learning experience of the groups you are in. Extroverted people can create a situation in which like-minded people have an enhanced learning experience. Introverted people quite often come back with questions that voice difficulties shared by many of the group, and the answers gained help everyone.

6.5   Steps for using MBPT insights to help with dyslexia/ SpLD

You need to have a basic understanding of MBPT principles and an acceptance that working out of type can make dyslexia/ SpLD worse.

I then:

- listen attentively to the flavour of the discussion, and the comments that a student is making
- propose and try possible adaptations to the way information is being communicated
- monitor and refine the adaptations until a satisfactory way forward is found.

Exercise: Using MBPT insights

Working on your own, you could:

- record yourself describing a task you can't do

- play back the recording, listening for characteristics that belong to different mental functions and attitudes

- reflect on changes you could make to be more in tune with what you know about yourself

- see how well the changes work for you, and modify them until you have an approach that works and feels right for you.

Remember:
We can all use the different mental function and attitudes; don't rule any of them out; just find out what you need to use to make the more difficult tasks and situations go better for you.

7 Multiple Intelligences (MI)

Multiple Intelligences is a theory researched and proposed by Howard Gardner in *Frames of Mind* (1983) and later extended by him in *Intelligence Reframed* (1999). Many subsequent resources have been developed based on his theory.

Gardner (1983, 1999)

Gardner was a member of a small research team that was asked to research into The Nature and Realisation of Human Potential. His 'goal was to come up with a view of human thought that was broader and more comprehensive than that which was then accepted in cognitive studies.' (Gardner, 1993, p xi)

Gardner (1993, p xi, his capitals)

4 Thinking Preferences

Originally, Gardner defined intelligence as:

> 'The ability to solve problems or create products that are valued within one or more cultural settings.' (Gardner, 1999, p 33)

Gardner (1999, p 33)

Later he recognised that one could be intelligent without using the intelligence, and he modified his definition of intelligence to:

> 'A biophysical potential to process information that can be activated in a cultural setting to solve problems or create projects that are of value in a culture.' (Gardner, 1999, p 33)

The theory was called 'Multiple Intelligences' to emphasise the separate nature of the different strands of human thinking and to put the new intelligences he was defining on an equal footing with those that are measured by IQ tests.

There is overlap between MI and the other thinking preferences discussed in this chapter, but I think this is also a useful framework for you to understand.

- It incorporates ways of thinking beyond the initial perception of information by the *SENSES* and *RATIONALE OR FRAMEWORKS*.

SENSES: p 197

RATIONALE OR FRAMEWORK: p 216

- I think the core operations, the end-product and the activities suitable to each intelligence are useful summaries.

- The naturalist intelligence I also find very important in working with dyslexic/ SpLD people. It contains ways of using intelligence that I don't think are contained in the other systems I have discussed in this chapter. It made sense of characteristics that I had noticed in some of my dyslexic/ SpLD students and which I couldn't fit into the other ways of discussing thinking preferences.

Originally the theory contained seven intelligences. Subsequently Gardner considered three other possible intelligences, but decided only one of them fully satisfied his criteria. Currently, the theory contains eight intelligences (Smith, 2002, 2008).

Smith (2002, 2008. Accessed 19 Feb 2021)

7.1 Summary of Multiple Intelligences

The theory establishes 8 independent intelligences. In order to be classified as one of the multiple intelligences, an intelligence has to satisfy eight criteria, which make up a body of knowledge that establishes the independence of the intelligence. For instance, the evidence from brain damage is that a) the intelligence can be impaired on its own without affecting any other form of intelligence and b), at the other extreme, it can be left intact while other intelligences are biologically harmed.

I've grouped the eight criteria in terms of four academic disciplinary roots:

biological:
1   potential of isolation by brain damage
2   an evolutionary history and evolutionary plausibility (i.e. an evolution with evidence)

logical analysis:
3   an identifiable core operation or set of operations
4   susceptible to encoding in a symbolic system (one can think using the core operations)

developmental psychology:
5   developmental history, along with a definable set of expert 'end-state' performances
6   the existence of 'idiots savants', prodigies and other exceptional people

traditional psychology:
7   support from experimental psychological tasks
8   support from psychometric findings

For the purposes of using the intelligences in work with dyslexic/ SpLD people, the most useful criteria are the core operations (number 3) and the end-state performances (number 5), including activities suitable to the different intelligences.

idiots savants have an 'area of stunning strength along with other ordinary abilities or even marked deficits' (Gardner, 1999, p 39)

7.2 Eight Intelligences

The Intelligences are listed in the table that follows. As a result of wondering how to present MI theory to students, I noticed some aspects that were shared by pairs of the intelligences, which gives rise to the column 'origin' in the table.

Origin	The Intelligences	
aural domain	Linguistics	Music
the world of objects	Logical - mathematical	Spatial - visual
physical environment	Body - kinaesthetic	Naturalist
personal domain	Intrapersonal	Interpersonal

Linguistics and Music have sound in common. Intrapersonal and Interpersonal are both thinking in the personal domain. It seemed to me that Body - kinaesthetic and Naturalist are focusing on the physical environment. Logical - mathematical has its origin in objects, although the advanced thinking is often very abstract; Spatial - visual is a root through which objects are discerned, although the intelligence can be used beyond initial vision, and objects can be discerned through other intelligences; 'the world of objects' reflects a common theme to do with objects between these two intelligences.

Gardner (1999) makes the point that no intelligence is better than any other and that they can all be used for benefit or harm.

Gardner (1999)

7.3 Core operations and end-state performance

Core operations (criterion 3) are the thinking processes that are characteristic of each intelligence as it is used; they develop (criterion 5) during the growth of a person through childhood to maturity. The end-state performance (criterion 5) represents how the intelligence can be used when it is fully developed. Exceptional people (criterion 6) are those whose mastery of an intelligence is highly developed.

The table that follows gives the core operations of the intelligences and the end-state performances. The roles and use of the fully developed intelligence are given under the name of each intelligence.

Table: MI Roles, Fully developed use, Core operations and End-state performance

Linguistics:

Roles, Fully developed use: poets, creative writers, general use

Core operations	End-state performance
sensitivity to:	rhetorical use of language – the ability
the meaning of words	to convince others
the order of words	mnemonic use of language
sounds, rhythms, inflection & metres of words	role in explanation
	meta-linguistics – to be used to explain
different functions of words, their potential to excite, convince, please, stimulate....	its own activities

Music:

Roles, Fully developed use: composers, players, listeners

Core operations	End-state performance
ability to discern:	compose
pitch (or melody)	play
rhythm	appreciate
timbre (quality of a tone)	
horizontal relationships (tunes and themes)	
vertical relationships (harmony & discord, etc.)	

Logical - mathematical:

Roles, Fully developed use: mathematicians, scientists, accountants

Core operations	End-state performance
sense of:	make patterns with ideas and concepts,
permanence of objects	solve problems systematically
class or set of objects	accounting, time-keeping
abstraction from objects	
number	
variables	
operations about variables, functions of variables	
functions of functions	

Table: MI Roles, Fully developed use, Core operations and End-state performance

Spatial - visual (a spatially intelligent person who is blind can use touch to explore space):

Roles, Fully developed use: communication via spatial analogies, e.g. Darwin's vision of a tree of life.

Core operations	End-state performance
perceive the spatial world accurately	orientation of space, recognition, working with graphs
transform and modify initial perception	problems can be solved through the
recreate aspects of one's spatial experience	manipulation of spatial dimensions, of spatial internal representations or
produce spatial and visual images	of graphical coding

Body - Kinaesthetic:

Roles, Fully developed use: mime artists, actors, sports men & women, craftsmen, musicians, surgeons

Core operations	End-state performance
ability to control the motion of one's body	non-verbal communication, undertake many kinds of practical work
capacity to handle objects skilfully	with competence, solving
capacity to express ideas and communicate through the body	practical problems, inventing, innovating in practical ways

Naturalist:

Roles, Fully developed use: people with extensive knowledge of the living world and ability to care for the world around

Core operations	End-state performance
recognition and classification of species of his/her environment (flora & fauna, & artificial ones), including:	leads to the coding/classification of flora, fauna and artificial bodies
value of species, dangerous ones, new or unfamiliar ones	
chart out relationships in the classifications	

Table: MI Roles, Fully developed use, Core operations and End-state performance

Intrapersonal:

Roles, Fully developed use: wise elders, writers who are skilled about inner feelings

Core operations	End-state performance
ability to:	integrated people
access one's own feelings	
affect discrimination among the feelings	
label them	
develop a code for them	
draw on them as a means of understanding and guiding one's behaviour	

Interpersonal:

Roles, Fully developed use: respected leaders; good team members; those with the skill to motivate and nurture others

Core operations	End-state performance
ability to notice and make distinctions among other individuals, in particular, their moods, temperaments, motivations and intentions	people good at working with groups and with others, in-tune with the culture or society behaviour of work and everyday life

Table: Activities suited to the intelligences

The following lists are not exhaustive, but they give the flavour of activities suitable to each intelligence.

Linguistic
  story-telling
  verbal debate
  writing plays, TV scripts, novels
  describing situations or places
  writing directions or instructions

Music
  using music, musical imagery
  teaching songs, musical
    instruments
  creating sound effects
  playing, conducting, composing
  using rhythm in many forms
  relaxation through sound

Logical - mathematical
  problem solving through logic
  using time-lines
  outlining
  analysis of differences and similarities
  following instructions or recipes

Spatial - visual
  graph work
  visualisation for memory or
    problem-solving
  mind-mapping spatially
  using diagrams and flow charts

Body - kinaesthetic
  role-play
  miming, drama
  acting, sports
  non-verbal communication
  field trips, crafts
  experiments

Naturalist
  collecting objects and data
  observing the environment
  classifying information
  labelling objects
  organising collections
  detailed record-keeping

Intrapersonal
  self-reflection activities
  time-line of own life
  journal-writing
  writing autobiography
  meditation

Interpersonal
  group learning
  face-to-face work and activities
  co-operative projects
  empathy-building initiatives
  giving and receiving feedback

7.4   The 8th Intelligence: Naturalist

The collection of thinking preferences that are discussed in this chapter grew as a result of listening to many dyslexic/ SpLD students describe how they approached various tasks, together with reading about thinking in general. The test of any categorisation was always "Can you build on this insight to make study or tackling tasks easier?"

For a long time there were some students whose thinking did not fit any of the patterns I'd uncovered, until I read *INTELLIGENCE REFRAMED* (Gardner, 1999) and discovered the naturalist intelligence. In my experience the most obvious characteristic is the way they see parallels so quickly and are instinctively sorting information into categories.

Gardner (1999)

Insight: Naturalist student

As I talked to one student, he kept interjecting "You mean it's like ...". I could be suggesting a strategy to try, or explaining part of his dyslexia. It was so obvious that his brain was immediately bringing up ideas or situations that had something in common with what I was saying.

For example:
MIND SET was "like breathing exercises before singing in a concert".
Searching for *KEY WORDS* was "like finding the melodies and
        counter-melodies in a piece of music".
The structure of a course was "like a building plan".
Not having the basics of a course was "like having no foundation
        for a building and everything falls down".

MIND SET: p 152

KEY WORDS: p 340

7.5 Multiple Intelligences in practice

RECORDINGS:

Exercise: Multiple Intelligences in practice

- Read the tables of the core operations, the end-state performances, the roles and the activities.

- Notice which items attract your attention. Which ones do you already use?

- Also notice which ones you rarely use.

- Is there a group in which you use many of the examples but which contains other processes that would be worth exploring?

- Assess which intelligences you think you use most of the time, and which ones you rarely use.

- Are you held back in any way by not using the intelligences you rarely use? Can you strengthen these through the use of the ones you mostly use?

- How well do your job, hobbies or study fit with the intelligences you use well or most frequently?

8 Sundry extras

This section contains a few ideas that are to do with thinking well, but which are not so clearly a preference. The first idea highlights the possibility of more options than are contained in this chapter.

'Other'

Very early on I learnt the value of a boxed area in my notes labelled 'other'. The ways people said or did things simply didn't fit what I already knew. As you work through the thinking preferences described in this chapter, remember that your ways of thinking might belong in 'other'; use the *TEMPLATE: E7 - THE BOX 'OTHER'* to collect your experiences.

TEMPLATE

The more you can *OBSERVE WITH AN OPEN MIND*, the more confident you will be in the recognitions of your strengths – and your weaknesses – and the better you will be able to achieve what you want to.

OBSERVE WITH AN OPEN MIND: p 45

Episodic memory

For some people, episodic memory is a key part of how they think. It can be used as a strength for linking information and understanding together. It can hamper progress when learning is supposed to take sections of a memory and put them together in a different way. EPISODIC MEMORY is discussed in some detail elsewhere in this book, but it does need to be considered when you explore your thinking preferences.

EPISODIC MEMORY:
p 118, 131

Other-referenced vs. self-referenced NLP

One interesting idea from NLP is more useful as a thinking preference component than as part of THINKING CLEARLY. If ideas and thoughts are perceived from someone else's position you are 'other-referenced'; if they are perceived from your own position you are 'self-referenced' (Hoag, www.nlpls.com accessed 15 Feb 2021, O'Connor and Seymour, 2002).

Self-referenced is not the same as being self-centred.

ⓖ p 353: NLP
NLP: p 279

Hoag, www.nlpls.com accessed 15 Feb 2021, O'Connor and Seymour (2002)

Examples: Other-referenced and self-referenced

Other-referenced thinking: how OTHERS express ideas
a scientist focuses on the work of others, how they carried out research, what
    problems they were trying to solve
a social worker is primarily thinking from the stand-point of the people he/she is
    helping.

Self-referenced thinking: what YOU think about something, how YOU evaluate it
a scientist is motivated by his own joy in working out problems, his own understanding
    of theories
a social worker enjoys the practical work of looking after others.
Neither of these examples is about the person concerned.

Self-centred thinking, for comparison
a self-centred attitude can be expressed in either a self-referenced or other-referenced
    way:
"I'll tell you what I want." (self-referenced)
"Do you know what you can do for me, you can ...." (other-referenced).

In helping dyslexic/ SpLD people to think well, it has sometimes been useful to work with the reference point of the person; it allows ideas to be held together more easily and therefore the person's thinking can be more effective. The other-referenced perspective is the usual stand-point of most information sources and text books, so other-referenced dyslexic/ SpLD people are well catered for. It is usually the self-referenced dyslexic/ SpLD people who need to see that they naturally have a different point of reference. They may need to appreciate the different approaches of other-referenced people.

Anecdotes

Anecdotes can be used to link ideas and information together in such a way that they are much more memorable. They can be used with any thinking preference and they help to chunk ideas and information together so that working memory can be used more efficiently.

anecdote: a narrative of an interesting or striking incident. ('anecdote, n 2a' OED Online, 2021)

CHUNKING: p 154

Insight: Anecdote to show chunking

One student was about to fail a module for the last allowable re-sit. All her other modules had been successful and she would fail her whole degree if she didn't pass this re-sit. Her tutor had told me that her exam scripts made no sense and yet she had worked in the sector for some time.

She explained what she knew to me and it was all in stories from her working life, not in the form of academic issues. We realised she had to use stories to chunk the issues together.

To outline the difference between marketing issues for local shops and those for supermarkets, her story was (with the module issues in brackets):

> A friend comes to stay. They go for a walk and pass the local shop (local shops are in residential areas). They go in.
>
> They see the shelves stacked with produce (stock issue). They see notices of this week's best offer (pricing issues).

They come round to the counter and see Mr. X packing a box for a customer (*local shop keepers can help local people). They also see Mr. X's choice hams (*local shops often have specialities).

(*marketing issues that change with time)

With stories like this, she was able to chunk the issues together and pass the module.

Telling this story when teaching about chunking makes the concept more understandable.

9 Thinking preferences in practice

For many dyslexic/ SpLD people, thinking preferences

- are a key component of managing the dyslexia/ SpLD effectively
- enhance many of the techniques described in TECHNIQUES TO ASSIST USING YOUR MIND
- give subliminal learning a better chance of operating
- can be maintained through the insights and practices of THINKING CLEARLY.

TECHNIQUES TO ASSIST USING YOUR MIND:
p 151

THINKING CLEARLY:
p 254

References

Edwards, Betty, 2008, *The New Drawing on the Right Side of the Brain*, HarperCollins, London

Gardner, Howard, 1983, *Frames of Mind,* Fontana Press, London

Gardner, Howard, 1993, *Multiple Intelligences: The Theory in Practice,* Basic Books, NY

Gardner, Howard, 1999, *Intelligence Reframed,* Basic Books, NY

Morton, John and Frith, Uta, 1995, *Causal Modelling: A Structural Approach to Developmental Psychopathology*, in *Developmental Psychopathology*, Ch 13, Vol 1, 357-390

O'Connor, Joseph, 1987, *Not Pulling Strings: A Book of Instrumental Teaching and Music Education,* Lambent Books, London

O'Connor, Joseph and Seymour, John, 2002, *Introducing NLP Neuro-Linguistic Programming,* Harper Element, London

Russell, Peter, 1979, *The Brain Book: Know Your Own Mind and How to Use It,* Routledge, London

Stacey, Ginny, 2005, *A Taste of Dyslexia DVD,* Oxfordshire Dyslexia Association, Oxford

Stacey, Ginny, 2020, *Development of Dyslexia and other SpLDs,* Routledge, London

Stacey, Ginny, 2021, *Gaining Knowledge and Skills with Dyslexia and other SpLDs,* Routledge, London

Williams, Linda Verlee, 1983, *Teaching for the Two-Sided Mind,* Simon & Schuster, NY

Further reading

The Senses

Bell, Nanci, 2007, *Visualizing and Verbalizing: For Language Comprehension and Thinking*, Gander Publishing, San Luis Obispo, CA

Vitalle, Barbara, 1982, *Unicorns Are Real*, Jalmar Press, CA

Language

Burchfield, Robert, 1985, *The English Language,* Oxford University Press, Oxford

Dykes, Barbara, 1992, *Grammar Made Easy: A Guide for Parents and Teachers,* Hale & Iremonger, Alexandria, New South Wales

Gee, Robyn, 2004, *The Usborne Guide to Better English*, Usborne, London

Truss, Lynne, 2005, *Eats Shoots and Leaves,* Profile Books, London

Myers-Briggs Personality Type

Briggs Myers, Isabel, 1989, *Gifts Differing,* Consulting Psychologists Press, Palo Alto, CA

Lawrence, Gordon, 1993, *People Types and Tiger Stripes,* Centre for Applications of Psychological Types, Gainsville, FL, 3rd ed.

<u>Website information</u>

OED Online, December 2020, Oxford University Press. Accessed 15 February 2021.
Series website: www.routledge.com/cw/stacey

Multiple Intelligences

Smith, Mark K., 2002, 2008, *Howard Gardner and multiple intelligences*, The encyclopedia of informal education, http://www.infed.org/mobi/howard-gardner-multiple-intelligences-and-education Accessed 15 February 2021

NLP

Hoag, John David, www.nlpls.com/articles/metaPrograms.php Accessed 15 February 2021

5 Thinking Clearly

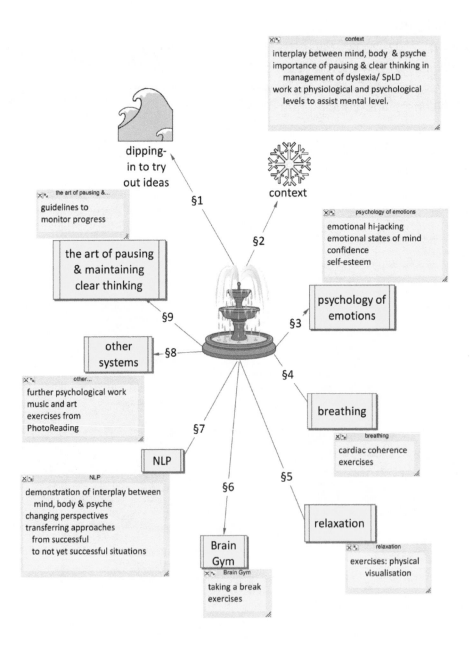

context
interplay between mind, body & psyche
importance of pausing & clear thinking in
management of dyslexia/ SpLD
work at physiological and psychological
levels to assist mental level.

dipping-
in to try
out ideas

§1

context

§2

psychology of emotions
emotional hi-jacking
emotional states of mind
confidence
self-esteem

the art of pausing &...
guidelines to
monitor progress

the art of pausing
& maintaining
clear thinking

psychology of
emotions

§3

§9

other
systems

§8

§4

other...
further psychological work
music and art
exercises from
PhotoReading

breathing

breathing
cardiac coherence
exercises

§7

NLP

§6

§5

NLP
demonstration of interplay between
mind, body & psyche
changing perspectives
transferring approaches
from successful
to not yet successful situations

Brain
Gym

relaxation

Brain Gym
taking a break
exercises

relaxation
exercises: physical
visualisation

Contents

Vital for dyslexic/ SpLDs, good practice for all

Most of this chapter could be useful to anyone. There is only one section that really applies only to dyslexic/ SpLD people. It is marked by the fountain chapter icon and the gold margin line. Even the paragraph *PAUSING AND THINKING CLEARLY AS PART OF DYSLEXIA/ SPLD MANAGEMENT* could apply to any situation that someone found difficult.

Section applying only to dyslexic/ SpLD people: p 260

Tip: Record the instructions

For any of the exercises in this chapter, you may find it helpful to record the instructions. Either you can put the steps in different sound files and move on at a pace that suits you. Or, you can leave pauses between instructions so that you don't have to stop what you are doing to change the sound file. The aim is to allow you to concentrate on the exercise without diverting attention to find the next instruction.

RECORDINGS are on the *WEBSITE*

Working with this chapter

Whether you dip-in or read straight through:
> Think about the times when you need:

1   to pause
2   to make choices about your frame of mind or the way you are thinking.

Be aware of what you already use. You may have well-established routines in one area of your life that you haven't thought of using in other situations. Notice new suggestions; they may help you in the future to pause well or to change your frame of mind.

Use *THE ART OF PAUSING AND MAINTAINING CLEAR THINKING* to help you monitor your approach to keeping your thinking clear.

THE ART OF PAUSING AND MAINTAINING CLEAR THINKING: p 297

Templates on the website

TEMPLATES

A1   *JOTTING DOWN AS YOU SCAN*
A4   *JOTTING DOWN AS YOU READ*
B1   *COLLECTING IDEAS THAT RELATE TO YOU*
B3   *COMPARE EXPECTATIONS AND REALITY*
B4   *ACTION, RESULTS, NEXT STEP*
B11   *MONITORING PROGRESS*

All the *TEMPLATES* suggested in this chapter are shown in the *LIST OF TEMPLATES*.

LIST OF TEMPLATES: p 362

Appendix 1 Resources

The general resources will help you to gather information together.

APPENDIX 1: p 300

Appendix 2 Individual, Personal Profile and Regime for Managing Dyslexia/ SpLD

As you gather insights about pausing, add them to your profile and regime.

APPENDIX 2: p 314

Appendix 3 Key Concepts

This appendix has a summary of the key ideas I cover when doing an audit of skills and knowledge with a dyslexic/ SpLD student. It shows which of the 4 books in the series covers each idea in full.

APPENDIX 3: p 328

1   Dipping-in to try out ideas

Read *CONTEXT, §2,* to see how this chapter helps you deal with difficult situations.

Read *A LITTLE PHYSIOLOGY AND PSYCHOLOGY OF EMOTIONS, §3,* to gain some understanding of the role of emotions in dyslexia/ SpLD management.

Read *BREATHING,§4,* to learn about, and practise, good breathing techniques; these are very important. Look at the diagrams about coherent breathing and full use of the mind.

§2: p 257

§3: p 260

§4: p 266

Skim through

RELAXATION, §5	*BRAIN GYM, §6*
NLP, §7	*OTHER SYSTEMS, §8*

§5: p 270
§6: p 275
§7: p 279
§8: p 294

2   Context

There are often times when you need to be able to think at your best. It may be that you are engaged with something that you want to go really well; it may be some unexpected situation that needs careful attention; it could be that something to do with your dyslexia/ SpLD is demanding attention; or something else is happening that would proceed better if you were thinking at your best, i.e. thinking clearly.

5 Thinking Clearly

Interplay between mind, body and psyche

Thinking clearly can involve body and psyche as well as mind; these can be thought of as three levels of being that make up a whole, single person. Thinking clearly can be helped by work at any of these three levels of being:

- The mind level involves choosing your thinking preferences and knowing the pitfalls of your dyslexia/ SpLD.

- The physical level can be worked on by physical relaxation, good breathing and physical movement.

- The psychological level involves changes in perspective, self-esteem and confidence.

There's an analogy that is helpful when considering the interplay between these different levels. You have a mind, a body and a psyche. Your mind is the thinking and feeling that results from activity in the networks of the brain. The body is the physical form that you have, including the physical components of the brain. For some people the psyche is the soul or spirit, for others it is the accumulated memories of your life. The precise way you understand these levels of being doesn't matter for the analogy below which is about the way that they interact with each other and how tension or relaxation pass from one level to another.

Figure 5. 1 Beach

The three levels, mind, body and psyche, can be seen as analogous to water, earth and air. Think of a beach, *FIGURE 5.1*. As the air moves over the water, it creates ripples, waves or even storms in the water. As the water moves over the sand on the beach, again ripples or sandbanks are created. The process works in both directions in that

psyche: there are several subtly different interpretations. The one used in this book is 'the collective mental or psychological characteristics of ... people' ('psyche, n. 1d', OED Online, 2021)

Ⓖ p 353: levels of being: the three levels of being (mind, body and psyche) are helpful concepts used in this chapter.

the shape of the earth affects how water and air move. The air, water and sand interact with each other; they each move differently because of the effects of the other two; but they don't change into each other because of the movements.

The analogy is that the state of tension or relaxation of mind, body or psyche is like the ripples or the waves, so that tension and relaxation are passed between the levels of being; thus thinking clearly can be assisted by work done at the physical and psychological levels. To experience the interaction between mind, body and psyche, try the *EXERCISE: SIT-STAND*.

EXERCISE: SIT-STAND: p 281

2.1 Pausing and thinking clearly as part of dyslexia/ SpLD management

In any situation when clear thinking would be beneficial, the steps in *REGIME FOR MANAGING DYSLEXIA/ SPLD* can be used to good effect. This chapter has suggestions for the second step: pausing.

There are various ways of pausing: learning to breathe well; being able to relax; taking breaks that assist your concentration. These ways mainly operate on the physical level of being; they are discussed in *BREATHING, RELAXATION* and *BRAIN GYM.*

MARGIN NOTE: The steps for *REGIME FOR MANAGING DYSLEXIA/ SPLD*, p 71, are:	
Step	*Further discussion*
SEE POTENTIAL DYSLEXIC/ SPLD PITFALLS, p 74	*OBSERVE WITH AN OPEN MIND*, p 45 *METHODS FOR OBSERVING*, p 55
PAUSE AND KEEP THINKING CLEARLY, p 76	*BREATHING*, p 266 *RELAXATION*, p 270 *BRAIN GYM*, p 275
KNOW HOW YOUR MIND WORKS, p 77	*THINKING PREFERENCES*, p 188
KNOW WHAT YOUR GOALS ARE, p 78	Stacey (2021)

Another element that may help in thinking clearly is being able to change your perspective of a task or topic; this is work at the psychic level of being. For example, you may be reluctant to write an essay or report, but if you can find a creative or positive outcome for the report, you may find you increase the ease with which you write it. Some possibilities for such changes are discussed in *NLP*.

NLP: p 279

5   Thinking Clearly

There are other processes that can help you think clearly, some of which are briefly discussed in OTHER SYSTEMS. The last section, THE ART OF PAUSING AND MAINTAINING CLEAR THINKING, has guidelines for monitoring your progress.

OTHER SYSTEMS:
p 294

THE ART OF PAUSING AND MAINTAINING CLEAR THINKING:
p 297

The chapter starts with a discussion of some physiological and psychological ideas about emotions, since understanding more about emotions can help with keeping a balanced perspective.

3   A little physiology and psychology of emotions

There are four aspects from the physiology and psychology of emotions that I think it is important for dyslexic/ SpLD people to be aware of.

1) Emotional hi-jacking: it can be very helpful to understand the way in which something can trigger an emotional memory and you can find yourself dealing with dyslexic/ SpLD issues that you thought were well under control.

2) Emotional states of mind and clear thinking: it can be helpful to realise that thinking in general is more difficult in highly charged emotional states of mind.

3) Confidence: a lack of confidence is often a side effect of dyslexia/ SpLD and makes matters worse; it is possible to deliberately alter how you think about your capabilities.

4) Self-esteem: often dyslexic/ SpLD people undervalue themselves, and taking steps to change the evaluation can result in significant changes in perspective and achievement.

 It can be helpful to appreciate the difference between self-esteem and confidence, and to practise some ways that help you to keep either frame of mind positive.

MARGIN NOTE:
Emotions are processed by the hedonic detector in Baddeley's model of working memory, see HEDONIC DETECTOR,
p 112 and p 128

The impact of stress is also important:
Stacey (2020)

3.1   Emotional hi-jacking

There are occasions when we all have a very fast, strong emotional reaction to information received by our senses. The reaction is faster than rational thought; Goleman (1996) called the reaction "emotional hi-jacking".

Goleman (1996)

FIGURE 5.2 shows neural pathways through the brain from signals received by the eyes, as an example. The solid route is signals going from the eyes to the thalamus, then to the visual cortex.

The signals are interpreted visually in the visual cortex and then sent to other parts of the brain for further processing. One of the other parts is the neocortex which rationally assesses the signals before they get to the amygdala. The amygdala is the emotional storehouse of the brain. Using this route, the brain has had time to find a considered response to the initial signal.

At the same time, a small signal from the information is passed straight from the thalamus to the amygdala for immediate emotional processing;

neocortex: the most recently evolved part of the brain (OED, 1993)

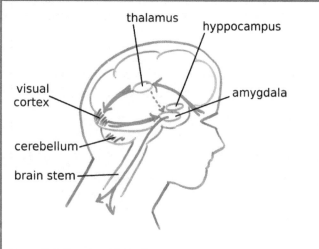

Figure 5. 2 Emotional hi-jacking.
The route of emotional hi-jacking is the dotted red line

this is a much quicker route, shown by the dotted red line in FIGURE 5.2. This route allows the amygdala to act as an emotional watchdog. If there is something that the amygdala recognises as dangerous, it will immediately send signals out to the brain and the rest of the body to prepare for immediate strong reaction to the incoming signals. This fast reaction is part of the flight or fight or fright system which can be vital for survival. As a result, people can move very fast, and before they've had time to think; the heart rate probably goes up, breathing will change, and the hormonal balance in the body will be affected.

The amygdala can also send out alarm signals if something in the present situation triggers the memory of some situation that happened in the past, often a highly emotional one but not always.

Story: Emotional hi-jacking

One person was 56 minutes late for a meeting with a friend for lunch. He thought he was 4 minutes early and was very pleased with himself. The friend's fury triggered memories of being so late as a child and he didn't function well for the rest of the afternoon.

The story in *Unpredictable Pitfall* when memories of exams suddenly hit a colleague is another example of emotional hi-jacking.

Another example: after 30 years, I found my smart early-maternity clothes; I instantly had the sensation of morning sickness.

Unpredictable Pitfall: p 74

The reaction isn't always as clear-cut as these two examples. Sometimes you get a sudden drop in confidence; you aren't sure why, but you know you are unable to do something that you would normally have no problem with.

When your experience of dyslexia/ SpLD includes various difficulties, anything in your present life has the potential to trigger the memory of a past difficulty and hence to generate a reaction by the amygdala, with all the accompanying physiological changes.

It is not difficult to see how the emotional hi-jacking can produce a moment of dyslexia/ SpLD; and because of the physiological reactions it can take some time for the whole brain and body to reset to normal processing.

Insight: Good and bad days

Dyslexia/ SpLD people talk about having 'good' or 'bad' days (Miles and Varma, 1995). Some know that once they have got into a 'bad day' frame of working, they might just as well leave the task in hand and do something totally different because anything they try to do for the current task will just make things worse until their brains and bodies have reset, as above in the first *Story: Emotional Hi-jacking*.

Miles and Varma (1995).

Story: Emotional Hi-jacking: p 261

3.2   Emotional states of mind and clear thinking

Baddeley (2007) discusses three divisions of psychology that were recognised in the early part of the twentieth century:

> cognitive psychology: the study of knowledge;
> oretic psychology: the study of emotion;
> conative psychology: the study of will.

He suggests that oretic and conative psychology have not been studied as much as the cognitive branch because it is difficult to do laboratory experiments to measure their effects.

He discusses some experiments that were carried out into the clarity of thinking under extreme emotional states and the results that showed poorer ability on cognitive tasks when high states of emotion were induced in participants.

In *Dyslexia and Stress*, Miles and Varma (1995, p vii) point out that there is plenty of evidence from case studies to show that 'dyslexics experience more than their fair share of stress'. The book covers different situations in which dyslexia causes extra stress, and includes personal contributions from several dyslexic adults.

The work of Miles and Varma considered in the light of that of Baddeley (2007) supports the idea that stress makes the effects of dyslexia worse and that knowing how to deal with stress is an important part of managing dyslexia effectively.

Baddeley (2007)

Miles and Varma (1995, p vii)

Baddeley (2007)

Story: Decision to think clearly

The moment I discovered my bank debit card was missing, my heart rate shot up and my breathing became rapid. I thought about the preceding day and decided where it was most likely to be. I needed to phone the place, and to phone the bank and check what to do. I had to get my heart rate down and my breathing back to normal, otherwise I would not have put the right numbers into the phone, nor would I have spoken coherently to anyone nor listened properly.

Exercise: Stress

Stress is rather a broad term and it could be useful to be more precise about it.

Make a list of emotions that can produce it: frustration, dis-satisfaction, worry...

Think of several situations that you find stressful: Have you included all the emotions that produce the stress?

Precise naming of an emotion can be the beginning of doing something to reduce its difficult effects, especially any damaging effects on thinking.

RECORDINGS:

3.3   Confidence

Confidence is a state of feeling certain about your ability to do something. Often the things that dyslexic/ SpLD people are good at are not valued by the present culture, which results in dyslexic/ SpLD people lacking confidence.

confidence: assurance arising from reliance on oneself
(OED, 1993)

Insight: Use your individuality

Many have said that they have stopped using a technique that worked for them because no-one else seemed to be using it. So they have thrown away a skill that could have given them confidence.

They need to give themselves permission to enjoy and value what they are good at, and to allow their confidence to increase.

Several of the exercises in *NEURO-LINGUISTIC PROGRAMMING (NLP)* are about changing your psychological state so that you can operate with more confidence.

NEURO-LINGUISTIC PROGRAMMING (NLP):
p 297

3.4 Self-esteem

Self-esteem is about valuing yourself, knowing that you have an intrinsic worth which is independent of what you can or cannot do; it is not the same state of mind as self-confidence.

For example, take laying the table.
With confidence in your ability to lay the table, you might say
> "I can lay the table"
with low self-esteem, you might say
> "All I can do is lay the table"
with high self-esteem, you might say
> "It's great; I can lay the table".

The two states of mind aren't necessarily linked, either. A very competent person can still have low self-esteem. Someone with high self-esteem can still rate their skills at a particular job as not being very good, even when to other people the skill level would seem to be high.

It is worth recognising the impact of stress on dyslexia/ SpLD and the resulting effect on self-esteem.

self-esteem: esteem: value, worth, favourable opinion; hence self-esteem is valuing oneself (OED, 1993).

Story: Finding the root of stress

A student had broken up with a long-term friend; the knock-on effect on study was serious. His language became vulnerable and more dyslexic than usual. Therefore, study could not help to restore equilibrium after the break-up. The student was in a situation where nothing would work well to re-establish confidence and self-esteem and nothing in life had any meaning. It was important to realise that the friendship break-up was at the root of the problem, that it was increasing the dyslexic effects and making study hard but that enjoyment of the subject was still there.

By contrast, someone with secure language ability would be able to use study as a way to 'get over' the friendship problems.

5 Thinking Clearly

Working with Dilts' levels allows you to observe your level of self-esteem in particular situations and to see whether a shift in perspective will improve it.

NEUROLOGICAL LEVELS – DILTS' LEVELS: p 290

4 Breathing

Many years ago I heard a doctor giving a talk about good breathing. One of the things he mentioned was the toggle switch (on/off) between deep breathing and panic. In other words, you cannot panic at the same time as breathing deeply. On many occasions I have tested this, as in the previous bank card story, *DECISION TO THINK CLEARLY*. Initially, I found that, providing I was in charge of my breathing ahead of a difficult situation, maintaining deep breathing through the difficulty made an enormous difference. While it is still better to take control of breathing well in advance, I can now improve my equilibrium when I start to breathe well in the middle of a difficult situation.

STORY: DECISION TO THINK CLEARLY: p 263

4.1 Cardiac coherence

Watkins (2014)

Research work has been done into 'cardiac coherence', and the capacity to think clearly (Watkins, 2014). Cardiac coherence occurs when the heart and breathing systems beat in a smooth, coherent rhythm, bottom diagram in *FIGURE 5.3*[1]. The rhythm can be measured with a probe clipped to the ear lobe. You can be given a task to do and the coherence of your heart and breathing systems is monitored through the task. If it's a task that you find difficult, for example speaking to an unknown, possibly critical audience, then your heart and breathing can go into chaotic rhythm with many jagged peaks, top diagram in *FIGURE 5.3*.

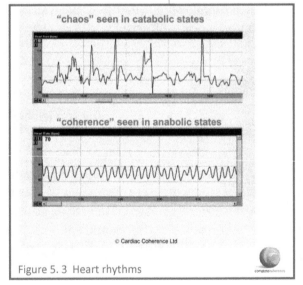

Figure 5. 3 Heart rhythms

---

[1] *FIGURES 5.3* and *5.4* are used with permission from Dr Alan Watkins. They are former versions of diagrams in Watkins (2014).

According to the researchers, when they also monitor brain activity with electrodes placed on the surface of the head, they find very little mental activity in the frontal lobes of the brain when the heart and breathing systems are showing chaotic rhythms, right hand diagram in *FIGURE 5.4*. In contrast, there is mental activity in the frontal lobes when the heart and breathing systems have coherent rhythms, left hand diagram in *FIGURE 5.4*. Their punch line is that you are performing a self-lobotomy (an operation which cuts off part of your brain) when you allow your breathing and your heart systems to beat chaotically, rather than coherently.

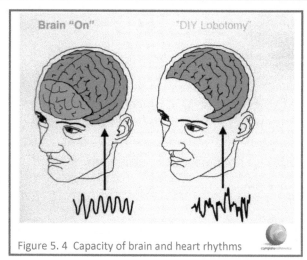

Figure 5. 4 Capacity of brain and heart rhythms

Under the chaotic conditions, dyslexia/ SpLD gets worse.

4.2 Good breathing

Tip: Good breathing

There are many activities which allow you to learn good breathing: singing, swimming, many forms of sport, martial arts, yoga, playing certain musical instruments, and acting, to name but a few. When students have learnt any breathing techniques, I recommend they use those techniques to assist study situations.

If you have never learnt to breathe deeply and be in control of your breathing, you can try the exercises given here. You need to be aware of where your breathing is taking place, and if you find that your chest is moving a lot, don't persist. Shallow breathing in the upper chest can have bad side-effects. Similarly, if you feel uncomfortable in any way doing the following breathing exercises, stop them. Find some other way that suits you better to be in control of what is happening to you, or consult a teacher who is professionally trained to teach breathing.

Tip: CAUTION

If you feel dizzy, get up and walk about, or hold your breath for a count of 10. Dizziness from poor breathing is caused by too much oxygen, and you need to use it up by walking about or to retain CO_2 by holding your breath a while.

Exercise: Breathing 1

Lie on the floor, with a book or cushion under your head; place a book on your chest; have your hands comfortably beside you on the floor.

Breathe deeply from your stomach; watch the book on your chest and try to breathe so that the book is not moving.

Notice how you are moving the muscles of your stomach.

When you feel confident about this way of breathing, try to do it when sitting or standing.

Experiment with imagining the breath flowing downwards as you breathe out, or with it flowing horizontally from the level of your heart. Personally, I find I go to sleep easily when the breath flows downwards and I stay alert when I imagine it flowing out horizontally.

First, see the *TIP: CAUTION:* above

RECORDINGS:

Tip: Suggestions for recording for *EXERCISE: BREATHING 2*

For the first cycle: start from 'Sit comfortably..' and read until '.. let it relax further.'
Don't read too fast.

For the second and third cycles: only say the parts of the body, but leave time to feel the sensations in each part and to relax it.

Leave the recorder to run for the duration of another 5 cycles, then say: 'When you are ready, come back to this room and open your eyes.'

If you carry a lot of tension in your body, you may find it more useful to work through the relaxation *Exercise: Physical 1* before attempting the following exercise.

Exercise: Physical 1: p 268

First, see the *Tip: Caution:* p 268

Recordings:

Exercise: Breathing 2

During the exercise, as you breathe in you feel the sensations in different parts of your body, as you breathe out you let go of the sensations. You can imagine the out-breath flowing easily into that part of the body.

Sit comfortably and close your eyes. Breathe naturally while doing the exercise.
As you breathe in,
feel the sensations in your:

face	and let go
neck and shoulders	and let go
arms and chest	and let go
stomach	and let go
buttocks and legs	and let go
whole body	and let it relax further.

Repeat the cycle several times.

First, see the *Tip:*
CAUTION: p 268

RECORDINGS:

Exercise: Breathing 3

This exercise only involves 2 breaths to complete the cycle. When I'm trying to go to sleep, I find I haven't got enough concentration to do exercise 2, but I can work with this one.

Lie flat on your back, on a bed or on the floor. Have your arms beside your body with palms down. On the floor you may need a book under your head in order to keep your neck long and straight.
Be comfortable.

Take 4 deep breaths.

On the next in-breath, tighten the muscles of your feet, legs and buttocks.

On the out-breath, press your hands into the bed or floor, and tighten your stomach muscles.

On the in-breath, tighten the muscles of your chest, upper arms, neck and face.

Pause for a moment.

On the out-breath, slowly let go of all the tension in your whole body and relax completely.

Repeat the cycle once or twice more. (By that time I've gone to sleep.)

5 Relaxation

Relaxation can be mental or physical or belonging to the psyche, as explained in *CONTEXT,* and the three levels of being will influence each other.

CONTEXT: p 257

It can be surprising to notice how much physical tension we generate in our bodies when thinking. How useful the tension is differs from one person to another. Some people find they thrive on some physical tension and energy to get them going; for others the tension is wasted energy. Experimenting and noticing the differences that happen for you is the only way to decide your optimum level of tension or relaxation; use the guidelines in *THE ART OF PAUSING AND MAINTAINING CLEAR THINKING* to compare different levels of tension and relaxation.

THE ART OF PAUSING AND MAINTAINING CLEAR THINKING: p 297

The exercises and suggestions in this section include relaxation using the body and visualisation. The best state of relaxation is that which allows you to be comfortably alert without excess mental or physical or psychic stress.

Story: Pain indicating a need to relax

Working on these books involved long hours at a computer. I eventually complained of neck ache. My Pilates teacher said a lot of neck pain is from tense shoulders and gave me some tips about relaxing.

I took to sitting in an armchair every hour. The chair-arms took the weight of my arms and allowed me to relax my shoulders. I found I had much more mental energy for working on the book.

5.1 Physical exercise

Many people have a routine of physical exercise: they run, walk, swim, go to the gym; they play team sports. Their general sense of well-being improves through the exercise and it affects other parts of their lives. It is often very important to keep to these routines.

It is also important to be able to relax physically, which is the purpose of the following two exercises.

Exercise: Physical relaxation 1

RECORDINGS:

Sit comfortably and close your eyes.
Tighten

| the muscles | of your face | and let go |
| " | of your neck and shoulders | " |

tighten

the muscles   of your arms, clench your hands   and let go

    "   of your chest   "

    "   of your stomach   "

    "   of your buttocks and legs   "

Tighten your whole body and let go.
Repeat this cycle several times.

Exercise: Physical relaxation 2

When you can relax fairly quickly, you can use the following cycle.
Sit comfortably and close your eyes.
Feel

the sensations   in your face   and relax.

    "   in your neck and shoulders   "

    "   in your arms, and your hands   "

    "   in your chest   "

    "   in your stomach   "

    "   in your buttocks and legs   "

Feel the sensations in your whole body and let it relax further.
Repeat this cycle several times.

 RECORDINGS: COMPANION @ WEBSITE

5.2 Visualisation

It is possible to relax through using a positive visualisation. You don't
have to use internal vision; it is possible to use other senses or other
ways of processing thoughts to engage with visualisation. In the
exercise below, only one instruction suggests using sight. If you are
following a different exercise and it seems to be mostly in terms of
sight, decide what the purpose of the instruction is and follow it in
your own best way.

RECORDINGS:

Exercise: Visualisation of a happy event

Sit comfortably; while reflecting on each suggestion have your eyes closed. Be as relaxed as possible; maybe use either of the exercises above or a breathing exercise, or something similar, before starting.

> Think of various happy or good events, any time in your life......
>
> Choose one of them to reflect on at some length.
>
> How old are you at the time of the event?
>
> Where does the event take place?
> Picture it or remember it as clearly as possible.
>
> What time of day is it? What's the weather like?
>
> Who is with you or are you alone?
>
> Why are you happy? Do you feel anything else with your happiness?
>
> How did you respond to the happiness? Can you treasure it now?
>
> Remember the good feelings ... keep them with you now, if you can.
>
> Look at the place and the people one last time and let them go back into memory.
>
> Come back to the present, the room where you are, the people around you (if any).

MARGIN NOTE: This exercise can be modified to relive being in a beautiful place.

You simply need to replace some words: 'beautiful places' for 'happy or good events' 'time you were in the place' for 'time of the event' 'What is happening in the place?' for 'Where does the event take place?'

Many other adaptations are possible.

When you relive a good experience in this way, it is possible to regain the good state of mind and being that you had, and then take those forward into what you are doing now.

RECORDINGS:

Exercise: Building a garden, a house or landscape

This exercise is a way of taking stock of good qualities as well as relaxing.

Sit comfortably. While reflecting on each suggestion, have your eyes closed. Be as relaxed as possible; maybe use either of the exercises above or a breathing one, or something similar.

You are going to create a garden for people you know and like, a garden you can enjoy with them.

What sort of garden do you want to create? Large, small, one area or many? ..... Where in the country or world is it?

Start with a place in your garden ... what are you going to put there? Which of your friends is this part for? What will you do there?

Move to another place ... what are you going to put here, who will come here and what will you do together?

Settle in either place and enjoy it. Enjoy anticipating being here with the friends you have created it for. What does the place mean for you? People arrive to be with you in the garden ... who are they? What do you all do? Watch for a while. How do you feel about creating a place for others?

Leave your friends and the place. Come back to the present, the room you are in and anyone around. When you are ready open your eyes.

MARGIN NOTE: Change the wording to suit building a house or a landscape.

Once you become familiar with this style of visualisation, there are many other ways you can use it.

6 Brain Gym

Brain Gym is a set of physical movements devised by Paul Dennison (Dennison and Dennison, 1986). The idea behind the movements is that the physical exercises improve many different tasks, especially learning ones. There is controversy about Brain Gym and not everyone feels any benefit, but it is one of those systems that I have come across and used without spending lots of money. When I introduced students to some of the exercises, they told me how they benefited and that in turn encourages me to pass the exercises on to others. My approach is: try these, some people have liked them … use the exercises you like.

Dennison and Dennison (1986)

The idea of using movement to assist thinking makes sense to me because:

- I'm a kinaesthetic thinker and, before I heard about Brain Gym, I already knew that movement is an important part of working with my memory, both in retaining memories and accessing them

- I am left-moused, but otherwise right-handed: I cannot access the spatial thinking needed to control a mouse with my right hand, with my left hand it's easy

- I often don't think in words and I struggle to translate ideas into language, so the two sides of my mind need to be connected; moving my hands as I talk allows my ideas and speech to remain coherent

- a problem that others have is being able to co-ordinate the two sides of their body and of the environment: it's as if crossing the plane (the mid-line) running down the middle of the body produces a discontinuity in spatial awareness (Springer and Deutsch, 1989).

Springer and Deutsch (1989)

Brain Gym is very good for short breaks. Many dyslexics tell me that taking a break can be a disaster because they forget they are taking a short break and it turns into a very long one, often with serious consequences, like missing a deadline. Brain Gym exercises only take a few minutes; you don't need to leave the place where you are; they are fun to do; so they make excellent short break activities.

Story: Brain Gym would have been a better break

One student took a break from a boring task, running a bath, and decided to have some breakfast. She discovered there was no milk and went out to get some. On the bus to the shops, she remembered the bath tap running. It cost £500 to sort out the damage to the electrics.

The full set of exercises is found in *Brain Gym* by Paul and Gail Dennison (1986). I've set out below the ones I particularly like to pass on, with comments by me and others.

Dennison and
Dennison (1986)

Exercise: Double doodle, *FIGURE 5.5*

You need
- two things to draw with, one in each hand: pen, crayon, pencil
- something to draw on: A3 paper is good, a whiteboard is great, A4 paper is OK

Draw using both hands together. Let your drawing be random movements; the hands should mirror each other (though sometimes people can't do that, and the hands move together rather than in mirror directions).

Don't talk as you draw.

Figure 5. 5 Double doodle

I find it clears my mind.

A student comment: he found he could write more fluently after doing double doodle, so he did it every time he sat down at the computer.

Most students feel very positive and calm after trying double doodle.

Exercises: Lazy 8s

RECORDINGS:

In these exercises you are drawing the figure 8 on its side, as if lying down ∞, hence the name. You start the movement upwards from the middle. I do one of them when stuck with thinking. The following are different ways of drawing Lazy 8s:

> Put your hands together at arm's length in front of you; draw ∞ out in front of you, sweeping from one side of your body to the other. Complete the figure several times.

> Move your eyes in ∞, covering the full range of possible movement, again several times.

> Put your cheek on your shoulder as you stretch one arm out in front of you, to the finger tips; bend your knees and move your whole torso as your finger draws ∞ in the air several times; repeat with the other arm.

Version 2 can be done invisibly, so it's the one I use mid-conversation or in a lecture when I'm finding it really hard to follow what's being said.

Exercise: PACE

RECORDINGS:

PACE contains three exercises and a recommendation to drink enough water. I use these exercises when stuck with writing. They take 3 minutes; I just expect them to be an excuse to move, but 20 minutes back at work after using them, I find I'm thinking: "It's worked again!" The log-jam of my thinking has freed up, and I'm usually wondering why I didn't do them before I got so frustrated.

Exercise: PACE 1: Cross crawl

Stand up; you lift each knee in turn in front of you, as high as you can comfortably, and you touch it with the hand on the other side. You do it 30 times, i.e. 15 times with each knee.

You can do it sitting, just by touching each knee with the other hand as you sit; swing your body a little from side to side as you do it.

RECORDINGS:

Exercise: PACE 2: Brain buttons

Hunch your shoulders forwards and, with finger and thumb of one hand, find the hollows just below each collar bone; you find there are a couple of places that feel more sensitive as you apply pressure. Relax your shoulders and apply pressure with finger and thumb. Rest the other hand over your navel, in your lap. Count to 30.

RECORDINGS:

Exercise: PACE 3: Cook's hook-ups

Part 1
Sit in a chair; raise one leg and place the ankle or lower leg over the other, cross your hands at about the wrists; place your crossed hands on the raised leg so that one hand is holding the toes and the other the ankle. Hold the position for a count of 30.

Part 2
Sit straight in the chair, with feet on the ground. Put the tips of your fingers and thumbs together and rest your hands in your lap for a count of 30.

RECORDINGS:

MARGIN NOTE enough water: the debate about how much water to drink and what quality is needed seems to go in cycles; Brain Gym isn't the only source of 'Drink more water. You should drink 2 pints a day.'

'Exercise': PACE 4: Enough water, see MARGIN NOTE

I get restless working with words; it is a struggle. Comfort eating just means I put on weight, so I'll drink water or a hot drink that suits me instead.

My practical experience is that for some people doing the exercises makes a difference to their achievement. It may be that taking the break and moving is allowing something else to happen which really makes the difference to your thinking. As with everything in this book, it is a question of trying different approaches and observing what works for you.

7 Neuro-Linguistic Programming (NLP)

'What is NLP? Its title gives one answer. 'Neuro' refers to the mind and how we organise our mental life. 'Linguistic' is about language, how we use it and how it affects us. 'Programming' is about our sequences of repetitive behaviour and how we act with purpose.' (O'Connor and McDermott, 1996, p xi) Again there is the understanding that we have mind, body and psyche; that these affect each other and that our deliberate work at one level will affect the others, as discussed in INTERPLAY BETWEEN MIND, BODY AND PSYCHE.

Some books on NLP are listed in the bibliography, p 298

O'Connor and McDermott (1996, p xi)

Ⓖ p 353: psyche

INTERPLAY BETWEEN MIND, BODY AND PSYCHE: p 258

This section is based on the ways I have used and developed ideas from NLP:

- to help the dyslexic/ SpLD people I have worked with, myself included
- as part of dyslexia/ SpLD workshops.

SIT-STAND is based on an exercise that demonstrates the interplay between mind, body and psyche.

SIT-STAND: p 280

SOME NLP CONCEPTS outlines a few concepts that help you to understand these exercises and benefit from them.

SOME NLP CONCEPTS: p 281

RE-FRAMING CLASSIFICATION explores ways in which different perspectives can change the way you experience a situation with your senses; the perspectives are shown by the language you use in relation to the situation.

USING CHALLENGES SHOWS HOW TO use challenges that you've dealt with to assist with those you haven't yet resolved.

NLP AND MEMORY discusses how the movement of the eyes can show which sense you use when thinking; you may be able to use the movement to activate memory.

NEUROLOGICAL LEVELS – DILTS' LEVELS are a system for working on attitudes that affect behaviour. The section discusses a process of investigating how to make changes of perspective; working with these levels allows you to change attitudes that may be blocking your progress.

USING NLP includes TIP: HOW TO USE NLP which sums up using NLP to establish and maintain clear thinking and positive attitudes.

The exercises allow you to explore your inner perspectives. There are external instructions that guide you to observe certain things. The exercises have been written as if two people are involved. If you are doing them on your own, they will probably work better if you record the guide's text. Or, find a suitable other person with whom you can do them.

These exercises are often good to do in a group. People work in pairs and then share what they have experienced. The different reactions that people have widen your understanding of the way NLP works.

7.1 Sit-stand

To demonstrate the connection between mind, body and psyche, I use the following exercise from an NLP trainer. If you are working on your own with a recording, replace the discussion instructions with prompts to stop and notice your reactions and feelings.

Exercise: Sit-stand

RECORDINGS:

One person, A, sits on a chair, the other, B, stands slightly behind on the left.

In the exercise, A doesn't need to describe what s/he is remembering, s/he just needs to indicate that the memory is as vivid as possible.

B: Ask the sitter to get up and sit down again, then use the following text:

"On a scale of 1 - 5 (bad to good) remember a time when you were in a bad situation, about level 2

"Remember how you felt .....

"What do you see? .... See any colours, see any movement

"Are there any sounds? ... Really hear them

"Notice how your body feels....

"Notice how you feel about yourself ...

"Now get up ...... and sit down again.

"What was it like to stand up?"

Discuss what you both noticed:

A: the quality of the memory;

both: the effects on A's physical state of being;

anything else worthy of note.

B: Stand on the right, and use the following text:

"On a scale of 1 - 5 (bad to good) remember a time when you were in a good situation, about level 4".

use the same prompts as above to help A remember as well as possible.

Discuss what you both noticed, as above.
Discuss any differences between the two states of being and any difference in standing up.

MARGIN NOTE:
Person B: Emphasise the second and third 'see' so that person A pays attention to what s/he sees.

When working with a group, the exercise can first be carried out as a demonstration with a volunteer; ask the group what they observe. Then allow people to work in pairs taking turns to be sitter or talker. It's useful to take both roles.

Most often, the volunteer experiences physical heaviness in the first situation; people watching can see that the posture is hunched, or closed-in in some way; the movement to stand up is slow and reluctant; the facial expression is not happy. In the second situation, the person feels lighter; the posture is upright; there's a smile on the face; standing is smooth.

Again, you have to ask the person what it is like for them; one person moved out of the bad situation fast, out of relief to get away from it. The quality of the sensations remembered is often different: there is usually a contrast between the amount of colour seen; how wide the view of the scene is; the quality of the sounds is different; the way in which sensations are felt in the body can be different.

The exercise brings home the relationship between the mental, physical and psychological levels of being discussed in *INTERPLAY BETWEEN MIND, BODY AND PSYCHE*. The difference between the good and bad situations is generated simply by one person asking another to remember as vividly as possible a couple of situations from their past.

INTERPLAY BETWEEN MIND, BODY AND PSYCHE: p 258

Insight: You can choose to change how you feel

You can change the dynamics of a situation, or of the way you tackle a task, simply by the way you are standing. Standing upright, at ease but alert is more beneficial than being hunched over and down-trodden.

It is worth checking your posture from time to time, especially when something is difficult.

You can combine the insights of the *SIT-STAND EXERCISE* with the *EXERCISE: EXPLORING CHANGES IN SUB-MODALITIES DEPENDING ON CLASSIFICATION*.

EXERCISE: SIT-STAND: p 281

EXERCISE: EXPLORING CHANGES IN SUB-MODALITIES DEPENDING ON CLASSIFICATION: p 284

When you notice from your posture that you are in a situation on the bad side of neutral, you can use the classification ideas to change your mental attitude towards the situation.

7.2   Some NLP concepts

These are some of the useful concepts of NLP. They relate to the exercises presented here.

Internal representation

The world around us is external to our thinking, and our thinking is an 'internal representation' of this reality. The internal representation is a map; it is never complete: 'the map is not the territory'. Exploring the details of that internal representation can be a useful tool in thinking clearly.

'The map is not the territory' originates from Alfred Korzybski. It is discussed in O'Connor and McDermott (1996)

Modalities and sub-modalities

The ways in which we sense the world around us, namely seeing, feeling, hearing, tasting and smelling are called modalities in NLP. Our memories often use particular modalities which will not be the same from one individual to another. Each modality has fine detail, called sub-modalities. For example, seeing is a modality; included in the visual sub-modalities are: colour, sharp or fuzzy; moving or still; framed or without boundary. What you experience in the exercises in this section will show you other sub-modalities for seeing, as well as for the other modalities.

Modal operators

The language we use about a situation can indicate our attitude towards the situation; this is true even in our internal thoughts. I am speaking; I ought to speak; I could speak; I can't speak. All these sentences indicate different expectations or perspectives in relation to speaking. The expectations are modal operators in that they operate on verbs (what we are doing, have or are) and change the mode of the verb. See below *RE-FRAMING CLASSIFICATION* for further examples and a list of modal operators.

RE-FRAMING CLASSIFICATION: p 284

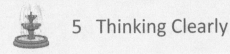

7.3   Re-framing classification

The way we think about something will alter our approach to it. For example:

People	object	attitude
to most people	*Jane Eyre* is a novel	'I would like to read it'
to an English student	it can be a set book	'I have to read it'
to some shoppers	shop floor design is not worth attention	'I won't notice the design'
to other shoppers	attractive floor design	'I'll notice the design'
to shop floor managers	attractive and efficient shop floors relate to business productivity	'I have to notice the design'

The perspective changes the approach and the modal operators.

Sometimes the perspective can be negative or heavy, in which case the approach can become much more laboured than it need be.

It is useful to see how the perspective alters the way the mind processes a situation, which can be done by observing the sub-modalities of the visual, auditory and kinaesthetic senses.

RECORDINGS: COMPANION @ WEBSITE

Exercise: Exploring changes in sub-modalities depending on classification

For two people:

> 1st person, A: You choose an everyday event, e.g. eating breakfast, and remember yourself doing it or being there.

> 2nd person, B: You help A to explore the event by using the questions in the following 3 boxes.

A doesn't describe the event to B.
B's job is to make sure A is able to explore the event.

To start, try to find out which modality is the strongest. Is A seeing the event more clearly or are the sounds stronger, or are movements and a sense of physical reactions strongest? You can choose to work with the strongest modality or you can work with all three.

The next 3 boxes suggest questions for the different modalities.

These questions are only a guide. Explore in more detail if that seems helpful.

Questions to explore the visual modality and its sub-modalities:

Can you see the situation? Is it vivid or hazy? Is it 2-dimensional or 3-dimensional? Is it sharply focused or blurred? Is it a movie or still picture?	Are there any colours, or is it black & white? Is it framed or going to the edge of vision? Where is the picture, high or low, in front or to one side, near or far?

Auditory modality and its sub-modalities can be explored with questions such as:

Can you hear the situation? Can you hear distinct sounds or general noise? Are the sounds loud or soft, harsh or melodious?	Is the sound dynamic or gentle? What are the sounds? music - voices - general noise - what? Does the sound belong to one object or person, or many?

Kinaesthetic modality and its sub-modalities can be explored with questions such as:

Can you feel yourself in the situation? Does any part of your body register a sensation? What is it? How are your feet, legs, buttocks, stomach, breathing, arms, shoulders, head?	Do you need to move to feel it? What's behind the movement? Are you light or heavy? In each part: What is the sensation? Is there any movement, or desire to move? Notice any feelings.

Stay with the same everyday event and explore the changes in sub-modalities depending on the following modal operators. Keep with the same set of questions while exploring the effect of the modal operators, unless you discover the modality changes dramatically with a change of modal operator. Examples are given below for eating breakfast.

· **Impossibility**: impossible, unable to, incapable, couldn't, can't
· **Possibility**: can, could, may, might, able to, possible, yet
· **Capability**: able to, capable of, can, could
· **Desire**: wish, would like to, want, choose, hope
· **Necessity**: need to, have to, must, ought to, should, necessary
· **Certainty**: shall, will, won't, am, is, am going to

An example of one event with different modal operators:

I *am eating* breakfast. (neutral, first time through)

I *can't* eat breakfast.   (impossibility)

I *might* eat breakfast. I have yet to eat breakfast. (possibility)

I *am able to* eat breakfast.   (capability)

I *choose to* eat breakfast.   (desire)

I *ought* to eat breakfast.   (necessity)

I *shall* eat breakfast.   (certainty)

The differences that people notice are individual. Examples are:

Positive	*Negative*
More colour, the field of view is wider, light	Black and white, restricted field of view, muted or dark
Vivid sounds, clear	No sounds, very quiet
Light, fluid movements, relaxed	Heavy, tense

You can use the quality of the sub-modalities to indicate when you need to re-frame a situation, a task, an event.

Tip: Value of re-framing classification

By changing the classification of an event or situation, one re-frames it and converts bad to good, impossible to possible etc. (or vice versa!) Re-framing your classification can have a significant effect on your thinking and on any action you take.

The following stories show how re-framing and using sub-modalities can help you maintain clear thinking.

Story: Shifting feelings using movement

As a kinaesthetic thinker, I notice where in my body I register feelings and what those feelings are; I will move that part to change the way I'm feeling about something. For example, too much to do sits on my shoulders and I have to move them around as if trying to shift a harness. If I'm happy, I get a burst of energy that wants to dance. I have no internal vision (however, visual sub-modalities are part of my learning strengths) and no deliberate use of internal sound, so I have to work with the feeling sensations.

Story: Re-framing using visualisation

One student would plan actions he needed to do and he would see himself doing those actions; then he found his mind registered those actions as having taken place; and they were removed from his mental to-do list. From the insights of NLP, we devised the strategy of mentally putting a frame round actions yet to be done. The frame distinguished the 'yet-to-be-done actions' from those already completed, and they remained on his mental to-do list.

Here the student was altering the internal representation to bring clarity and to aid memory.

Story: Re-framing using other memories

I had a long essay to write for a course and I knew the tutor was not going to make positive comments about anyone's work. My dyslexia was getting steadily worse. I re-framed my classification: I put a sub-title on my essay: 'To All My Lovely Tutors'. After a while, I found a tune running through my head that related to one of the tutors, my thinking was clear and my writing was much more fluent.

Tip: How you think and what you do

Think 'I will forget ...', and you probably will forget. Think 'I will not remember ...' and you will probably remember.
If I think 'How do I spell ...<a word>?' I will get random answers for a spelling, since that's what I do. However, if I think 'How have I seen ... <a word>?' I am much more likely to remember the right spelling.

Other examples of the way in which thinking preferences affect how you recall are described in *Example: Checking Spelling and Thinking Preferences*.

Example: Checking Spelling and Thinking Preferences: p 193

7.4   Using challenges

Often it is possible to pick up the memory of a challenge that has been successfully accomplished and use it to face something that is not going well.

Story: The challenges of mountaineering and exams

One student had failed her final year, taken a gap year, re-taken the final year and was facing the final exams again. The academic tutor and I were worried that she would fail again. I used NLP questioning, as above, to look at tough challenges the student had faced (in this case mountaineering), to understand what it was that brought success (she liked a challenge, the excitement of the unknown); we brought that attitude to exams just 9 days before the first exam (they were a challenge to be surmounted, not a black horror to be feared). She got a first in all her exams, except one for which she got a good 2:1. It was just seeing the exams alongside the mountaineering that brought the necessary change of perspective.

7.5 NLP and memory

In my work, I don't often deal with learning spelling, but one adult basic learner I worked with was helped by NLP ideas of accessing memory (O'Connor, 1987, p 16). The direction of the eyes indicates which sense is being activated: up visual, sideways sounds, downwards feelings or talking to oneself. To the left for up and sideways is remembering, to the right for constructing; downwards left is for accessing feelings, downwards right is for internal dialogue, talking to oneself.

O'Connor (1987, p 16)

Story: Spelling aided by NLP

The student in question had incredibly small writing: the height of the letters was less than 1mm. He was so unsure of his spelling that he didn't want anyone to see it. We worked with his eyes going up to his left. At first I held up a board with words written on it, later I held up a clean board with him remembering the words and becoming confident of his spelling. His writing very quickly got larger, though that was not the object of our work.

7.6 Neurological levels – Dilts' levels

Compare these two attitudes to mistakes:

> You got that wrong!
>
> Well … that didn't work, shall we try something else?

MARGIN NOTE: no difference is intended between attitude and perspective; it would just be stylistically irksome to use one word all the way through this section.

In the first, 'you' are at fault. In the second, mistakes can be viewed as opportunities, as part of effective learning. For many people, this is a more creative attitude than one in which mistakes are to be avoided at all costs.

Some problems persist and get worse because an unhelpful attitude gets re-enforced. The ideas in this section can be used to shift perspectives and bring about change. I use the exercise below when I feel there is an attitude that is blocking a student's progress and that it will continue to do so until it is at least seen. Releasing unhelpful attitudes contributes to maintaining clear thinking.

Dilts' levels are a hierarchy of neurological levels that affect behaviour, as in the left column below. Relationships in a situation occur at these different levels; a way of thinking at one level will affect what happens at another level. Compare the analysis of the two attitudes to a keep fit class:

Dilts' levels	Creative attitudes	Destructive attitudes
Environment: where, when	many people, large hall seems large enough	many people, large hall doesn't seem large enough
Behaviours: what is done	friendly, co-operative	manipulating space to get the best place, non-co-operative
Capabilities: how	physical ability, motivated to have fun while keeping fit, discipline	physical ability, determined to be in prime condition
Values: why 1	giving time, money & companionship	self-centred: this is for me

capability relates to CONFIDENCE: p 264

Beliefs: why 2	fitness adds to the quality of life	fitness adds status with respect to others
Identity: who	person capable of fitness	I am better than the others
Goal: ultimate why	healthy level of fitness	to win no matter who gets damaged

beliefs relate to *SELF-ESTEEM:* p 265

There are influences between these levels so that what happens at one level affects what happens at others. In reality, the attitudes can be mixed, so that one person will have both creative and destructive attitudes.

Exercise: Walking through Dilts' levels

Aim: to see and understand a situation that you choose to work with.

You reflect on your reaction at each level, starting at the environment level and working up to the goal. At any level, you may decide that what you see is not what you want, and you can change it. Therefore, you usually gain a fresh insight into the situation. As you work back down from goal to environment, you usually find there are differences in your reactions somewhere along the way; you may have a new perspective; you may realise there is a change you want to make; or you will see something else that helps you understand what is happening in the situation.

For two people: The *Explorer* explores the Dilts' levels.

    The *Guider* is guiding the *Explorer* by using the questions.

The *Explorer* chooses a situation, one that he'd like to change.

Both people stand at one end of a room.

The *Guider* uses the questions in the table below (and any others that seem useful) to guide the *Explorer* through the levels.

The *Explorer* doesn't say what he's thinking, but just indicates when he's clearly identified what's happening at a level.

RECORDINGS:

Start at the *'Environment Level'*:

When you move from one level to the next, both of you take one step forwards.

When you have done *'Goal Level'* turn round. The *Explorer* looks at the situation from the *'Goal Level'*.

Then you move back down the levels using the same questions.

A problem at one level is usually resolved by a change in a higher level.

Exercise: Walking through Dilts' levels *continued*

Dilts' levels	Description – what happens at any level depends on the situation considered	Questions for moving through the Dilts' levels
Environment: where, when	the context surrounding the situation	Remember the situation: What is it like? See the colours. Hear the sounds. Feel the movements
Behaviours: what is done	how people interact	How do you behave? How are others behaving?
Capabilities: how	what a person can do	What are you capable of doing or being? Include capabilities you don't use.
Values: why 1	what has values, or is important – attraction & repulsion	What do you think is important? What attracts you? What repels you?
Beliefs: why 2	relates to a person's beliefs	What do you believe about the situation?

Identity: who	how a person identifies himself	How do you see yourself? Who do you say you are? Make several 'I am ....' statements about yourself.
Goal:	what a person wants to achieve	What is your aim or goal?

Story: Dilts' levels and taking part in a class

A student was not progressing well on a module, especially in the classes. We walked through the Dilts' levels for a class situation. He realised where the problem lay and how to connect with another student to make the situation better. He realised what sort of preparation could make his performance in the class more confident.

It was also obvious that part of the problem was caused by being with a group of students who were a year or more ahead of him, which meant they knew that much more of the material.

Understanding the issues more clearly gave the student choices he could make to improve the situation, as well as highlighting unrealistic expectations that were producing lack of confidence.

7.7   Using NLP

There is much more to NLP than is presented here; these are ideas that have been most useful in changing attitudes and perspectives of many of those I've worked with.

As with many ideas in this book, I don't expect someone to simply believe me that an idea will work. *Sit-Stand* is often the first exercise I use, just to let people see for themselves how easy it is to make changes in the physical and psychological energies. *Re-framing Classification* and *Walking through Dilts' Levels* are useful when someone is defeatist in some way. *Using Challenges* is particularly

Sit-Stand: p 280
Re-framing Classification: p 284
Exercise Walking through Dilts' levels: p 291
Using Challenges: p 288

helpful with exam nerves. Working in groups is beneficial as people can see the changes in someone else and it is reassuring to hear other people's stories or experiences.

Tip: How to use NLP

When you have a more open, positive perspective towards a task, you are more likely to succeed with it and it will be easier to manage your dyslexia/ SpLD, i.e. it is easier to keep your thinking clear.

The exercises in this section will help you see:

how much mind, body and psyche influence each other

how different modal operators change the internal representation
of a situation

how you can transfer your attitudes that bring success to
situations that are problematic

how you can alter your perspective on a situation and resolve
issues.

All these insights help to establish and maintain the desired open, positive perspective.

---

8   Other systems

NLP gives you ways of making changes at the psychic level without deep exploration. However, sometimes you need to do the deep exploration and you may need to work with a counsellor[2] or therapist for a longer period of time. You might find resources such as *The Artist's Way at Work* (Bryan, 1998) help you.

Bryan (1998)

Music and art

Playing a piece of music while looking at a piece of art work can be an effective way to realise something about your state of mind. I was

---

[2] Counsellors and therapists: make sure you work with someone who will take into account the pitfalls of your dyslexia/ SpLD (Stacey, 2021). Ⓖ p 353: pitfall

introduced to this idea while training for the SpLD diploma and I used it with classes on the module I taught for dyslexic students at Oxford Brookes University. I had prints of work by Cézanne and Monet and played *Prélude à l'Après-midi d'un Faune* by Debussy. The combination gives an opportunity for quiet reflection. Something important can emerge from the quiet, or you find there is a restorative quality to the calm.

Physical exercise

Many people find exercise is a good way to assist clear thinking. They either establish a routine of regular exercise; or they go for a run, walk or go to a gym, particularly when they are stuck with how to think through some issue. Researchers are looking at the hormones produced by exercise, in particular serotonin, and looking at the benefits produced.

PhotoReading[3] (Scheele, 1999)

Scheele (1999)

PhotoReading is a method of reading which works well for some dyslexics. It is beyond the scope of this book, but it includes two useful exercises for altering the state of your mind and allowing you to think more clearly.

Exercise: The ideal state of mind

This exercise is used before surveying any material to be read. The idea is to stay as an observer and not get absorbed by detail.

The image I use to explain the state of mind is that of an observer standing on a cliff looking down on a beach. You can see the activities happening on the beach: a family picnic; dog-walking; rock-pooling; kite-flying; but you are not part of any scene, you stay above as an observer.

RECORDINGS:

The wording of these two exercises is adapted from the book by Scheele (1999)

---

[3]Comments on the web about PhotoReading show people either think it is the best technique possible or that it is rubbish, i.e. the techniques work for you or they don't. The students I've worked with have been at both extremes. They haven't fallen in between. The main process of PhotoReading might not work for you, but many of the preparation techniques are worth investigating.

Sit comfortably and straight; close your eyes.

- Hold an imaginary tangerine in your hand. Experience its weight, temperature, texture, smell. Place it in the other hand; again feel the weight, texture, smell and temperature. Move it backwards and forwards. Really feel the tangerine with each hand.

- Hold it in your dominant hand and take it to the top, back part of your head. Touch the area with your hand gently. Imagine the tangerine staying on your head while you bring your arm down and relax your shoulders. Pretend it's magic and will stay there.

- Let the tangerine balance on the back of your head. Notice your physical and mental state as you do this. With eyes still closed, imagine your field of vision opening up.

- Maintain the relaxed feeling of alertness, open your eyes and begin the task in hand.

Exercise: Accelerated state of learning

RECORDINGS:

A relaxed, alert, receptive mind results when the following exercise works well:

- Lie down (beginner), sit well in a chair (non-beginner)

- Experience full physical relaxation: take in a deep breath and hold for a moment. As you exhale slowly think "3" and "relax"; this is the signal for physical relaxation. Progressively relax the major muscle groups from head to toe.

- Calm your mind: take a deep breath and hold it for a moment; exhale slowly thinking "2" and "relax"; this is the signal for mental relaxation. Let go of past and future; focus on the present. As you breathe in, let peace and tranquillity flow into every part of you.

- Take in another deep breath and hold it for a moment, exhale slowly and hear "1"; as you do so, picture a beautiful flower. This signals that you've focused your awareness and entered the resource level of mind – a state of creativity and ability to learn.

- Imagine yourself in a beautiful quiet place; become fully aware of it. Imagine an hour is elapsing. Let yourself rest. Let go of any remaining tensions – physical, mental. Maintain this state as you engage with learning or any other task.

9 The art of pausing and maintaining clear thinking

It is an art to be able to push the pause button on your thinking and to keep it clear. When you are good at dyslexia/ SpLD management you recognise the hallmarks of situations that challenge your dyslexia/ SpLD and you take action before anything happens.

Guidelines for monitoring progress

There may be times when you need to monitor how you are pausing and how you are working on keeping your thinking clear. You can use any of the suitable suggestions for observing that are given in *METHODS FOR OBSERVING*. You may find it helpful to pay particular attention to the following:

- Knowing about the interplay between different levels of being:
  - o Does the interplay help you notice events that need careful attention?
  - o Does it help you recognise what your particular reactions are?
- Knowing your good states of mind:
  - o Are you using these as a resource to draw on when you need to?
- Being alert for the onset of a challenging situation:
  - o Are you taking action early, and hence, minimising the impact of the situation?

METHODS FOR OBSERVING: p 55

Useful *TEMPLATES:*

B11 - MONITORING PROGRESS

B4 - ACTION, RESULTS, NEXT STEP

B3 - COMPARE EXPECTATIONS AND REALITY

- Rehearsing your best ways into a pause and to thinking clearly:
  - Are you practising these tools in less challenging situations?
  - Are they secure so that you trust them?
- The experience of situations that you have managed well:
  - Do you remember these easily?
  - Do you need to keep a record of them?
  - Are you building a collection of memories that gives you the confidence to keep using the tools and to keep exploring new ones too?

There are always those times that come unannounced. Gradually you get to recognise earlier and earlier the necessity for pausing and taking preventative action. As you get more confident, you will be able to pause well and extricate yourself with dignity. As your experience of dealing well with situations grows, then those that don't go so well will have less power to undermine your confidence and self-esteem; gradually you will be able to maintain clear thinking.

Being clear about your identity, how you communicate, what you bring to any situation and what you want to achieve can all be influential components of THINKING CLEARLY.

References

Baddeley, Alan, 2007, *Working Memory, Thought, and Action*, Oxford University Press, Oxford

Bryan, Mark, 1998, *The Artist's Way at Work*, William Morrow & Co., NY

Dennison, Paul and Dennison, Gail, 1986, *Brain Gym*, Edu-Kinesthetics, Ventura, CA

Goleman, Daniel, 1996, *Emotional Intelligence*, Bloomsbury, London

Miles, T R and Varma, Ved, eds, 1995, *Dyslexia and Stress*, Whurr, London

O'Connor, Joseph, 1987, *Not Pulling Strings: A book of Instrumental Teaching and Music Education*, Lambent Books, London

O'Connor, Joseph and McDermott, Ian, 1996, *Principles of NLP*, Thorsons, London

OED[4], Brown, Lesley Ed in Chief, 1993, *The New Shorter Oxford English Dictionary on Historical Principles*, Clarendon Press, Oxford

Scheele, Paul, 1999, *PhotoReading*, Learning Strategies Corp., Minnetonka, MN, 3rd ed.

Springer, Sally and Deutsch, Georg, 1989, *Left Brain, Right Brain*, WH Freeman & Company, NY

Stacey, Ginny, 2020, *Development of Dyslexia and other SpLDs,* Routledge, London

Stacey, Ginny, 2021, *Gaining Knowledge and Skills with Dyslexia and other SpLDs,* Routledge, London

Watkins, Alan, 2014, *Coherence: The Secret Science of Brilliant Leadership,* Kogan Page, London

Further reading

NLP

O'Connor, Joseph and Seymour, John, 2002, *Introducing NLP Neuro Linguistic Programming,* Harper Element, London

Sinclair, Joseph, 1992, *An ABC of NLP,* Aspen, London

Bandler, Richard and Grindler, John, 1975, *The Structure of Magic I,* Science and Behaviour Books, Palo Alto, CA

Grindler, John and Bandler, Richard, 1976, *The Structure of Magic II,* Science and Behaviour Books, Palo Alto, CA

Breathing

Williams, Mark and Penman, Danny, 2011, *Mindfulness: A Practical Guide to Finding Peace in a Frantic World*, Piatkus, London

Website information

OED Online, December 2020, Oxford University Press. Accessed 25 February 2021.

Series website: www.routledge.com/cw/stacey

---

[4] The online OED has been consulted every time, and the meanings are consistent. Sometimes the words used in the hard copy of OED (1993) are clearer, or more to-the-point in the context of this book, in which case, the reference is to the hard-copy edition.

Appendix 1: Resources

Contents

Templates on the website

TEMPLATES

300

1 General resources

This is a collection of resources and ideas that will help you to capture any ideas that seem important to you. Ideas that are captured will then be available to you for use later on.

Notice anything that doesn't work for you, and use it to design your own way to capture and use information that seems relevant to you.

Tip: Margin

You can use the right-hand margin to jot down your ideas as you scan or read the book.

I have used it for cross-referencing and for references to help you find these when you want them.

2 Collecting information together

- Create a mind map of the information; there are examples in the book. Experiment with different styles to find which work well for you. (Don't use mind maps if you don't like them.)
- Use a digital recording device; make sure you label the files so that you can remember what they are about.
- Create tables of information; this section has several suggestions for using tables.
- Use electronic note-collecting devices.

B1 - COLLECTING IDEAS THAT RELATE TO YOU

This *TEMPLATE* will help with building your *INDIVIDUAL, PERSONAL PROFILE OF DYSLEXIA/ SPLD* and your *REGIME FOR MANAGING DYSLEXIA/ SPLD*.

Column 4 allows you to reflect whether you are learning more about
1 your profile
2 your regime for managing dyslexia/ SpLD.

Column 5 allows you to note which elements are involved:
thinking preferences
pausing
pitfalls
accommodations
goals.

TEMPLATES

G p 353: profile, regime

B3 - COMPARE EXPECTATIONS AND REALITY

If you are going to observe objectively you need to keep a record of your expectations and what actually happens. The *TEMPLATE: COMPARE EXPECTATIONS AND REALITY* is one way of doing this. It can be easier to rule horizontal lines after writing in the template than forcing yourself to keep within lines already printed.

The template suggests you record the *situation* and *date*. It has 4 columns headed: *Events, Expected, Actual, Comments.*

TEMPLATES

For example:

Situation: to have everything ready for football on Saturday morning (include the date), in order to arrive on time.

Events	Expected	Actual	Comments
wash kit	Tuesday		
assemble kit	Friday		
put boots with kit	Friday		
get up	8.30 am Saturday		
breakfast	9.00		
leave house	9.45		
arrive at *venue*	10.15		

The Actual column would be filled in as close to the event as possible. The Comments could then reflect pleasure at success or any adjustments needed to achieve the desired result.

B4 - ACTION, RESULTS, NEXT STEP

This *TEMPLATE* is very similar to *COMPARE EXPECTATIONS AND REALITY*. In *COMPARE EXPECTATIONS AND REALITY* you are planning ahead and monitoring how well the plan was executed. In *ACTION, RESULTS, NEXT STEP,* you are observing the results of actions, whether planned or not, and considering any implications for the *Next Step*, whenever that might be.

TEMPLATES

For example:

Event	Action	Results	Next Step
conversation with friend	I created pictures in my mind as we talked	I remembered the details next day	try putting pictures on my lists
shopping	I drew some of the items on the list and left the list at home!	I remembered the drawings and some connected items; forgot others	see what other line drawing I can use

TEMPLATES

B5, B6 - RECORDING TEMPLATES - 1 AND - 2

These templates can be used for a number of different purposes.
In *B5 - RECORDING TEMPLATE - 1* the columns are uneven, which is
suitable for those times when you want to use one column for a lot of
detail while the others are only needed for brief information.
B6 - RECORDING TEMPLATE - 2 has 4 equal columns.

B7, B8 - RECORDING TEMPLATES - 3 AND - 4

These templates are similar to *B5, B6 - RECORDING TEMPLATES - 1* and - *2*,
but with a 5th column. Often the fifth column is very useful for a brief
key word or symbol. It allows you to code the information you are
collecting so that you can find sections that belong together. For
instance, if you are exploring how you use different senses, you can
put visual/ aural/ smell/ taste/ kinaesthetic or V/ A/ S/ T / K in the fifth
column. Then you only have to look for the V/ visual to find all the
notes about the way you use your vision.

Useful headings for linear lists or text notes

Any of the column headings suggested for tabular forms of collecting
information could be used as headings for lists or a sentence-based
way of collecting information.

You might divide a page into spaces for different categories of
information and label the spaces.

You might write down the information you are gathering and leave
space to add in the headings later.

MARGIN NOTE: when
these 4 templates are
recommended,
headings are usually
suggested.

3 Prioritising

Given a collection of tasks, situations or topics (not an exhaustive list),
what are the priorities for you?

1   You might have to prioritise bearing in mind limited time and
     resources.
2   You might be trying to decide the relative importance of each of a
     set of topics.
3   You might be deciding the order in which to do a series of tasks.

You can use any form of note-taking to collect the information
together. The suggestions here use a calendar, a mind map and a
tabular form.

Step 1   With limited time or resources

First you have to establish the constraints:

- Do you have enough time or resources to do everything?
- Does anything depend on another thing being done first?

Assessing the constraints first stops you trying to do more than you possibly can.

TEMPLATES

The *TEMPLATE: B9 - A CALENDAR MONTH FOR PRIORITISING* allows you to mark deadlines and block out sections of time. You can often then decide the priority of the various tasks and the order in which to do them.

Put everything that is happening in your life onto the calendar. In particular, include time for the ordinary, everyday tasks.

It can be helpful to highlight the beginning and end of the month, whether using paper or an electronic device.

You then continue with the second stage below.

Step 2   What is involved?

A second stage is simply to brainstorm about the tasks, situations or topics under consideration. You can use any of the shapes of mind map used in the book. You could make lists of ideas.

See the *INDEX*, p 379, for a list of mind maps

In terms of reading a book, a useful set of questions might be:
>What do I know already?
>Why have I picked up this book?
>What do I think it might give me?
>What am I interested in? or Who am I interested in knowing more about?
>What aspect would it be interesting to know more about?
>What do I really want to know?

MARGIN NOTE: GENERATING USEFUL QUESTIONS, p 306, could help you find the right questions.

If you are prioritising actions, a set of useful questions might be:
>What do I want to achieve?
>What equipment do I need?
>Who else is involved? How? Why?
>What individual tasks are there?
>What do I need to find out?

Step 3   Deciding relative priorities

When you have decided what is involved, you can put the information together in a table and then decide the relative priorities of the tasks.

B5, B6 - RECORDING TEMPLATES - 1 AND - 2 can be adapted to gather the information.

TEMPLATES

Title = the reason for sorting out a set of priorities.

       A = the priority assigned to each task once you've assessed them all

       B = name of a task

       C = details of the task

       D = resources or time requirements.

B7, B8 - RECORDING TEMPLATES - 3 AND - 4 could be used if a 5th column is useful.

TEMPLATES

       E = vital/ important/ non-essential.

This information would help in assigning the priorities that are written in column A.

Step 4   Plan of action

Use the priorities list in column A and the calendar to make a plan of action. Keep monitoring your progress. Adapt your plan as necessary.

4 Generating useful questions

Making a list of questions can be a very useful way to guide yourself through many different situations or tasks. The purpose of the list is to clarify what you are attempting to do, to help you be realistic and to help you achieve the end goal. Discussion around these ideas has come under: useful questions, ultimate goal, know your goal, research questions and probably a few other terms too.   It is hard to pick out any common themes that lead to a direct set of principles. However, the idea of useful questions is sufficiently important that there is an *INDEX* entry: *QUESTIONS, USEFUL: EXAMPLES.*

INDEX: p 379

TEMPLATE: B10 - QUESTIONS TO ASK ONESELF TO HELP OBSERVATION is an example of a good set of questions.

The style and wording of the questions will be slightly different depending on the circumstances, for example:

> When you're organising something, you might think about how you're going to organise it and why you're organising it in a particular way.

> When you are reading something or listening, having some questions you want answered gives a structure to the material. You then understand it faster.

> When you're writing an essay, doing a presentation, or communicating by some means, the purposes for your work need to be defined clearly. This approach usually gives a coherence to the work.

> When you are making major decisions for your life, you can be helped by a set of questions about what you want to do, what you are most interested in, how your decisions will affect others. The list is not exhaustive.

> When you need to keep your attention focused on a specific task and stop yourself getting diverted, you can use a set of questions to:

> a) define the specific task

> b) relate what you are doing at any moment to the specific task.

> Pulling yourself back from distractions can make a task more enjoyable, or it can shorten a task you don't really want to do.

TEMPLATES

The Basic Set of
USEFUL QUESTIONS:
Why?
Who?
When?
Where?
How?
What for?

Exercise: To practise generating useful questions 1

You are going to use *USEFUL QUESTIONS* to search the book in order to find any discussion on a specific topic:

- Think of a topic that interests you.
- What questions need answering to help you find out about the topic?
- List your questions.
- Use them as you scan the *INDEX ENTRY: QUESTIONS, USEFUL, EXAMPLES.* Then scan the rest of the *INDEX,* the *CONTENTS* and the book to find topics that are similar to the one you have in mind.
- How good were your questions? Did they help you to find the sections that deal with the topic you had in mind?
- What changes would you make to the questions for the next time?

MARGIN NOTE: this exercise could be applied to all 4 books in the series (Stacey, 2020a, 2020b, 2021a, 2021b)

INDEX: p 379
CONTENTS: p XVIII

Exercise: To practise generating useful questions 2

You are going to use *USEFUL QUESTIONS* to search the book in order to find the nearest match to a specific task:

- Think of a task that needs doing.
- What questions need answering to help you find the best match, in the book, to your task?
- List your questions.
- Use them as you scan the *INDEX ENTRY: QUESTIONS, USEFUL, EXAMPLES.* Then scan the rest of the *INDEX* the *CONTENTS* and the book to find tasks that are similar to the one you have in mind.
- How good were your questions? Did they help you to find a good match to the task you had in mind?
- What changes would you make to the questions for the next time?

MARGIN NOTE: this exercise will work best with *Organisation and Everyday Life with Dyslexia and other SpLDs* (Stacey, 2020a) and *Gaining Knowledge and Skills with Dyslexia and other SpLDs* (Stacey, 2021)

INDEX: p 379
CONTENTS: p XVIII

Tip: The skill of generating useful questions

This skill is worth developing until it becomes natural. You could add the *Exercise: To Practise Generating Useful Questions 1 & 2,* above, to the card index for *Systematic Review*. It is a skill that could be usefully practised once a week until it is easy to use.

Systematic Review: p 164

---

5 Surveying

In surveying you are looking over material to find out, in broad terms, what the material contains and where certain ideas are. As part of the process you will probably decide your priorities for exploring the ideas. 'Material' could be instruction manuals for household goods, books, articles, web pages.

Step 1 Key ideas

You need to establish a set of key ideas that you want to find out about. These will be your focus of attention as you survey any material.

Margin Note: Exercise: Initial Purpose for Reading, p 14 is a good example of surveying.

You can use one of the *Exercises: To Practise Generating Useful Questions.*
You can brainstorm around the associated topics to see if key ideas emerge.
You can look at other examples using *Questions, Useful: Examples* in the *Index*, and see if any of them help you to recognise the key ideas you want to read about.

Exercises: To Practise Generating Useful Questions: p 306

ⓖ p 353: brainstorm

Index: p 379

You can discuss your interest with someone else and use ideas that come out of the conversation.

It doesn't matter how you do it, but find a set of key ideas.

The set of key ideas will still be helpful, even when they are not quite right. They will help you to focus your mind as you survey. You will be more attentive to the material than if trying to read with a wide open mind that is not looking for anything specific.

Step 2   Recording your survey

TEMPLATES

Use *B5 - RECORDING TEMPLATE - 1.*

Headings   A = key topic   B = where in the book

C = main ideas   D = order to read.

(Complete D at the end of Step 3)

Step 3   Survey (as applicable to this book)

INDEX: p 379
CONTENTS: p XVIII

- Use the *INDEX* and *CONTENTS* of the book to find sections of the book that cover the topics you want to find out about.
- Scan the book for useful indications of important material, such as headings, words in bold or italic; scan graphs and other visual material.
- Cover all the topics you have identified in the key ideas list.
- Have a quick look at each section to gather its main ideas.
- Write in column D the order in which you would like to read the various sections.

Surveying other books

Some books don't have an index or contents list. You can use chapter headings. You may have to use introductions and conclusions to chapters. You may have to scan the beginnings of paragraphs every few pages.

Surveying can be used with any source of information. It can be extended to work with several sources at the same time. Column B would then be headed: Source, and where in the source. Or you could use the *B7 - RECORDING TEMPLATE - 3.*

TEMPLATES

6 Recording as you scan

Scanning a section: you can randomly move through a section deciding roughly what it is about. You don't try to understand the ideas.

Several times in this book you are recommended to scan several sections to find material and ideas that are relevant to you.

It is frustrating to see something interesting or useful and not be able to find it again.

TEMPLATE: A1 - JOTTING DOWN AS YOU SCAN allows you to make brief comments as you scan.

If you want to write more, and a landscape page would suit you better, use *B5 - RECORDING TEMPLATE - 1*.

The headings would be:

A = Source and page   B = Section/ Keywords

C = What is interesting   D = Priority.

Drawing a line after each entry can help to separate the ideas that you want to record.

TEMPLATES

7   Monitoring progress

It's really useful and encouraging to see how well you are doing. It's useful to see anything that isn't working so well, because then you can do something about it.

You might want to see:

> your progress with a skill
>
> knowledge you are gaining
>
> how a situation is developing
>
> how you are managing a task
>
> other ... the list is not exhaustive.

You can collect the information by any means that suits you:

notes	on paper or electronic device
voice recordings	art work.

Use the ideas below, in *USING TEMPLATES ON THE WEBSITE*, to help you decide what to record and how to label or annotate your information. You want to remember the key ideas and your reflections so that you can use them again later.

You can gather the information together by category, e.g. keep all the information about situations together.

Using the templates on the website

If you collect information using the *TEMPLATES: B3 - COMPARE EXPECTATIONS AND REALITY* and *B4 - ACTION, RESULT AND NEXT STEP*, you can use the last columns, *Comment* and *Next Step* respectively, to reflect on your progress and anything you want to change.

The *TEMPLATE: B11 - MONITORING PROGRESS* has 5 columns.

1	= date
2	= focus of interest
3	= current state of play
4	= last application
5	= reflection.

Comments about the columns:

1   It is almost always useful to have the date recorded.
2   A few words that capture what you want to monitor.
3   Record your summary of how far you have progressed.
4   Describe what happened when you tried out your progress to date.
5   Reflect on your progress; maybe think about the next step; anyone you could usefully consult; anything that will bring further progress or satisfaction.

TEMPLATES

TEMPLATES

References

Series: *Living Confidently with Specific Learning Difficulties (SpLDs)*
Stacey, Ginny, 2020a, *Organisation and Everyday Life with Dyslexia and other SpLDs*, Routledge, London
Stacey, Ginny, 2020b, *Development of Dyslexia and other SpLDs*, Routledge, London
Stacey, Ginny, 2021a, *Finding Your Voice with Dyslexia and other SpLDs*, Routledge, London
Stacey, Ginny, 2021b, *Gaining Knowledge and Skills with Dyslexia and other SpLDs*, Routledge, London

Website information

Series website: www.routledge.com/cw/stacey

Appendix 2:
Individual, Personal Profile of Dyslexia/ SpLD
and
Regime for Managing Dyslexia/ SpLD

Contents

Series: *Living Confidently with Specific Learning Difficulties (SpLDs)*

Book 1: *Finding Your Voice with Dyslexia and other SpLDs*

Book 2: *Organisation and Everyday Life with Dyslexia and other SpLDs*

Book 3: *Gaining Knowledge and Skills with Dyslexia and other SpLDs*

Book 4: *Development of Dyslexia and other SpLDs*

Stacey (2020a, 2020b, 2021a, 2021b)

Templates on the website

1   Living confidently

The aim of the whole series *LIVING CONFIDENTLY WITH SPECIFIC LEARNING DIFFICULTIES (SPLDS)* is that, as a dyslexic/ SpLD person, you have ownership of your dyslexia/ SpLD; therefore this appendix is addressed to you and is essentially the same throughout the series.

2   Building up insights

The table shows the overlap between the elements of your individual profile and your regime for managing dyslexia/ SpLD. It also shows the key way for developing and testing each element.

Element	Individual, personal profile	Regime for managing dyslexia/ SpLD	For developing and testing processes	Covered in book (or see Appendix 3 for summaries)	Page
Thinking preferences	1	3	recall & check	1	188
Pausing	2	2	practise & reflect	1	254
Pitfalls	3	1	observe & reflect	2 & 4 partly in 1	69
Accommodation	4		negotiate, use and reflect	2, 3 & 4 partly in 1	71
Goals		4	via applications	3 partly in 1	78

The aim is to build up the insights into a *TOOL BOX FOR LIVING CONFIDENTLY*. The tool box will develop and expand over time, see *UPDATING THE TOOL BOX*.

If you keep your records in a way that you can easily review, you will build on your insights in an effective way. You will be able to use them and discuss them with others.

B1 - *COLLECTING IDEAS THAT RELATE TO YOU - TEMPLATE*

Collect the stories, insights, examples, etc. from the book that relate to you. Collect what happens when you try any of the exercises.

To fill in the 4th column, write 'profile' or 'regime/ managing'.
Use the elements in the table above to fill in the 5th column.
It is then easy to scan these two columns to bring your insights together.

TOOL BOX FOR LIVING CONFIDENTLY: p 319

UPDATING THE TOOL BOX: p 322

TEMPLATES

Look at the layout for the summary templates:

TEMPLATES

> D3 - REGIME FOR MANAGING DYSLEXIA/ SPLD (SPATIAL)
>
> C1 - INDIVIDUAL, PERSONAL PROFILE OF DYSLEXIA/ SPLD (SPATIAL)
>
> E2 - TABLE OF THINKING PREFERENCES
>
> D4 - REGIME FOR MANAGING DYSLEXIA/ SPLD (LINEAR)
>
> C3 - INDIVIDUAL, PERSONAL PROFILE OF DYSLEXIA/ SPLD (LINEAR)

Which do you think will suit you best?

Which do you think would be worth trying out?

You can use them as soon as you start gathering insights. They may well change as further insights are gained.

Observe and reflect

Templates that can be used for gathering insights are:

TEMPLATES

> B2 - KNOW YOUR OWN MIND
>
> B7, B8 - RECORDING TEMPLATES - 3 OR - 4
>
> D1 - MANAGING DYSLEXIA/ SPLD (MIND MAP)
>
> D2 - MANAGING DYSLEXIA/ SPLD (LINEAR)

Suggestions for headings for the RECORDING TEMPLATES - 3 OR - 4 are:

A = date   B = situation   C = what I was trying to do

D = details, including strategies being used

E = notes on success or otherwise.

Column E could either be narrow for a single word that rated your success or it could be wider for more detailed notes. Choose the template depending on whether you want column E to be narrow or wide.

E4, E5 - THINKING PREFERENCES, one spatial, one linear, are two useful TEMPLATES for recording brief notes as you build your profile.

TEMPLATES

Appendix 2   Profile and Regime

Examples from a log book

A log book is another way of recording incidents and reflections. You can pull the insights together by using key words in columns down the edges of the pages. You gradually have confidence in your insights because you have experience and evidence, which you are recording in a systematic way.

These notes were taken over several weeks while observing behaviour patterns:

MARGIN NOTE:
I usually shorten my headings to fit the columns
e.g. Th-Pref for Thinking Preferences

Date	Details	Other	Pitfall	Th-Pref (Thinking Preference)
DD/ MM/ YY	Total absorption in what's current in my mind – nothing rings any bells to warn me that something else needs attention. (Example) Focusing on writing reports before a deadline meant I missed an evening class		frequent problem	
DD/ MM/ YY	Can't remember from top of stairs to bottom that I need to add something to the shopping list. Crossing my fingers at top of stairs will remind me at the bottom that I have to remember something (that's enough to remember what to add).		poor short-term memory	kinaesthetic
DD/ MM/ YY	A friend explained the mechanism of blood circulation and capillary healing; now I know how to look after my ankle injury. I had forgotten the list of instructions. When there is no logic behind information, I forget what I'm told; or I modify half-remembered instructions by trying to make sense of incomplete information.		poor short-term memory	logic needed

Date	Details	Other	Pitfall	Th-Pref (Thinking Preference)
DD/ MM/ YY	Total confusion in my paperwork. If it isn't organised and doesn't stay organised, I've had it. I won't remember where any relevant other pieces of information are; I won't remember if it exists. Not having a printer in this room is causing major problems. I can't multi-task when paper is involved.		reading problem & recall	
DD/ MM/ YY	After I've been reading black-on-white intently for a while, my vision has the black print lines across it. Bright images also leave a strong imprint.	eyes: after images		

3 The tool box for living confidently

If you consistently work through the ideas in this book and build a picture of how you think well, how you take-action well and how you manage your dyslexia/ SpLD well, you will accumulate a body of knowledge and skills. You can summarise what you learn in three templates:

Ⓖ p 353: taking-action

> D3 - REGIME FOR MANAGING DYSLEXIA/ SPLD (SPATIAL)
>
> C1 - INDIVIDUAL, PERSONAL PROFILE OF DYSLEXIA/ SPLD (SPATIAL)
>
> E2 - TABLE OF THINKING PREFERENCES

TEMPLATES

or use the linear alternative templates:

> D4 - REGIME FOR MANAGING DYSLEXIA/ SPLD (LINEAR)
>
> C3 - INDIVIDUAL, PERSONAL PROFILE OF DYSLEXIA/ SPLD (LINEAR)

If some of the insights are more important than others, add this information to the summaries.

Make cross-references to any notes you have about the insights you put on the summaries. For example, you could have a log book entry which gives a good example of you using your kinaesthetic thinking. You list 'kinaesthetic' in your thinking preferences table with cross-reference '(log book, date)'.

You could also have:

> a collection of stories that reflect your experiences

> a log book or other systematic collection of evidence that you can easily access.

What you know about yourself will change and develop over time, which is the same for everyone. Any summary should be dated so that you know when it was the current one.

Even when nothing is causing you to update your tool box, it is worth reflecting on the whole tool box from time to time, to see whether any element needs to be developed further.

This accumulated knowledge and skills is your tool box for living confidently with your dyslexia/ SpLD.

You can use the *A3 - BOOKMARK – PROFILE AND TECHNIQUES* to record your profile and the techniques that help you. Then use the bookmark when you are reading to make sure you are doing everything possible to ease your reading.

TEMPLATES

Examples of insights of some other people are in *TEMPLATES*:

TEMPLATES

> *D5 - EXPERIENCES FOR MANAGING DYSLEXIA/ SPLD (LINEAR EXAMPLE)*

> *C2 - EXAMPLE: INDIVIDUAL, PERSONAL PROFILE OF DYSLEXIA/ SPLD (SPATIAL)*

> *C4 - 2 EXAMPLES OF INDIVIDUAL, PERSONAL PROFILES OF DYSLEXIA/ SPLD (LINEAR)*

> *E3 - EXAMPLE: TABLE OF THINKING PREFERENCES (SPATIAL)*

It can be useful to see what insights other people have gained.

General letter to employers

It might be possible and useful to have a general letter in your tool box from someone who has given you dyslexia/ SpLD support. These are extracts taken from a single page for a student (PG) with dyslexia. He had decided that he wanted any future employer to know he was dyslexic.

Example: Extracts from a letter to employers

To Whom It May Concern (with qualifications of author somewhere)

Re: PG and dyslexia in the workplace

Dyslexia
Short paragraph about dyslexia and giving a reference to a book that shows a positive approach to dyslexia.

Dyslexia in the Workplace
Short paragraph about management rather than cure of dyslexia and that suitable environment allows dyslexic people to be as effective as any others.

PG's choice of career
PG wants to work in pharmaceutical and medical marketing. PG has done a biology and chemistry degree at Y University. He has also discovered that he likes dealing with people and that he has appropriate, interpersonal skills. He has chosen pharmaceutical and medical marketing as a career because he will be able to use both his degree and his interpersonal skills.

Most of the time in this job, PG does not expect his dyslexia to hinder him. He may find certain electronic devices extremely useful, such as a voice recorder and an electronic organiser. The one task he may need to take extra care with is report-writing. He has found at university that he can deal with coursework assignments providing he leaves adequate time, does not work right up to the deadline and gets someone else to read his work before the final stage. He will need to use the same strategies for any report-writing at work.

Conclusion
A couple of sentences about dyslexics in general having intellectual strengths.
PG should be able to contribute his knowledge and thinking strengths to any employer provided his different ways of working are accommodated so that he can effectively manage his dyslexia.

4 Updating the tool box

Any time the tool box seems to be unhelpful:

- look after your confidence
- check you are pausing in ways that help you
- read (re-read) about fluctuations between the *4 LEVELS OF COMPENSATION*.

4 LEVELS OF COMPENSATION: p 342

Observe and reflect

Use any of the formats that have worked for you in building your tool box to find out what is undermining the management of your dyslexia/ SpLD and to develop any necessary new skills and knowledge.

In particular, the following could be table headings or arms of mind maps:

Date, situation	*Insights as to why the strategy didn't work
What I want to do	*What was going well
Strategy I thought would work	*Insights as to why the strategy worked
*What was going wrong	What to try next.

*In a table, I would combine these headings into one column, 'Details'. It would be wide enough to write quite a bit. I'd have a narrow column beside it which would categorise the details:

✓	or	OK
✓ ?		OK/ why?
x		not OK
x ?		not OK/ why?

Working in this way, you can find new insights about the contents of your tool box. You may simply be adding to it. You may find some of the insights you had were not as robust as you thought they were. You may be replacing them or developing them. You may find the source of your decreased management had nothing to do with the dyslexia/ SpLD. The processes set out here should help you to identify the root of the problem.

Tip: Adding new significant insights to the tool box

Whenever something significant comes to light:

- add it to the summaries

- date it.

Keep the stories that led to the new insight.
Make sure you can connect the summary to the stories.

Progress report

Progress reports can be useful.

- They can show you what you have achieved so far; they can demonstrate how those achievements have come about and what skills or capability you have.

- They can state the problems that remain.

- They can make the case for accommodations and continued support. They can contribute to updating the tool box.

- They should have a declared benefit, especially for you. The issues addressed need to be pertinent to you.

Example: Extracts from a progress report

Name XX - Progress report on dyslexia support tuition

This report outlines the progress that XX has made in study skills, and the support she is likely to need to complete her course successfully.

Five areas relevant to XX have been covered recently:

1) time management

2) organisation

3) reading and note-taking

4) essay-writing

5) exams stress control.

For example: Reading and note-taking

XX has learnt to read more effectively. She now scans contents lists and headings to get an overview and to find the sections of immediate relevance; she no longer works her way slowly through every word. She continues to have difficulty understanding some texts, and benefits from translating them with the help of pictures. For note-taking, she now uses mind maps. She still needs support to group notes by topic. She has developed various personal 'shorthand' symbols and also uses colour very effectively.

[Any significant comments about the other areas.]

General conclusion

XX has made considerable strides towards becoming a confident student, able to use appropriate strategies to overcome the range of difficulties caused by her dyslexia. She has become much more willing to try new approaches. Her results in a number of modules show that she has the potential to achieve a good degree.

5 Negotiating accommodation

It is fairly hard to negotiate accommodation for yourself. You may need to get someone, your advocate, who has been working with you or who knows you well, to put your case.

These are suggestions as to how to make the case for accommodation. The request might be in a formal letter or in an email from your advocate.

Ⓖ p 353: accommodation

The role and expertise of the advocate need to be stated, and the contact they have with you in relation to the case being made. If these details are already known, they could be excluded.

The advocate should:

Propose the requested accommodation directly and simply.

Explain the situation that prompts the request. Include any information about dyslexia/ SpLD that may be relevant.

Give any comparisons with the experiences of other people (if possible and useful).

Explain any solutions that you have tried in order to deal with the situation and why nothing has worked.

Give evidence of your capabilities (if not known to the person who would agree to the accommodation).

Re-state the request, possibly in greater detail.

End as fits the document being written.

Example request for accommodation

Situation: dyslexic mathematician receiving support at university, including:
notes taken by a fellow student at lectures;
a university department organising support;
a support tutor;
a system of feedback between support tutors and the university department.

It was necessary for the student to attend the lectures in order to be eligible to receive the notes from the note-taker.

Email request: with copy going to subject tutor

Dear [name of person, or person's job title],

Can XX opt out of lectures and still receive the notes from the
note-taker?

I had email contact with XX before the beginning of term and
then didn't hear from him. Last week I contacted him, asking
whether the silence meant everything was OK or whether he
was drowning. It was the latter.

He came to see me this morning. Last week he got so
demoralised that he was considering giving up the course.

He has 9 lectures a week and is getting nothing from them. He
has compared experiences with a couple of other students.
One doesn't understand the lectures either, but she gets
enough so that she is able to use the relevant sections to
help her complete the problem sheets. The other finds that
in the end everything falls into place, and that the maths
doesn't all have to make sense immediately.

XX doesn't work like this; as I mentioned in the feedback sheet
last term, he needs to understand everything as he goes, to
build up the whole subject, and he cannot make progress
when there are gaps in his knowledge. He has tried to use
the on-line handouts before lectures so that he has some
framework to listen with, but the lecturers don't follow the
handouts and XX can't work out quickly enough how the
lecture relates to the printed pages. Also, the handouts are
very wordy so trying to understand them takes XX a long
time. He records the lectures and finds that a bit useful. At
the moment XX is spending 9 hours at lectures without
understanding them, and is getting nowhere.

On Sunday he decided to go back to his preferred way of
working and he solidly worked through all the maths relating
to his problem sheets, making sure he understands
everything. He managed to get the problem sheets done,
albeit one was late.

He used the notes made by the note-taker. They are bullet points, succinct and clear. Just occasionally he has had to find extra information from the on-line lecture handouts. They are a very good resource for him.

We have worked on trying to find a solution to the problem of the lectures, but I am not very hopeful within the current situation; the lectures are really 9 hours that take time and destroy his motivation and morale.

Can XX receive the lecture notes if he doesn't go to the lectures? Is an understanding of the way he needs to work and of the problems he is having with the lectures sufficient evidence? Can receiving the notes without going to the lectures be accepted as suitable accommodation for his dyslexia?
Best wishes
Support Tutor

Result of this request

XX was allowed to have the notes from the official note-taker even though he didn't go to the lectures. He had a conversation with the subject tutor, which resulted in a radical change to the way he worked on his course. He finished his degree.

References

Stacey, Ginny, 2020a, *Organisation and Everyday Life with Dyslexia and other SpLDs*, Routledge, London

Stacey, Ginny, 2020b, *Development of Dyslexia and other SpLDs*, Routledge, London

Stacey, Ginny, 2021a, *Finding Your Voice with Dyslexia and other SpLDs*, Routledge, London

Stacey, Ginny, 2021b, *Gaining Knowledge and Skills with Dyslexia and other SpLDs*, Routledge, London

Website information

Series website: www.routledge.com/cw/stacey

Appendix 3:   Key Concepts

Contents

<table>
<tr><td colspan="2">

Series:
Living Confidently with Specific Learning Difficulties (SpLDs)

</td></tr>
</table>

Book 1		*Finding Your Voice with Dyslexia and other SpLDs* (Stacey 2021a)

Book 2		*Organisation and Everyday Life with Dyslexia and other SpLDs* (Stacey 2020a)

Book 3		*Gaining Knowledge and Skills with Dyslexia and other SpLDs* (Stacey 2021b)

Book 4		*Development of Dyslexia and other SpLDs* (Stacey 2020b)

Useful template on the website:

B1   COLLECTING IDEAS THAT RELATE TO YOU

TEMPLATES
COMPANION @ WEBSITE

Appendix 3   Key Concepts

Templates on the website

B1   *COLLECTING IDEAS THAT RELATE TO YOU*
E1   *LIST OF OPTIONS FOR THINKING PREFERENCES*

TEMPLATES

Context

The books in this series are written to be used individually, but people's lives can't be separated quite so neatly. In any situation, you may need information from more than one book.

THINKING PREFERENCES are highlighted in orange in this appendix.

This appendix has summaries of many of the skills and knowledge that I cover when going over all that is useful in managing dyslexia/ SpLD. It has been included to allow the books to be used individually.

The book that covers each key concept is indicated by the icons and the coloured lines in the *CONTENTS*, and the coloured lines on the left hand side of the text.

1   Thinking clearly (pausing)

INDIVIDUAL, PERSONAL PROFILE OF DYSLEXIA/ SPLD: p 64

Pausing is the second element in both your *INDIVIDUAL, PERSONAL PROFILE OF DYSLEXIA/ SPLD* and your *REGIME FOR MANAGING DYSLEXIA/ SPLD. Finding Your Voice with Dyslexia and other SpLDs* (Stacey, 2021a) discusses the benefits of thinking clearly and gives you several different methods for doing so.

REGIME FOR MANAGING DYSLEXIA/ SPLD: p 71

Stacey (2021a)

Thinking Clearly in *Finding Your Voice with Dyslexia and other SpLDs* also discusses confidence and self-esteem. Maintaining good levels in these two states of being is important.

You need to practise some of the methods for pausing in order to experience the benefits. As you work with the ideas in this series of books, you will be able to reflect on what is happening for you. You can add your insights to your *Profile* and *Regime*.

This section repeats 2 of the exercises from *Finding Your Voice with Dyslexia and other SpLDs*.

1.1   Breathing

If you switch on good breathing, you switch off panic, anxiety and many other unhelpful emotional states.   Focusing on your breathing allows you mental space to stop and step back from the immediate situation.

Tip: CAUTION

If you feel dizzy, get up and walk about, or hold your breath for a count of 10. Dizziness, from poor breathing, is caused by too much oxygen and you need to use it up by walking about or to retain CO_2 by holding your breath for a while.

If you carry a lot of tension in your body, you may find it more useful to work through the relaxation *EXERCISE: PHYSICAL RELAXATION* before attempting the following exercise.

EXERCISE: PHYSICAL RELAXATION: p 333

Exercise: Breathing

First, see the *TIP: CAUTION* above.

During the exercise, as you breathe in you feel the sensations in different parts of your body; as you breathe out you let go of the sensations. You can imagine the out-breath flowing easily into each part of the body.

Sit comfortably and close your eyes.
　　　　Breathe naturally while doing the exercise.
As you breathe in[1],

　　feel the sensations in your:

face	and let go
neck and shoulders	and let go
arms and chest	and let go
stomach	and let go
buttocks and legs	and let go
whole body	and let it relax further

Repeat the cycle several times.

RECORDINGS:

1.2   Relaxation

Being able to deliberately stop and relax is another way to give yourself the opportunity to pause well. Relaxation, however you do it, allows you to focus on the here and now and to step back from any situation that requires you to manage your dyslexia/ SpLD.

---

[1] When I lead this exercise, I usually say "As you breathe in" just once.
I say "feel the sensations in your (*name the part of the body*)" for at least the first cycle.
When it feels right, I just say the part of the body and "and let go".

Exercise: Physical relaxation

Sit comfortably and close your eyes.

Tighten the muscles	of your face	and let go
"	of your neck and shoulders	"
"	of your arms, clench your hands	"
"	of your chest	"
"	of your stomach	"
"	of your buttocks and legs	"

Tighten your whole body and let go.

Repeat this cycle several times.

RECORDINGS:

2   Using the mind well

Using the Mind Well is a chapter in *Finding Your Voice with Dyslexia and other SpLDs* (Stacey, 2021a) which discusses many techniques and skills for thinking. A selection of the techniques is summarised here.

Stacey (2021a)

2.1   Mind set

If your mind is expecting a particular subject, it is able to handle relevant information more effectively.

Take about 5 minutes to switch your brain onto the subject you are about to deal with. Recall to mind what you already know or what your most pressing questions are.

2.2   Chunking

Working memory stores information more effectively when it is linked together in some way that makes sense to you. The packages of linked information are known as 'chunks'.

Ⓖ p 353: chunking, working memory

Deliberately notice the links between pieces of information, or create your own links if necessary, or if you prefer. The process of making links is known as 'chunking'.

2.3   Recall and check

You strengthen your memory of information, knowledge or skills by recalling what you know and then checking against a reliable source. Re-reading material is not nearly as effective.

2.4   Memory consolidation

Your memories of knowledge are made much more permanent by having a pattern of repeated recall and check. You start by recalling your knowledge the next day, then after a week, then after a month, then after 6 months.

Done efficiently, memory consolidation is an extremely effective strategy.

The same memory consolidation is required for memories of skills. 'Little and often' is a better time scale for skills.

2.5   Concentration

Concentration is often a problem for dyslexic/ SpLD people. As you observe the way you do things more precisely, you should look out for those places, times and conditions when you can concentrate easily. Gradually build up your knowledge of the things that help you and see how you can use them when you find concentration difficult.

2.6   Metacognition

Metacognition is the awareness of the fact that you are doing or thinking something; it is not awareness of how or why. Just by noticing what is happening as you manage your dyslexia/ SpLD you will be developing the skill of metacognition. Be positive about the things you notice: enjoy those things you do well; find ways that enable you to be positive about anything you don't do so well.

2.7   Objective observation

Ⓖ p 353: objective

Observation is most effective when it is objective. If you keep factual records and reduce any emotional aspect to a minimum, the way forward with anything you want to change will be clearer.

2.8   Reflection

Once you have collected some observations on a common theme, you can look at them all together and see what sense to make of the whole group together. This is the skill of reflection, which is helpful in making decisions.

2.9   Prioritising

PRIORITISING: p 304

PRIORITISING is also a skill for using the mind well. It is a section in *APPENDIX 1*.

2.10   A model of learning

There are various stages in learning when you need to pay attention to how you are processing information, these are:

Input: any time new information is given.

Immediate use: very shortly after input.

Feedback loop: when what is being learnt is checked against what is intended to be learnt.

Recall: information is brought back from memory some time after input.

Direct use: information and skills are used exactly as they were given.

Developed use: knowledge and skills are modified in some way.

Long-term memory: knowledge and skills are established in long-term memory, and can be recalled.

Understanding: an appreciation of significant concepts has taken place.

You might use different ways of thinking:

- for each stage of a task
- for different tasks
- at different times for any particular task.

You need to experiment to find out what works for you. You will often have to be quite determined about what's right for you, and not let others persuade you to adopt ways that you know don't suit you so well.

3 Thinking preferences

THINKING PREFERENCES are part of both the *PROFILE* and *REGIME* (Stacey, 2021a). They are often key to a dyslexic/ SpLD person being able to function well. Often in this series there is a section on *THINKING PREFERENCES*.

It is unusual for people to pay attention to how they think, so the usual – orthodox – approach is to ignore how anyone is thinking. These thinking preferences can be seen as unorthodox simply because they are outside the orthodox approach.

The *TEMPLATE: E1 - LIST OF OPTIONS FOR THINKING PREFERENCES* has suggestions for using the different preferences.

One way to find out about your *THINKING PREFERENCES* is to use *RECALL AND CHECK*, together with *MEMORY CONSOLIDATION*; then to reflect on your ways of thinking.

Make sure you know what your preferences are and that you have the confidence to use them.

Attention is often given to visual and verbal aspects of communication and education. The same attention should be given to kinaesthetic processing and to the *RATIONALE OR FRAMEWORK*. If kinaesthetic processing and the need for a framework are part of your thinking preferences, do find ways to make sure these needs are met.

3.1 Sense-based: visual, verbal and kinaesthetic

The five physical senses are vision, hearing, taste, smell and kinaesthesia. The use of taste and smell to help use information is not covered in this series, although they are important for some people.

Kinaesthesia is used as an umbrella term for the physical senses, touch, position and movement. The term also includes experiences that are primarily remembered through a connection with the physical part of the experience.

The visual thinking preference uses spatial awareness and other visual patterns to process thinking.

Stacey (2021a)

INDIVIDUAL, PERSONAL PROFILE OF DYSLEXIA/ SPLD: p 64

REGIME FOR MANAGING DYSLEXIA/ SPLD: p 71

TEMPLATES

RECALL AND CHECK: p 62

MEMORY CONSOLIDATION: p 160

RATIONALE OR FRAMEWORK: p 216

ⓖ p 353: kinaesthesia

See *INDEX* for examples in this book.

The **verbal** thinking preference uses language and words to process thinking.

The **kinaesthetic** thinking preference uses the kinaesthetic sense as the basis for thinking processes.

See *INDEX* for examples in this book.

To facilitate discussion of kinaesthetic thinking processes, 'doing' and 'taking-action' are used for acquiring and applying knowledge and skills, in parallel with reading, writing, listening and talking:

Acquiring	Applying
Reading	Writing
Listening	Talking
Doing	Taking-action

3.2   Rationale or framework

Some dyslexic/ SpLD people do not keep hold of information or understanding if they don't know what the overall rationale or framework is. Their minds don't retain the seemingly random information long enough for the framework to emerge; it has to be given in advance.

Ⓖ p 353: rationale, framework

3.3   Holistic vs. linear

'Holistic thinking is happening when a large area of a topic is held in the mind and processed simultaneously. An example is when you look at a scene in front of you, you see that scene as a whole. This type of thinking doesn't involve words, but you are definitely thinking.' (Stacey, 2021a)

Stacey (2021a)

'Linear thinking involves analysing and breaking topics into their component parts. Linear thinking is thought to be localised to definite areas for specific tasks, whereas holistic thinking is diffused over larger areas.' (Stacey, 2021a)

3.4   Motivation

Two schemes for looking at individual differences between people are used in *Finding Your Voice with Dyslexia and other SpLDs* (Stacey, 2021a):

Stacey (2021a)

Myers-Briggs Personality Type

Multiple Intelligences.

In the context of this appendix, the most interesting characteristics from both schemes are the motivations that people have, and which some dyslexic/ SpLD people can use to help themselves think well.

3.4.1   Myers-Briggs Personality Type (MBPT)

The Myers-Briggs scheme is based on 4 mental functions and 4 attitudes. The scheme characterises people as:

MARGIN NOTE:
Judging is used in the sense of being able to make decisions, not in judging right or wrong.

4 mental functions:	*4 attitudes:*
sensing	extroverted
intuiting	introverted
thinking	perceiving
feeling	judging (deciding).

The motivations of the different types come from their approach to the world around them.

Mental functions

- **Sensing** people are practical, pay attention to the here-and-now, like practical skills and learning with their hands.

- **Intuiting** people focus on concepts, ideas and plans.

- **Thinking** people tend to be logical, to like structures and organisation.

- **Feeling** people engage with people dynamics and feelings.

Attitudes

- **Extroverted** people sort out their ideas with the people and environment around them.

- **Introverted** people sort out most of their ideas on their own, before engaging with anyone else.

- **Perceiving** people like to carry on gathering information.

- **Judging** people like to come to a decision.

3.4.2   Multiple Intelligences (MI)

The Multiple Intelligences scheme includes 8 different, independent intelligences. Most of the intelligences have overlap with the Myers-Briggs system, as far as motivation is concerned, so I don't use them. However there is one intelligence that is distinct and worth noting.

The **Naturalist Intelligence** involves accurate observation of the world around. People skilled with this intelligence are able to see parallels between topics or within a group of objects. They are able to classify ideas or objects and they instinctively sort information into categories.

3.5 'Other'

The list of thinking preferences has grown as I have worked with dyslexic/ SpLD people and tried to make sense of what happens to or for them. There was no point in trying to make them fit already known patterns, so I have always worked with a category titled 'Other'.

'Other' is a holding category that allows you to keep hold of experiences that don't fit any category you already know.

---

4   Useful approaches

You will be managing your dyslexia/ SpLD during everyday events and while you tackle tasks. *Organisation and Everyday Life with Dyslexia and other SpLDs* and *Gaining Knowledge and Skills with Dyslexia and other SpLDs* deal with the practical application of using your PROFILE and REGIME. The approaches summarised here are those that help you make a good start with most tasks.

Stacey (2020a, 2021b)

4.1 Materials and methods

For many situations or tasks, you will want to collect information together. You should find out your best way of doing it. The options depend on how you think best.

Materials include: paper, recording device, computer; using colour; using pen or pencil with a suitable grip. You need to think how you manage your materials, e.g. being able to spread out can make a significant difference.

Methods include: making lists (**linear** thinkers); mind maps (**holistic** thinkers); doing for yourself (**kinaesthetic** thinkers); bouncing ideas off other people (Myers-Briggs **feeling**, **extroverted** people).

When something is working well for you, notice what you are using and how you are doing it.

4.2   Model for developing organisation

The model puts forward 5 steps that need attention in organisation:

Step 1   gather strengths

Step 2   assess hazards

Step 3   describe what needs organising

Step 4   recognise insuperable obstacles

Step 5   develop constructive ways forward.

Ⓖ p 353:
hazard, obstacle

By changing the text at step 3, this model can be adapted to work with different situations or tasks when no organisation is required.

As you work with the tasks and situations, record what happens for you. Have a system so that you can see what is working for you and you can deliberately make the progress you want.

4.3   Comprehension

To comprehend something is to have a mental grasp of it.

You need your mind to hold information together and for long enough so that you can understand, comprehend, what it is all about.

All the skills in this appendix will help with comprehension. Observe how you comprehend (understand) anything. Keep records so that you can reflect on your experience over time. Explore different approaches until you find the ones that work best for you.

4.4   Key words

Key words are the words that hold the essence of
          an idea, a paragraph, a subject ...

Take something that you are very familiar with. Jot down some words that are most important for describing it. Cut the number of words down and find the fewest words that you feel comfortable with. These words should be the key words of your chosen topic. Repeat the exercise over time, until you are good at producing a minimum collection of words to hold the essence of a subject.

When you can work well with key words, you can use them to give an overview of something or to help you sort out a main theme from minor details.

4.5   Know your goal

Knowing your goal is the 4th element of your *REGIME FOR MANAGING DYSLEXIA/ SPLD*. Quite often, when you are using *MENTAL ENERGY TO MANAGE DYSLEXIA/ SPLD*, you can do all the right things:

- observing what is happening

- pausing well

- deciding how to use your thinking preferences

but you still can't get matters under control and you still find yourself struggling in a circle.

Knowing what you want to achieve can help you to see the way out, or the way to resolve the situation.

Key words can help with knowing your goal. Learning how to hold your goal in a few key words means it is much easier to stay focused and not get lost in a maze of ideas.

REGIME FOR MANAGING DYSLEXIA/ SPLD: p 71

MENTAL ENERGY TO MANAGE DYSLEXIA/ SPLD: p 72

4.6   Planning

Planning is when you consider all the steps necessary to achieve a given outcome.

Almost all dyslexic/ SpLD people need to plan their work in order to minimise problems; for example, dyslexic people often write well when they have a good plan, but without a plan their writing will rarely reflect their ideas.

You need to find the level of detail that yields the result you want.

A big project can be broken down into smaller sections and separate plans constructed to achieve each section. This process makes the big plan less daunting and allows you to tackle it more readily.

5   Aspects of dyslexia/ SpLD

You need to stay confident and positive in order to manage dyslexia/ SpLD. The aspects summarised here help you to know more about the characteristics of dyslexia/ SpLD so you are prepared for the inevitable fluctuations; the full discussions are in *Development of Dyslexia and other SpLDs* (Stacey, 2020b).

Stacey (2020b)

5.1   Learned confusion

As a dyslexic/ SpLD person develops, certain patterns of confusion tend to become established in your brain, see *USEFUL PREFACE CONTEXT*. When you are older, you probably learn in better ways but you don't erase the original confused ways; they remain in your brain. They are there for your brain to activate.

USEFUL PREFACE CONTEXT: p 3

5.2   Oldest memory trace

When you unexpectedly need to think of something it is often the oldest memory trace that is used, not a later one. For example, you have learnt correct spellings, but when you use the words the older incorrect versions spring to mind.

5.3   Attention to learning

Most dyslexic/ SpLD people have to pay attention to all levels of a task; they do not learn subliminally. Reading a large number of books does not teach spelling.

Ⓖ p 353: subliminal learning

5.4   Average level of language skills a disadvantage

Intelligent students are often first recognised as being dyslexic/ SpLD at college or university, when they can no longer find ways round underlying problems. They have language skills that lift them above the group who are recognised as being in need of extra help at school, but those skills are not at the level of overall intelligence and the difference makes its mark in Higher Education.

5.5   4 levels of compensation

As you work on managing dyslexia/ SpLD, you gain skills and you become a 'compensated' dyslexic/ SpLD (McLoughlin et al., 2001).

McLoughlin et al. (2001)

There are different levels of compensation:

1   'People at level 1 are not aware of their weaknesses and have developed no strategies to overcome them.

2   'Those at level 2 are aware of their weaknesses but have not developed strategies to overcome them.

3   'People at level 3 are aware of their weaknesses and have developed compensatory strategies, but have developed them unconsciously.

4   'Finally, people at level 4 are aware of their weaknesses and they have consciously developed strategies to overcome them.'

The most important aspect is to realise that you do not remain consistently on any particular level. Even when you mostly operate as a 'compensated' dyslexic/ SpLD, i.e. on level 4, you may find you have dropped back into one of the less compensated ways of managing.

5.6   Pitfalls

('pitfall, n.4(b)', OED Online, 2020)

Gradually as you learn to manage your dyslexia/ SpLD, you will recognise certain things that often tip you into dyslexic/ SpLD functioning: these things are called pitfalls in the context of these books.

A pitfall is defined as 'a hidden or unsuspected danger, drawback, difficulty or opportunity for error' (OED Online, 2020).

I've divided pitfalls into 'hazards' and 'obstacles'. I've used the term 'glitch' for those moments when you notice a potential pitfall and deal with it immediately.

Ⓖ p 353: hazard, obstacle, glitch

5.7   Accommodation

Accommodations are adaptations put in place to address or reduce the problems caused by dyslexia/ SpLD; sometimes called 'reasonable adjustments' or 'provisions'.

There are certain situations in which a PITFALL of your dyslexia/ SpLD is very likely to be a significant issue, and it is known in advance. For some of these situations, e.g. exams and tests, accommodations are well established. Other situations may be specific to your circumstances.

5.8   Degrees of severity

Dyslexia/ SpLD is not like short- or long-sightedness: there is no equivalent pair of glasses that you can put on and find that the problems are reliably sorted. Learning 'coping strategies' gives you ways of dealing with issues, but you will constantly have to be putting effort into doing so.

I argue that 'degrees of severity' is not a useful concept. The statements usually used are that someone is 'mildly dyslexic/ SpLD' or 'severely dyslexic/ SpLD' as if this describes a static level of being dyslexic/ SpLD. The lived experience of dyslexia/ SpLD is that how you will be is variable and unpredictable.

It would be more useful to talk in terms of McLoughlin's 4 compensation levels (McLoughlin et al., 2001). For each person:

> What does level 4 consist of?
>
> How well can the person maintain level 4?
>
> How often does the person get triggered out of level 4?
>
> How much time and effort are required to get back to level 4?

4 LEVELS OF COMPENSATION: p 342

McLoughlin et al. (2001)

5.9   Stress

Stress usually makes the problems of dyslexia/ SpLD worse. You and those around you need to recognise this.

5.10   Benefits of recognising the problems

It is very difficult to do anything about problems that are not being recognised. When you know what your strengths are, and you realise you can make useful contributions, it is easier to acknowledge the problems and discuss them fruitfully with those around you.

References

McLoughlin, David, et al., 2001, *Adult Dyslexia: Assessment, Counselling and Training,* Whurr, London, 6th re-print
Series: *Living Confidently with Specific Learning Difficulties (SpLDs)*
Stacey, Ginny, 2020a, *Organisation and Everyday Life with Dyslexia and other SpLDs*, Routledge, London

Stacey, Ginny, 2020b, *Development of Dyslexia and other SpLDs,*
     Routledge, London
Stacey, Ginny, 2021a, *Finding Your Voice with Dyslexia and other
     SpLDs*, Routledge, London
Stacey, Ginny, 2021b, *Gaining Knowledge and Skills with Dyslexia and
     other SpLDs*, Routledge, London

Website information

OED Online, December 2020, Oxford University Press. Accessed 15
     February 2021.
Series website: www.routledge.com/cw/stacey

Appendix 4:   Group Work

Contents

1 Context

In the rest of the book, 'you' addresses an individual dyslexic/ SpLD reader. This appendix contains a resource for group leaders, support people and others, so 'you' addresses someone alongside dyslexic/ SpLD people.

2 Activities to explore Myers-Briggs Personality Type (MBPT)

MYERS-BRIGGS PERSONALITY TYPE: p 227

I found it worked well to explore the mental functions together in one activity and the attitudes together in a separate activity. Working with groups of people usually shows the differences within each category. It helps people to appreciate what they bring to a situation themselves and to see the value of other people's contributions. It helps people to recognise different approaches. The teaching on its own doesn't have the same impact.

While teaching about MBPT, I never told the groups I worked with what activity they would be doing, merely that they would be doing something that involved them using the next section of teaching. If I gave them the activity too early, they would just start thinking about it. Knowing they would be asked to use some part of the following teaching has the effect of allowing them to listen with a purpose.

Mental functions

1 Explain the mental functions of MBPT (without including the motivation from each).

2 Divide your group into subgroups of 4-8 people.

3 Assign one of the mental functions to each group.
  It also works to assign pairs of mental functions, making sure the combinations have one perceiving and one judging[1] (deciding) function.

4 Then give them a task to do using the characteristics assigned to the group; ask them to be prepared to tell the wider group how they would do the task. Allow them to act/ write/ draw as well as talk during their discussion.
  Possible tasks would be any that have no set structure to follow,
  e.g. organising and preparing for:
      either some task that is relevant to the individual group
      or a party, a trip, a holiday, an outing.

  Each group needs to have exactly the same task so that the activity highlights the impacts of the different mental functions.

5 After sufficient time, let each group describe how they would do the task set. If possible, write up the essence of the descriptions.

Motivation, from mental functions, included

6 Teach about the motivations that each mental function gives.

7 Keep the groups the same as before. Ask each group to discuss how the motivations from their assigned mental function(s) had an impact on how they decided to do the task.

8 Repeat step 5 above.

---

[1] Judging in the context of Myers-Briggs Personality Type is the process of making decisions; it is not about judging success or failure, good or bad, etc. I think this distinction is so important that I have put 'deciding' in brackets whenever 'Judging' is mentioned.

Appendix 4   Group Work

MBPT attitudes

1   Teach about the attitudes, or re-cap them if they have been introduced while discussing the mental functions.

2   Divide your group into subgroups of 4-8 people.

3   The task is to decide how the members of each group are going to act as a team on a project. This time the projects can differ from one group to another. In their discussion, each person needs to pay attention to the different MBPT attitudes. Discussion can again involve acting, drawing or writing.

Projects:

○   People in a group may already be working together before learning about MBPT. In this case, you could ask them to come to the session with a set of questions about that work. The MBPT project is then to decide how they will act as a team to research the answers to the questions.

○   When people are not working together outside the MBPT session, you can ask them to decide how they will act as a team to make progress on a local issue, an issue in the news, understanding a different country or culture, or any other project of your choosing.

One of the elements of this activity is to find how to keep to the task, which is to organise themselves as a team and to bear in mind the MBPT attitudes. They should not be working on the project itself. If possible, display the activity question: How do you as a team organise yourselves on the project given?

4   After sufficient time, let each group describe how they would organise themselves into a team, and how they made use of the MBPT attitudes.

Questionnaires for MBPT

I use a questionnaire from *People Types and Tiger Stripes* (Lawrence, 1993). At some point I suggest groups answer the questionnaire while thinking about any learning or situations that are new for them.

Lawrence (1993)

References

Lawrence, Gordon, 1993, *People Types and Tiger Stripes,* Centre for Applications of Psychological Types, Gainsville, FL, 3rd ed.

Glossary

Contents

1 Table: Symbols

Symbol	Explanation
§	Symbol used to denote a section.
Ⓖ	Symbol used to indicate an entry in the GLOSSARY. The page number is to the beginning of the appropriate section of the glossary.
COMPANION @ WEBSITE	The symbol signifies material on the companion website, www.routledge.com/cw/stacey. The section of the website is indicated.
Book icon and blue line	Used in Useful Preface to show text that is significantly different from one book to another.
Chapter icon and yellow line	In Chapter 2, there are sections marked as being significantly important for dyslexic/ SpLD people. In Chapter 5, a section is marked that summarises four issues that can be important for dyslexic/ SpLD people.

2 Table: Specific Learning Difficulties (SpLDs) descriptions

Dyslexia/ SpLD is used in most of this book because dyslexia is the most researched and recognised form of SpLD and because the dual term keeps the variations in mind.

SpLD	Definitions from DfES Report (2005)
Dyslexia	'Dyslexia is a combination of abilities and difficulties; the difficulties affect the learning process in aspects of literacy and sometimes numeracy. Coping with required reading is generally seen as the biggest challenge at Higher Education level due in part to difficulty in skimming and scanning written material. A student may also have an inability to express his/her ideas clearly in written form and in a style appropriate to the level of study. Marked and persistent weaknesses may be identified in working memory, speed of processing, sequencing skills, auditory and/or visual perception, spoken language and motor skills. Visuo-spatial skills, creative thinking and intuitive understanding are less likely to be impaired and indeed may be outstanding. Enabling or assistive technology is often found to be very beneficial.'
Dyspraxia / Developmental Co-ordination Disorder (DCD)	'A student with dyspraxia/ DCD may have an impairment or immaturity in the organisation of movement, often appearing clumsy. Gross motor skills (related to balance and co-ordination) and fine motor skills (relating to manipulation of objects) are hard to learn and difficult to retain and generalise. Writing is particularly laborious and keyboard skills difficult to acquire. Individuals may have difficulty organising ideas and concepts. Pronunciation may also be affected and people with dyspraxia/DCD may be over/under sensitive to noise, light and touch. They may have poor awareness of body position and misread social cues in addition to those shared characteristics common to many SpLDs.'
Dyscalculia	'Dyscalculia is a learning difficulty involving the most basic aspect of arithmetical skills. The difficulty lies in the reception, comprehension, or production of quantitative and spatial information. Students with dyscalculia may have difficulty in understanding simple number concepts, lack an intuitive grasp of numbers and have problems learning number facts and procedures. These can relate to basic concepts such as telling the time, calculating prices, handling change.'

Glossary

SpLD	Definitions from DfES Report (2005)
Attention Deficit Disorder ADD AD(H)D reflects the first sentence in the description	'Attention Deficit Disorder (ADD) exists with or without hyperactivity. In most cases people with this disorder are often 'off task', have particular difficulty commencing and switching tasks, together with a very short attention span and high levels of distractibility. They may fail to make effective use of the feedback they receive and have weak listening skills. Those with hyperactivity may act impulsively and erratically, have difficulty foreseeing outcomes, fail to plan ahead and be noticeably restless and fidgety. Those without the hyperactive trait tend to daydream excessively, lose track of what they are doing and fail to engage in their studies unless they are highly motivated. The behaviour of people with ADD can be inappropriate and unpredictable; this, together with the characteristics common to many SpLDs, can present a further barrier to learning.'

3 Table: Acronyms

Acronym	Explanation
ADD, ADHD, AD(H)D	Attention Deficit Disorder with or without Hyperactivity
DCD	Developmental Co-ordination Disorder
DfES	Department for Education and Skills
MBPT	Myers-Briggs Personality Type
MI	Multiple Intelligences
NLP	Neuro-Linguistic Programming
OED	Oxford English Dictionary
SAS	Supervisory Attentional System, part of Baddeley's model of Working Memory
SpLD	Specific Learning Difficulty

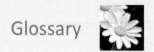

4 Table: Words and phrases, alphabetical list

Entry	Explanation
Accommodation	Accommodation refers to adaptations put in place to address or reduce the problems caused by dyslexia/ SpLD; sometimes called 'reasonable adjustments' or 'provisions'.
Autonomy autonomous	Control over your life by self-determination: acting and thinking for yourself; independent; free; self-governing. An autonomous person has autonomy.
Blueprint	Used in this book to refer to a set of notes against which you check your knowledge. More usually, it is the working instructions for a project.
Body See also LEVELS OF BEING	Used in contrast to mind and psyche, body is the physical nature of a person. The brain is included in the term 'body'.
Brain In contrast to MIND	Is the physical material: the structures of the brain, the neurons, the chemical reactions, etc. The brain is part of the body of a person.
Brainstorm	Collect all your ideas or thoughts about something; collect them in a concrete way, either on paper or on a whiteboard, etc., straight into a computer or using a recording device; the collection of ideas is then available for further processing. The initial stages of brainstorming are often not selective; all ideas are captured even if they don't seem very relevant.
Chaotic chaos theory	Chaos theory is a field of mathematics. 'Behaviour of a system which is governed by deterministic laws but is so unpredictable as to appear random owing to its extreme sensitivity to initial conditions' ('chaos, n.6' OED Online, 2020).

Glossary

Entry	Explanation
Chunk	A chunk is 'a package of information bound by strong associative links within a chunk, and relatively weak links between chunks' (Baddeley, 2007). The capacity of working memory is discussed in terms of chunks that can be stored.
Chunking	The process of making strong links between pieces of information so that more can be stored in chunks in working memory (Baddeley, 2007).
Concrete	Concrete in contrast to abstract: anything that has a physical reality. Abstract ideas are always in the mind; they do not have a physical presence. Concrete includes: people, animals, buildings, water, air. Abstract includes: happiness, self-confidence, theories, expectations.
Confidence	Assurance arising from reliance on oneself (OED, 1993).
Doing See also *KINAESTHESIA* and *SENSES*	In this series of books, 'doing' is used to refer to acquiring knowledge and skills using kinaesthetic thinking.
Focus of mind	The ability to bring your mind back to the selected topic rather than letting it wander following random associations.
Framework	A structure made of parts joined to form a frame; especially one designed to enclose or support; a frame; a skeleton ('framework, n.1a', OED Online, 2020).
Glitch	A sudden short-lived irregularity in behaviour ('glitch, n.a', OED Online, 2020). A glitch is a time when dyslexia/ SpLD has an effect on your behaviour, but you see it immediately and correct it. Any error is short-lived and there is no impact to prolong dyslexic/ SpLD functioning.

Entry	Explanation
Hazard	A hazard is a danger or a risk which you can take steps to deal with. 'Hazard' is used to describe one category of the pitfalls of dyslexia/ SpLD.
Kinaesthesia kinaesthetic See also *PROPRIOCEPTION* and *TAKING-ACTION*.	Used as an umbrella term for the physical senses (touch, body-sense, movement), by comparison with the visual sense or the hearing sense. The term also includes experiences that are primarily remembered through a connection with the physical part of the experience.
Levels of being See also *BODY* *BRAIN* *MIND* *PSYCHE*	Three levels of being are used in the series: mind, body and psyche, where body also includes brain. Mind, brain and psyche are difficult to separate into clearly defined entities. Apologies if I haven't always been clear, but this is how I think of them: Brain is the physical material: the structures of the brain, the neurons, the chemical reactions etc. Mind is the thinking processes: the products or results of what happens in the brain. Psyche is the complexity of thinking and emotions that contributes to an individual person's characteristics.
Long-term memory	Those parts of the brain/ mind that store information for an extended period of time, which can be many years.
Mind In contrast to *BRAIN* See also *LEVELS OF BEING*	There are many interpretations for mind in the OED. The one used in this book is the seat of awareness, thought, volition (will to act) and feeling (OED, 1993).

Glossary

Entry	Explanation
Mind map	To map ideas in an organised, spatial way, with relationships shown by linking lines or branch structures. Sometimes called a spider diagram.
Mind set	A process of switching your mind on to the topic you are about to work on: for study, for a meeting, for planning a project, etc. It is the equivalent of warm-up exercises before vigorous exercise. (Mindset as one word is something quite different.)
Mnemonics	Memorable phrases, words or sounds that help you to remember something. For example: Naughty Elephants Squirt Water gives the directions north, east, south and west round a compass or map; HONC gives the four most common elements in organic chemistry, hydrogen, oxygen, nitrogen and carbon.
Neural networks	Neural networks are established when neurons repeatedly fire in set patterns. These set patterns are related to learning.
Neuro-Linguistic Programming (NLP)	NLP is about the mind and how we organise our mental life; about language, how we use it and how it affects us; about repetitive sequences of behaviour and how to act with intention. Some of the ideas from NLP are used in THINKING CLEARLY (p 254). For further information, see O'Connor and McDermott (1996).
Neuron	A basic cell of the nervous system.
Neuron firing	A neuron fires a signal along its axon when the conditions in the neuron rise above a certain threshold; the conditions depend on all the many other neurons that input to that neuron.

Entry	Explanation
Objective vs. subjective	Objective: existing as an object of consciousness, as opposed to being part of the conscious [person]. (OED, 1993)
	Subjective: of or belonging to the thinking [person]; proceeding from or taking place within the individual's consciousness.
Obstacle	An obstacle is something that blocks your way or prevents progress; you have to go round it, or avoid it. 'Obstacle' is used to describe one category of the pitfalls of dyslexia/ SpLD.
'Other'	'Other' is a useful category. Whenever I'm sorting something out, for myself or a student, I keep the category 'other' in mind or give it space on the sheet of paper I'm working on.
	I use it for anything that I don't want to forget and that doesn't fit into the categories I already have.
Paradigm	A conceptual or methodological model underlying the theories and practices of a science or discipline at a particular time; (hence) a generally accepted world view ('paradigm, n. 4', OED Online, 2020).
Pitfall	A hidden or unsuspected danger, drawback, difficulty or opportunity for error ('pitfall, n. 4(b)', OED Online, 2020). Used as part of an individual's profile with respect to dyslexia/ SpLD.

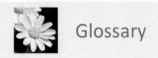

Glossary

Entry	Explanation
Profile: Individual or personal	A representation of a structured set of characteristics of someone or something. A description of a person, organisation, product, etc. ('profile, n.II.10', OED Online, 2020). The dyslexia/ SpLD profile used in this book is an outline of: 1 the thinking preferences 2 the dyslexia/ SpLD pitfalls 3 strategies for pausing 4 accommodations that need to be made. The profile is highly personalised and is the foundation for managing the dyslexia/ SpLD.
Proprioception	The reception of information by sensors which receive signals relating to position and movement ('proprioception , n.' OED Online, 2020); part of the kinaesthetic sense.
Pruning	Has been proposed as an idea to account for the reduction in synaptic connections that occurs during normal development (Kolb, 1995, p 154).
Psyche Also see LEVELS OF BEING.	There are several subtly different interpretations in the OED. The one used in this book is the collective mental or psychological characteristics of ... people ('psyche, n. 1d', OED Online, 2020).
Rationale	1 A reasoned exposition of principles; an explanation or statement of reasons 2 The fundamental or underlying reason for or basis of a thing; a justification ('rationale, n.2.1 and 2', OED Online, 2020).

Entry	Explanation
Regime	A way of doing things, esp. one having widespread influence or prevalence ('regime, n. 2a' OED Online, 2020). The regime for managing dyslexia/ SpLD used in this book includes: 1 recognising the pitfalls 2 pausing 3 using best thinking preferences 4 knowing the relevant goal. The regime is highly personalised.
Rehearsal, verbal	The verbal repetition that is often used to try to remember something, e.g. repeating 'petrol' endlessly when you need to fill up with fuel.
Schema	An (unconscious) organised mental model of something in terms of which new information can be interpreted or an appropriate response made (OED, 1993).
Self-esteem	Esteem: value, worth, favourable opinion (OED, 1993); hence self-esteem is valuing oneself.
Senses	The five physical senses are vision, hearing, taste, smell and kinaesthetic which is made up of touch, position and movement. The use of taste and smell to help use information is not covered in this book, although they are important for some people.
Short-term memory	Those parts of the brain/ mind that store information for time intervals of minutes or days. Short-term memory is still a useful term although, in recent research on memory, it is no longer seen to be an entity in its own right.

Glossary

Entry	Explanation
Subjective vs. objective	Subjective: of or belonging to the thinking [person]; proceeding from or taking place within the individual's consciousness.
	Objective: existing as an object of consciousness, as opposed to being part of the conscious [person]. (OED, 1993)
Subliminal Subliminal learning	Subliminal: below the level of consciousness. Subliminal learning is learning which happens without conscious effort or attention; it simply happens alongside other learning or through everyday life.
Taking-action	Used in this book to mean: 'applying knowledge and skills in a practical way through kinaesthetic thinking'. The hyphen is deliberate.

Taking-action is used in conjunction with 'doing' to facilitate discussing kinaesthetic processing and learning. It is used in parallel with reading, writing, listening and talking to give the following table for acquiring and applying knowledge and skills:

Acquiring	Applying
Reading	Writing
Listening	Speaking
Doing	Taking-action

Entry	Explanation
Thinking preferences	A major component of dealing with your dyslexia/ SpLD is to know how you think best.
Working memory	Part of the mind/ brain which has the capacity for complex thought; it has temporary storage and its workings can be monitored and directed by conscious attention.

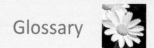
References

Baddeley, Alan, 2007, *Working Memory, Thought, and Action,* Oxford University Press, Oxford

Kolb, Bryan, 1995, *Brain Plasticity and Behaviour,* Lawrence Erlbaum Associates, Mahwah, NJ

O'Connor, Joseph and McDermott, Ian, 1996, *Principles of NLP,* Thorsons, London

OED[1], Brown, Lesley, Ed in Chief, 1993, *The New Shorter Oxford English Dictionary on Historical Principles*, Clarendon Press, Oxford

Website information

DfES Report, 2005, https://www.patoss-dyslexia.org/Resources/DSA-Working-Guidelines Accessed 10 June 2020

OED Online, December 2020, Oxford University Press. Accessed 15 February 2021.

---

[1] The online OED has been consulted every time, and the meanings are consistent. Sometimes the words used in the hard copy of OED (1993) are clearer, or more to the point in the context of this book; in which case the reference is to the hard copy edition that I have consulted.

List of Templates on the Website

This table lists the *TEMPLATES* on the companion *WEBSITE* that are recommended in each chapter.

The sections on the *WEBSITE* are:
  A: Aids for Reading
  B: Gathering Insights
  C: Individual, Personal Profile of Dyslexia/ SpLD
  D: Regime for Managing Dyslexia/ SpLD
  E: Thinking Preferences

There is no significant difference between ✓ and ◊; having 2 symbols just makes tracking easier.

Name of Template U-P is Useful Preface A1 – A3 are Appendices 1 – 3			U-P	1	2	3	4	5	A1	A2	A3
Jotting down as you scan	A	1	✓	◊	✓	◊	✓	◊	✓		
Bookmark – purpose	A	2	✓	◊		◊					
Bookmark – profile & techniques	A	3						◊		◊	
Jotting down as you read, with a few guiding questions	A	4	✓	◊	✓	◊	✓				
Collecting ideas that relate to you	B	1	✓	◊	✓	◊	✓	◊	✓	◊	✓
Know your own mind	B	2		◊			✓			◊	
Compare expectations and reality	B	3		◊	✓	◊	✓	◊	✓		
Action, results, next step	B	4		◊		◊	✓	◊	✓		
Recording template - 1 (4th column narrower for coding)	B	5				◊	✓		✓		
Recording template - 2 (4 equal columns)	B	6		◊		◊			✓		
Recording template - 3 (5th column narrower for coding)	B	7		◊		◊	✓		✓	◊	
Recording template - 4 (5 equal columns)	B	8					◊		✓	◊	
A calendar month for prioritising – 5 weeks	B	9							✓		
Questions to ask oneself to help observation	B	10							✓		
Monitoring progress	B	11		◊		◊	✓	◊	✓		

Name of Template U-P is Useful Preface A1 – A3 are Appendices 1 – 3			U-P	1	2	3	4	5	A1	A2	A3
Individual, personal profile of dyslexia/ SpLD (spatial)	C	1		◊			✓			◊	
Example individual, personal profile of dyslexia/ SpLD (spatial)	C	2		◊			✓			◊	
Individual, personal profile of dyslexia/ SpLD (linear)	C	3		◊			✓			◊	
2 Examples of an individual, personal profile of dyslexia/ SpLD (linear)	C	4		◊			✓			◊	
Managing dyslexia/ SpLD (mind map)	D	1		◊						◊	
Managing dyslexia/ SpLD (linear)	D	2		◊						◊	
Regime for managing dyslexia /SpLD (spatial)	D	3					✓			◊	
Regime for managing dyslexia /SpLD (linear)	D	4					✓			◊	
Experiences for managing dyslexia/SpLD (linear example)	D	5		◊			✓			◊	
List of options for thinking preference	E	1					✓				✓
Table of thinking preferences (spatial)	E	2					✓			◊	
Example: Table of thinking preferences (spatial)	E	3		◊			✓			◊	
Thinking preferences (spatial)	E	4					✓			◊	
Thinking preferences (linear)	E	5					✓			◊	
Visual, aural, kinaesthetic questionnaire	E	6					✓				
The box 'Other'	E	7					✓				

Website information

Series website: www.routledge.com/cw/stacey

Addendum:
A Role for Neurons

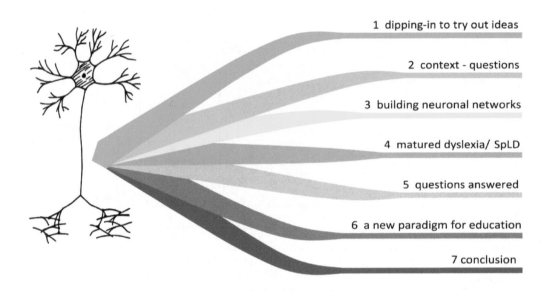

1 dipping-in to try out ideas

2 context - questions

3 building neuronal networks

4 matured dyslexia/ SpLD

5 questions answered

6 a new paradigm for education

7 conclusion

Contents

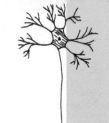

1 Dipping-in to try out ideas

Read *BUILDING NEURONAL NETWORKS*, §3, and *MATURED DYSLEXIA/ SPLD*, §4,
    to understand the proposed role for neurons.
Scan the list of questions in *CONTEXT*, §2, to find the questions that
    interest you.
Read the appropriate answers in *QUESTIONS ANSWERED*, §5.
Scan *A NEW PARADIGM FOR EDUCATION*, §6, to find topics that interest you
    and then read those parts.

§3: p 366
§4: p 369

§2: below

§5: p 370
§6: p 374

2 Context – questions

Between submitting the manuscript of this book and the start of
publishing processes, I realised how neuronal pruning and neurons
wiring together if they fire together resolve many of the issues that
are typically debated about dyslexia:

1. Does dyslexia exist?
2. Is there a cure?
3. What is dyslexia?
4. Does intelligence matter for the definition of dyslexia/ SpLD?
5. What is the difference between dyslexic people and non-dyslexic poor-readers?
6. Are the interventions the same or different for dyslexic people and non-dyslexic poor-readers?
7. Can one usefully talk about mild, moderate and severe dyslexia/ SpLD?
8. Why is there so much co-occurrence among the various SpLDs?
9. Why are there so many variations, of problems and solutions?
10. How useful are labels?
11. Does dyslexia/ SpLD have an impact beyond just reading and spelling?
12. Would the benefits of dyslexia disappear if we could avoid dyslexia developing?
13. Why should resources be diverted to support dyslexic/ SpLD people?

For discussion of the
issues, see:
Elliott and Grigorenko
(2014)
Gibbs and Elliott
(2020)
Ramus (2014)

The main debate is about dyslexia. As other syndromes have been
recognised as similar but different from dyslexia, 'specific learning
difficulties (SpLD)' has become an umbrella term. The hypothesis
proposed here applies to all the different SpLDs, even though the
debated issues are mainly about dyslexia.

Addendum   A Role for Neurons

In this addendum, I want to briefly and simply describe neuronal pruning and how neurons that fire together, wire together; then I will outline how dyslexia/ SpLD can mature out of these processes; next, I will set out how this understanding answers the questions listed above; and finally, I will address educational issues.

3   Building neuronal networks

In the *USEFUL PREFACE*, an analogy is described between park paths and learning. *FIGURE ADDENDUM 1* represents a) the random ways people walk when a park has no gates and b) the mass of neuronal

PARK PATHS AND PRUNING NEURONS: p 4

connections that a child has. *FIGURE ADDENDUM 2* represents both how people walk when there is one gate either side of the park and a neuronal path that is the result of learning. *FIGURE ADDENDUM 3* represents the experience that dyslexic/ SpLD people have that they can learn the right lesson – spelling or reading or something else – but that the dyslexic/ SpLD options have not gone away.

Figure Addendum 1 All paths possible through a park; many connections in a child's brain

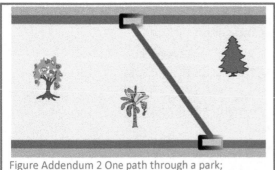

Figure Addendum 2 One path through a park; learnt neural pathway

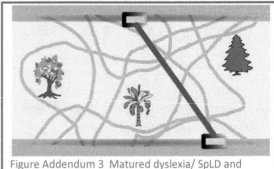

Figure Addendum 3 Matured dyslexia/ SpLD and one learnt neural pathway

Neuronal pruning is the process that reduces the many connections in a child's brain to those neuronal networks that have been acquired by repeated use. As the child makes sense of their world, certain neurons are used and others are not. Those that are used get fed nutrients and they continue to live. Those that are not used are not fed nutrients and they die (Kolb, 1995). This is a simplified description of neuronal pruning.

Kolb (1995)

Neurons wire together if they fire together. Donald Hebb proposed this idea in 1949 (Hebb, 1949). Kolb (1995) describes several different ways in which neurons connect with each other. For the purpose of this discussion, a simplified description is sufficient.

Hebb (1949)
Kolb (1995)

FIGURE ADDENDUM 4 shows a sequence in which (a) neuron A has reached its threshold for firing; (b) the signal has been transmitted to neuron B and has taken B over its threshold for firing; (c) resulting in B firing. The synapses involved are strengthened by such a reaction of two neurons firing together and the wiring together is represented by the enlarged synapses in *FIGURE ADDENDUM 5*. As the same route is used repeatedly, learning takes place and the neurons wire more firmly together, so that when A fires, the probability that B fires increases.

The parts of a neuron are labelled in *FIGURE 2.2:* p 95

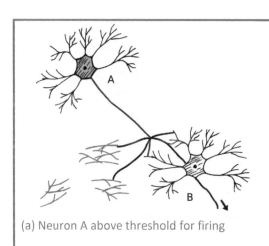

(a) Neuron A above threshold for firing

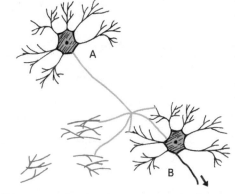

(b) Neuron A fired, B above threshold for firing

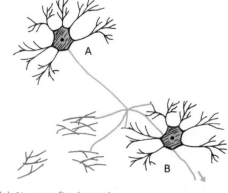

(c) Neurons fired together

Figure Addendum 5 Two neurons firing together

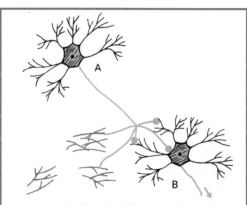

Figure Addendum 4 Two neurons wired together with enhanced synapses

367

Neurons are surrounded by a mass of others and are influenced by signals, some positive some negative, from many other neurons. It is the resulting sum of these influences on the body of a neuron that determines whether it reaches the potential for firing. In *FIGURE ADDENDUM 6*, we have another neuron, C, influencing neuron B. The wiring of B and C is stronger than that of A and B, as represented by the more enlarged synapses. If C is keeping the threshold of B down, the signal from A may be insufficient to take B over the threshold, as shown in *FIGURE ADDENDUM 7*. In other words, if A – B represents some intended learning, that learning may not happen unless other factors, represented by C, are assisting it.

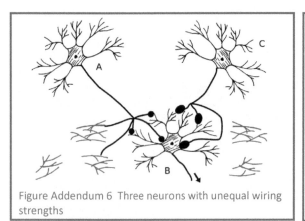

Figure Addendum 6 Three neurons with unequal wiring strengths

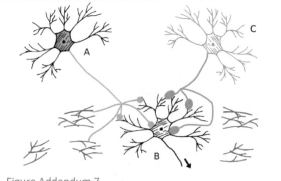

Figure Addendum 7
Neurons A and B firing together prevented by neuron C

When the intended route doesn't get established, other routes through the available connections are likely to be used. They may allow partial achievement, but they won't be systematically building to produce the desired network that constitutes the learned task. They will be used and fed so they won't die out, i.e. they will not be pruned.

One example of un-pruned but well used alternative routes through the mind would be the many spelling options that dyslexic people have, instead of the single, accepted spelling of a word.

As a support tutor, one is working with individual students to find the factors C that can either be used to assist the desired learning, or that need to be prevented from disrupting it.

One child thought that words changed depending on where he was when he had to read them, so that reading a word at school was not the same task as reading it at home.

A child who quickly sees patterns can do certain language exercises without learning the language component. For example, an exercise to practise apostrophes was:

> 'The nest of the robin' can be written as 'The robin's nest'.
> Change the following sentences:
> and then followed ten similar phrases.

The exercise can be done as:

> take the last word, add 's, write the 2ⁿᵈ word.

As the child does the exercise, the apostrophe is probably experienced only as a hand movement. A mind that likes patterns can do the exercise swiftly without any connection to the underlying language while apparently getting it completely right.

The first is an example of established alternative routes. The second, a misconception that was disrupting reading. The third, a task well done that did not connect with the intended language lesson. The second and third are ways that the alternative routes through the mind can be used, fed and not pruned out.

4   Matured dyslexia/ SpLD

FIGURE ADDENDUM 8 represents the dyslexic/ SpLD neuronal pathways that are allowed to mature because they have not been undernourished and allowed to die in the pruning process. When the right approaches to learning for a particular individual are found, it is possible to achieve the desired learning, as represented by the neuron path A – B, but that usually happens too late to

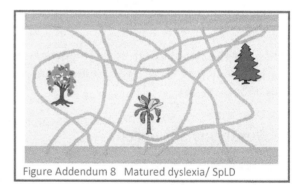

Figure Addendum 8   Matured dyslexia/ SpLD

remove the dyslexic/ SpLD network. So the two exist together, as in *FIGURE ADDENDUM 3*.

- A – B represents the task that should be learnt, see *FIGURE ADDENDUM 5*.

- C represents other factors that need to be addressed to enable learning for some people, see *FIGURES ADDENDUM 6 AND 7*.

- The un-pruned networks, *FIGURE ADDENDUM 8,* represent the matured networks of dyslexia/ SpLD.

FIGURE ADDENDUM 3:
p 366

FIGURE ADDENDUM 5:
p 367

FIGURE ADDENDUM 6:
p 368
FIGURE ADDENDUM 7:
p 368

There are many cognitive and physiological effects that have been researched as candidates for being the cause of dyslexia/ SpLD. Any and all of them could contribute to interrupting the wiring of A – B through the stronger influence of C on B; and hence to the failure of A – B to become a well established neural pathway. It is the relative strengths of the wiring together of A – B and C – B that will enable C to have more effect on the establishment of the A – B route.

The hypothesis presented here is that:

1. there are constitutional elements and psychological characteristics that mean a child can be 'at risk' of dyslexia/ SpLD developing in their brain and consequently in the way they think

2. dyslexia/ SpLD develop when the elements and characteristics through neuronal firing-and-wiring and neuronal pruning produce well established neuronal networks that do not conform to the expected outcomes of education

3. the developed dyslexia/ SpLD is observed through a variety of resulting behaviours

4. correct later learning does not replace the matured dyslexia/ SpLD.

Point 2 is the new hypothesis. The others provide the context. Points 1 and 3 are well known. Point 4 has been voiced before, though not widely discussed.

5 Questions answered

1 Does dyslexia exist?
2 Is there a cure?

Dyslexia/ SpLD doesn't exist initially but once it has matured the networks are always there to be activated. Initially, there is a child 'at risk' of becoming dyslexic/ SpLD. So eventually, dyslexia/ SpLD does exist and there is no cure, only strategies to avoid activating the dyslexic/ SpLD neural networks.

3 What is dyslexia?

Dyslexia/ SpLD is the collection of neuronal pathways that mature when appropriate pruning has not taken place, as represented by *FIGURE ADDENDUM 8*.

FIGURE ADDENDUM 8:
p 369

4   Does intelligence matter for the definition of dyslexia/ SpLD?

When the desired learning, A – B, is not developing through use, an intelligent mind will try to find other paths to perform tasks, which will eventually lead to dyslexia/ SpLD maturing. Any discrepancy between observed general intelligence and basic literacy or maths skills should alert educators to the possibility of an 'at risk' child. This is true at all levels of intelligence. Dyslexia/ SpLD can affect the processing skills of people with above-average language skills and whose general level of intelligence is very high. The debates about how to measure intelligence should not be used as an excuse to leave it out of the dyslexia/ SpLD definitions.

5   What is the difference between dyslexic people and non-dyslexic poor-readers?
6   Are the interventions the same or different for dyslexic people and non-dyslexic poor-readers?

The difference between dyslexic/ SpLD and non-dyslexic poor-readers is that there are no factors C slowing down poor-readers. The poor readers just need to go slowly along routes represented by A – B until the learning has been established, whereas the teaching and learning for dyslexic/ SpLD students needs to attend to the factors C that are preventing the desired learning.

7   Can one usefully talk about mild, moderate and severe dyslexia/ SpLD?

Mild, medium and severe dyslexia/ SpLD are not terms that fit well with the lived experience. A person can have many strategies for dealing with their dyslexia/ SpLD and so have it under control for most of the time, but certain situations may then make them as badly hampered by dyslexia/ SpLD as if they had no strategies (Stacey, 2020b). The more useful way of classifying the dyslexic/ SpLD experience would be to acknowledge how many of the behavioural characteristics might be affected by dyslexia/ SpLD for a particular person, how many strategies they have for dealing with the impacts of dyslexia/ SpLD, and the length of time it takes that person to re-establish their best functioning after an episode of dyslexic/ SpLD functioning.

Stacey (2020b)

8   Why is there so much co-occurrence among the various SpLDs?

9   Why are there so many variations, of problems and solutions?

The symptoms, causes, co-occurrence and interventions will depend on a wide range of factors that make up C. These will be very individualistic; they will depend on the experiences of each child or adult, as well as their innate strengths and weaknesses.

The subtypes of dyslexia/ SpLD can be accommodated in this hypothesis. A *MODEL FOR SPLD* is shown in *FIGURE 2.11*. It comes from a paper by Morton and Frith (1995). In their paper, they discuss competing causes of dyslexia, saying 'Another challenge is that we focused on a phonological deficit when there may be others (e.g. visual deficit) that underlie at least a subtype of dyslexia'.

FIGURE 2.11 MODEL OF DYSLEXIA/ SPLD: p 120

Morton and Frith (1995)

Researchers are looking for causes and suitable interventions to match to the causes. Specialist tutors are working with individuals and have to pay attention to solutions that work for those individuals.

If we look at neural pathways, all these variations in problems and solutions can be seen as factors that operate on a system and result in the shared description represented by *FIGURE ADDENDUM 3*. This hypothesis does not address causes but shows how different causes can impact on learning and produce a variety of problems. It also accommodates variety in the solutions that enable students to learn.

FIGURE ADDENDUM 3: p 366

10   How useful are labels?

SpLD is usually understood to include dyslexia, dyspraxia, AD(H)D and dyscalculia. They become grouped together because of similarities in the patterns of unexpected learning difficulties. It is the learning difficulties that are of interest here and in this series of books. These labels are useful since they should lead to different approaches for teaching and learning. They should not be used in a way that lowers expectations.

My work with students leads me to think:

- with dyslexia, the A – B routes experience disruption because other factors (e.g. thinking preferences) are not being utilised
- with dyspraxia, the lack of body stability and body image disrupts learning
- with AD(H)D, the frequent changes in focus of the mind cause disruptions.

The appropriate teaching practice includes many of the same elements, which have been discussed in *USING THE MIND WELL*. The focus of teaching is often subtly different:

USING THE MIND WELL: p 138

- for dyslexics: an exploration of thinking preferences and how to utilise them
- for dyspraxics: a major focus on organisation
- for AD(H)D: deliberate work on study skills and mind focusing techniques.

Dyscalculia is harder for me to discuss because the students with maths problems that I have supported have not had fundamental issues with maths concepts and their problems have been resolved through exploring thinking preferences. The most important supporting practice has been to observe very carefully where and how any lack of comprehension is being shown by the student. I think my own arithmetic-dyscalculia comes from being able to use patterns to do the work without paying any attention to the numerical consequences.

11   Does dyslexia/ SpLD have an impact beyond just reading and spelling?

Dyslexia/ SpLD does not relate just to reading and spelling but to learning any new subject and to doing tasks. We need many more case studies from adults in order to illustrate the impact to those who work primarily with children.

One purpose of this series of books is to show the wide range of experience that adults describe beyond the difficulties with reading and spelling (especially in Stacey, 2020a).

Stacey (2020a)

12   Would the benefits of dyslexia disappear if we could avoid dyslexia developing?

Many people have got their dyslexia sorted out and they are comfortable with how they manage it. Many famous dyslexic people use their experience to encourage others. Often they will say that their other qualities are so satisfying that if dyslexia is the price they have to pay for those other qualities, then it is a price worth paying. These other qualities are a person's inherent talents and thinking processes. They are the qualities that need to be harnessed to enable the desired learning to take place. They will not disappear if education is adjusted to cater most naturally for dyslexic/ SpLD people.

13   Why should resources be diverted to support dyslexic/ SpLD people?

The teaching that is VITAL for dyslexic/ SpLDs is also good practice for all. If the paradigm outlined below were adopted it would benefit all learners; there would be very little extra cost needed to address any remaining educational needs once cohorts of children have progressed through the school system.

6   A new paradigm for education

The tuition that suits different people can be quite individual, but it could easily be delivered in a way that caters for the needs of the majority of dyslexic/ SpLD children and adults, while at the same time providing good practice for all learners. This has been done by Henderson (1999) in two different state primary schools.

Henderson (2003)

Stacey (2020b)

In *Development of Dyslexia and other SpLDs* (2020b), I surveyed research papers looking especially for evidence that cognitive abilities were playing a major part in the dyslexia/ SpLD field. At the end of the survey, I proposed a new paradigm for education. Instead of looking for single styles of teaching and learning, I believe there are three elements that need to be brought together:

- a learner's abilities
- a range of different options for learning
- the outcome to be achieved, whether that is learning knowledge or skills or completing a task.

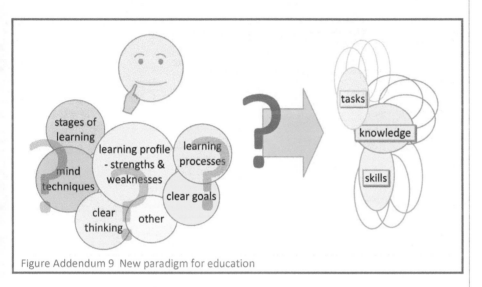

Figure Addendum 9 New paradigm for education

There needs to be a programme whereby there is much more focus on which choices each learner needs to make, see *FIGURE ADDENDUM 9*. We need to help people to have agency over their own learning processes and to be able to select those processes that suit them.

There are many learning and thinking processes that need to be taught overtly and in detail. The way the teaching should be delivered is described in *Gaining Knowledge and Skills with Dyslexia and other SpLDs* (Stacey, 2021). In particular, the skills and processes need to be named as they are taught, practised and used, otherwise they remain associated with the task and there is no realisation that they are transferable skills and processes.

Stacey (2021)

In one workshop, I was questioned as to how it would be possible to include the processes for learning in a crowded English literature curriculum and in a way that would suit dyslexic/ SpLD learners.
I suggested that a whole school approach would be possible.
The processes of learning that are VITAL to be taught overtly and
deliberately could be made into a poster that is on display in
every single classroom.
Then during lessons, these processes could be deliberately used in
class activities.
The teacher could draw attention to the fact that one of the processes
is being used.
In this way, teaching the different learning skills will be integral to
each subject and throughout the whole school.
They will not only serve the dyslexic/ SpLD students, but will also be
good practice for all students.

7   Conclusion

The hypothesis about the role of neurons in the development of dyslexia/ SpLD leads to a construct that:

- describes a physical system for dyslexia/ SpLD, including
  - how dyslexia/ SpLD matures
  - why it persists even after correct learning has been achieved
- includes all the research to date on
  - the constitutional origins of dyslexia/ SpLD
  - the psychological processing involved
  - the behavioural symptoms
  - the interventions for children
  - the work with adults
- resolves many of the issues that contribute to the doubts that dyslexia is a real phenomenon
- promotes educational changes that will allow mainstream education to adopt practices that are VITAL for dyslexic/ SpLD students since they are good practice for all.

Even while the hypothesis is being examined by others concerned about dyslexia/ SpLD, we have the opportunity to look at the new paradigm for education that it points to. The new paradigm is a cost-effective route to cater for dyslexic/ SpLD students in mainstream education with teaching that will benefit all students.

References

Elliott, Julian G., and Grigorenko, Elena L., 2014, *The Dyslexia Debate*, Cambridge University Press, NY

Gibbs, Simon J., and Elliot, Julian G., 2020, *The Dyslexia Debate: Life without the Label,* Oxford Review of Education, 46(4), pp 487-500

Kolb, Bryan, 1995, *Brain Plasticity and Behaviour,* Lawrence Erlbaum Associates, Mahwah, NJ

Hebb, Donald, 1949, *Organisation of Behaviour*, McGraw-Hill, NY

Henderson, Elizabeth, 2003, *How to Have a Dyslexic Friendly School*, Beacon Office, Oldfield School, Maidenhead

Morton, John and Frith, Uta, 1995, *Causal Modeling: A Structural Approach to Developmental Psychopathology*, in *Developmental Psychopathology*, Ch 13, Vol 1, 357-390

Ramus, Franck, 2014, *Should there Really Be a 'Dyslexia Debate'?,* Brain, 137, pp 3371-3374

Stacey, Ginny, 2020a, *Organisation and Everyday Life with Dyslexia and other SpLDs,* Routledge, London

Stacey, Ginny, 2020b, *Development of Dyslexia and other SpLDs,* Routledge, London

Stacey, Ginny, 2021, *Gaining Knowledge and Skills with Dyslexia and other SpLDs,* Routledge, London

Index

*in front of an entry marks a word or phrase that is in the GLOSSARY, Ⓖ, p 353

The following may be useful INDEX entries:
(sub-entries are shown in brackets)

Tip: To find a word in the text

If the word you are looking for doesn't show quickly, try running a ruler or envelope or other straight edge down the page. Doing this makes your eyes look at each line and you are more likely to find the word.

Occasionally, the entry refers to the context and not a specific word; so sometimes you need to read the text.

Index

Index

BBC SOUNDS

BRITISH LIBRARY

The BBC Listening Project records conversations between different people about many different kinds of experiences between people with a wide range of relationships.

Ginny and Sally — A Dyslexic Brain

Sally and I have enjoyed our journey working together on these four books and we recorded our thoughts about the experience for The Listening Project in April 2018. Though we are both dyslexic, our experience of dyslexia is quite different; we have different processing strengths and different ranges of problems. We are both positive about dealing with any problems and we both enjoy our various strengths. It has been huge fun working together, as we hope you can hear from our conversation.

An extract from our conversation is available on the BBC website at https://www.bbc.co.uk/sounds/play/b0b1tmbl

The whole conversation is archived at the British Library and will be made available later this year (2020) at https://sounds.bl.uk

Full details of the recording can be found on the British Library's Sound and Moving Image catalogue at http://sami.bl.uk (search for C1500/1554).

Ginny Stacey and Sally Fowler
Photo by Louise Pepper for the BBC Listening Project

Lightning Source UK Ltd.
Milton Keynes UK
UKHW052130130622
404387UK00003B/7